1986

WRITING AND READING IN HENRY JAMES

WRITING AND READING IN HENRY JAMES

Susanne Kappeler

Foreword by
Tony Tanner

First published 1980 by
THE MACMILLAN PRESS LTD
London and Basingstoke
Companies and representatives
throughout the world

Printed in Hong Kong

British Library Cataloguing in Publication Data

Kappeler, Susanne
  Writing and reading in Henry James
  1. James, Henry – Criticism and Interpretation
  I. Title
  813′.4   PS2124

  ISBN 0–333–29104–2

Contents

Foreword

We tend to think of the writer, the critic, the reader in terms of a descending hierarchy – privileged creation, parasitic redaction, passive consumption. Dr Kappeler's book changes all that – and changes it most decisively and constructively. She sets about achieving this in an unusual and very interesting manner. First she considers some of the current theories – deriving from V. S. Propp – that modern narratives, for all their complexity, are in some way derivatives of certain basic, generative structures to be found in folk tales. Drawing on her own extensive knowledge of linguistics, structuralism, and semiotics, she demonstrates that this is simply not true – for many reasons, but in large part because the function, expectation, and behaviour of the reader has changed radically from that of the notional 'listener' to the folk tale. Alluding to the insufficiently known work of Clemens Lugowski on the emergence of individuality in the novel, Dr Kappeler shows how the erosion of the collective audience of the folk tale created the modern reader, a figure who has learned suspicion, expects ambiguities, tolerates polysemic texts, indulges in reflective 'double' reading, and wants difference rather than repetition – the never-told, not the twice-told, tale. As in the detective story in which 'the reader is not a simple listener: he becomes himself an imaginary subject of his reading, traversing the narrative space along the traces and clues provided', and as, in a different way, in the *nouveau roman*, so in the Jamesian novel the reader is invited to join in the endless work – the endless game – of active and creative interpretation. We learn – if we read James as he invites his work to be read, as Dr Kappeler invites us to read him – what she calls 'the tricks of the hermeneutic', in particular of the 'second hermeneutic', i.e. not just the plot contained in the text, but the deeper plot of the construction of the text itself. As an example of this, Dr Kappeler offers an extended, detailed, and quite arrestingly brilliant, reading of *The Aspern Papers* which is itself something of a milestone in Jamesian criticism. Then in a second part she examines a number of James's works in which the relations between the writer, the critic – the editor, journalist, readers of all kinds – and the community, communities, at large are explored. She elicits James's sense and depiction of the problematical relationship between the artist, his work, and society's demands – and the related relationship between creativity, sexual passion, and marriage. There is also the problematical status of the literary product – a commodity which is never fully consumed; and she shows how, for James, there are 'conceptual' productions which partake of the nature of art even though they never find any external realisation or concretisation. One important part of this exercise is to decisively dissolve the established and accepted distinction, or opposition, between the artist as a passive observer, renouncing participation in life, and society as the realm of action and mating. As she shows, the terms can all be inverted according to the perspective you adopt and, in any case, art, beside being a substitute for love and marriage 'is itself of the very nature of passionate love' as James dramatises it. To explore and explain this further, in a third part Dr Kappeler offers a marvellously subtle and scrupulous reading of *The Sacred Fount* – a text which, as she shows in a long important appendix, has been quite excessively, even absurdly, mis-read, over-read and under-read by generations of critics. She compares the activity of the narrator of that story to that of the artist – as is usual; but then goes on to show how his activity is also like that of the anthropologist, the psychoanalyst, and the literary critic. Analyst and interpreter of the signs and symptoms of the society of Newmarch, penetrator of the secrets, not just of individual traumas, but the 'dissimulations of a collective unconscious', he also acts, paradoxically, as part of the 'collective suppression agency' knowing that, as it were, what he knows must not be made known. The important point is that his activity is not *just* para-creative, or *just* psychoanalytic (or pathological) – it is, in every sense, interpretative. If he is not quite a novelist he is not 'merely' a critic. Our old unexamined divisions are inadequate and false: 'the novelist is as much an interpreter of "the canvas of life" as the reader is an interpreter of the novelist's embroidery . . . the activities of writer and reader are singularly similar'. Dr Kappeler conclusively, and really quite dazzlingly, develops and demonstrates this conclusion by an examination of James's Prefaces in which he writes as a reader-critic of his own work, and in which there is nothing 'apart from some trivial biographical data of little interest, that we as readers should not be able to trace on our own'. As she trenchantly formulates it – 'thus it is that we can learn from the prefaces our job as critics, but not the master's craft'. But writer-critic-reader have by now become much more richly inter-related terms. All are 'reproducers', just as a novel itself is a text, a production, which precipitates endless further reproductions, reinterpretations. There are no final, definitive terminal readings. There are only endless re-readings and the all important thing is the 'how' of it, the how of the writing which is reproduced in the how of the reading. Dr Kappeler's own book is a beautiful example of just how rewarding, enriching, such an approach to the pleasure, the game, the play-work, of reading a complex literary text can be. As she says, using James's own terms, 'the critic should not fall into normative criticism, but shall, rather, "for the fun of it" "appreciate", "appropriate", "take intellectual possession" and make the thing criticised his "own"'. And as she says, she does. Drawing with admirable and informed lucidity on the whole range of con-temporary literary theory and, refreshingly, showing – by her own example – that its use must be demonstrated in practice, the creative reading of specific texts, Dr Kappeler has written a book which shifts Jamesian criticism into a new key of sophistication, scrupulousness – and pleasure.

TONY TANNER

Preface

I would like to thank the Master and Fellows of Jesus College, Cambridge, for the award of a Research Fellowship, which has made it possible for me to turn my thesis into the present book. I am also indebted to King's College, Cambridge, for the award of an External Studentship during the academic year 1973–74, which enabled me to begin research in linguistics and poetics. I am very grateful to the British Council, whose generous support with a Council of Europe Higher Education Scholarship from January 1975 to September 1977 allowed me to continue and complete the research for my thesis.

I acknowledge with gratitude Professor Frank Kermode's subtle supervision of my thesis, and his patience in reading parts and finally the whole of the draft. I would also like to thank Linda Gillman for reading the draft; and Dr Lisa Jardine for intellectual and moral support throughout. Special thanks go to Dr Tony Tanner, for reading the final draft of the book, and for invaluable encouragement.

Jesus College, Cambridge   SUSANNE KAPPELER
August 1979

Acknowledgements

The author and publisher wish to thank the following who have kindly given permission for the use of copyright material:

Associated Book Publishers, Ltd., for extracts from '*The Ambassadors*' and '*The Sacred Fount*: the artist *manqué*' by Bernard Richards in *The Air of Reality: New Essays on Henry James* (1973), edited by John Goode, and published by Methuen and Co., Ltd.

Suhrkamp Verlag for an extract from *Die Form der Individualität im Roman* by Clemens Lugowski.

Introduction

One of my major aims in this book has been to combine theorising and practical text interpretation. In literary studies the chasm has widened between those who practise criticism and those concerned with its theory, while it remains hard to say whether there is less harm in the theorist who neglects practice or in the practical critic who has no theory. It is certainly deplorable that the theoretical discourse has abstracted itself largely to a metacritical level from which direct application to literary texts is no longer easily made. Thus, rather than add to the metacritical discourse, I explore the meaning and the implications of some theoretical issues at a practical level.

I do not believe that literary texts have a definable nature which distinguishes them intrinsically from any other text, nor that they are written in a special 'poetic' language which itself could be systematically described. Rather, I regard literature as a social practice, like other arts or sciences, which is defined *by* its practice, and not by the corpus of its products. Both producers and receivers assume a literary or aesthetic disposition and acquire a special competence. It is as a consequence of this conception of literature as practice that the theory of reading forms a crucial part of the theory of literature, describing the attitudes the reader takes and the assumptions he makes.

From this perspective I review some traditional issues of literary criticism, such as the 'author's intention'. It has been so copiously discussed, however, that I could not pretend to survey it; instead, I try to show what becomes of the author's intention viewed from the reader's standpoint. If reading is a process established between the reader and his text, all he can do is infer an 'intention' from the text; he cannot read one into it. What he can also do is read out 'unconscious intentions' or 'unintentional meanings' if these are coded in the text. What he cannot do is separate an 'author's intention' from the text and compare the two, either claiming that the author's intention has not been achieved in the text, or that the text exceeds the author's intention.

It is clear that the term 'intention' is inadequate for the complex of phenomena it is supposed to cover. Since the writer's medium imposes its own constraints, it would be absurd to argue that every feature of the text is in a strong sense intended, or indeed demand that it should be; yet this does not allow us to call such features unintended. Rather than try to determine the degree of conscious design behind them, we ought to realise that we are entitled to use their significance in our interpretation.

A related issue concerns the 'message' of the literary work, often the tacitly assumed grail of the practical critic. The text *is* the message, not to be distilled into a shorter or quintessential message, but to be interpreted by the reader. He must act upon it independently, with no supplementary metacommunication. This leads to the definition of the literary practice as a 'game'.

Generally, my approach has been shaped by a longstanding preoccupation with linguistic techniques and the ways in which they can be used in literary interpretation, as well as an involvement in semiology and semiological criticism, communications theory, and the psychoanalytical approach to discourse. The starting point for this study is Roland Barthes's theoretical aphorism that the reader is properly the 'writer' or 'producer' of his text; its aim is the exploration of the 'reader's share' in his experience of reading. The justification of my method is intrinsic to the argument, and it accounts for the dominance of quotation over paraphrase.

I Analysis of Narrative

I The relevance of folkloristics to the analysis of modern narrative

It is well known that the literary analysis of narrative structure has derived inspiration from anthropological studies of verbal folklore, the most notable source being Propp's *Morphology of the Folktale*.[1] The felt relevance of such studies to the analysis of modern literary narrative, however, is based on intuition rather than on a careful consideration of the necessary premises. The adoption of folkloristic methods into literary narrative analysis occurred under the general influence of structuralism, Propp's morphology itself offering an essentially structuralist method, while its application to a different corpus, literature, seemed sanctioned by the interdisciplinary orientation of structuralist methodology. This folkloristically inspired tradition has been greatly developed and sophisticated, especially in France, and in combination with textual linguistics;[2] but rather than review the various current theories I wish to draw attention to their point of origin.

The assumption behind this methodological transference is that the relatively simple and uniform structure of the folktale provides a fundamental matrix for the analysis of the highly complex narrative structures of literary fiction. It is considered the essence of narrative, the archetype of story, if it is not indeed thought to embody universals of narrative that correspond almost to innate ideas of story in the human mind. But to assume that modern narratives are structural derivatives of the folktale is to confuse structural with historical ancestry. It is rather like trying to use the form of the sonnet in order to analyse and explain free verse. Indeed, it is worse than that, since folklore and modern literary fiction pertain to mutually remoter modes of cultural production than do the sonnet and free verse respectively. It has often been pointed out that the structuralist bias towards synchrony can lead to a serious neglect of the diachronic dimension. To treat folklore narrative and modern literary narrative as if they were instances of the same 'language' or 'grammar' – say, like Chomsky's early kernel and complex sentences – is a mistake of precisely this order. For in the process of this comparison a number of crucial factors are being overlooked, the most obvious of which will be discussed below. They are factors which mark the difference between the oral and the literate traditions, as well as the change in attitude towards artifice as it manifests itself in conventions of representation, and of narrative in particular; and which means by implication a change in the understanding of reality. The former are captured in the problem of the relationship between 'author', text and audience, and can be broached extrinsically in terms of the sociologies of folklore and of literate art. Discussion of this shall serve in the first instance to dispel the notion of simple kinship between the two modes of verbal production; but it will also lead us to intrinsic considerations of the second complex of problems, which is necessarily affected by the former.

Jakobson and Bogatyrev[3] pointed early to the different sociological backgrounds of oral and written literatures, and to the danger involved in ignoring them. Myths, legends, folktales etc., are anonymous with respect to their inventors, and are being recreated in many variant forms. In this aspect they resemble the performing arts, in which the individual articulations of an original – a score, a script, a choreography – have a status of their own, and not just that of performance in the Chomskian sense of competence *manqué*. It is the performance which bears the marks, if any, of originality and individuality, rather than the 'material' which is being recreated. But the existence of an oral work, unlike, say, a Beethoven symphony, depends entirely on these performances, since there is no script or other notation. Hence the reception by the public plays a crucial role, and neglect by the public may mean the death of any particular work. A work of literature, in contrast, may well survive periods of public neglect and be rediscovered by later generations, as the history of literature has repeatedly shown.

This active role of the public in the determination of its art may partly account for the relative uniformity of folk literature. Jakobson and Bogatyrev discuss what they call the 'preventive censorship of the community':[4]

the absolute reign of the preventive censorship, which makes any conflict of the work with the censorship futile, creates a special type of participant in poetic creation and forces the personality to renounce any attack aimed at overcoming the censorship.

(*my translation*)

(die absolute Herrschaft der Präventivzensur, die jeden Konflikt des Werkes mit der Zensur fruchtlos macht, schafft einen besonderen Typ von Teilnehmern am dichterischen Schaffen und zwingt die Persönlichkeit, auf jeden auf die Überwältigung der Zensur gerichteten Anschlag zu verzichten.)

The purpose of this passage is to dispel the romantic misconception of the folk poet being, like the modern poet, a social outcast or rebel. While the modern poet is allowed, if not expected, to be critical of his *milieu* and to disregard demands made by the public, and hence has the opportunity to influence both that *milieu* and those demands, the folk poet is entirely at the mercy of the 'preventive censorship of the community', which will strictly guard its values and suppress subversive tendencies.

While it is obvious that the advent of writing literature down, and later of printing, has significantly changed the sociological conditions of the work, it still does not mean that the earlier oral tradition has been completely superseded by our literary tradition. It is true that as a result individual authorship was able to develop the particular tendency towards avant-gardism in response to the pressure of originality which characterises our particular concept of canonical literature. Yet it is not an intrinsic or exclusive merit of the written medium as such. The same preventive censorship of the community may still be at work in a literate culture, only its efficacy is restricted, both to its own age, and in degree. Due to the permanence of the written medium censorship is no longer preventive in a strong sense, and its verdict is not final. But even such control as there is no longer lies in the hands of the community at large. Different instances of censorship are installed between the author and the public, the economic, aesthetic and political censors embodied by editors, publishers, patrons, public propagandists and critics, church and government. The limited censorship of the community at large, consequently, no longer acts as preventive, as this is beyond its scope, but in the way of positive selection. The phenomenon is perfectly familiar, only we have chosen, with our disposition for avant-gardism, not to call literature what has not passed the test of literary history in a strict sense. Common parlance divides literary products into 'art' and 'trash', 'highbrow' and 'popular', depending on the desired inflection. It is of course in itself characteristic that the critical vocabulary lacks a proper term for non-arty literature, say, like the concept of *Trivialliteratur* of German literary criticism. In conclusion it remains to point out, of course, that it is not to be taken as a sign of greater enlightenment if a literate community allows a wider ranging, less censored literature which it cannot prevent.

The differences between oral and literate art have been stressed particularly as a warning against the rash application of folkloristic analysis to literature proper. I now emphasise that we must further distinguish collective and individual production, as a further call for caution. For these factors are not just sociological, but they significantly influence the intrinsic constitution of the works themselves.

Speaking in terms of function, folklore is a vehicle for expressing the collective wisdom and taste, and is thus orientated towards moral content. In contrast, the modern 'high literary' interest has shifted more and more to the level of form and technique as the means for expressing individuality. Popular wisdom and existing mores need to be rearticulated, not innovated, and this is helped by a set of strict conventions. One way of looking at it shows how in the diachronic development of oral folklore actional 'content' turns into formal symptom, structuration and content thus mutually reinforcing each other and so doubly ensuring the conservation of values. For example, it is a general observation of folklorists that character attributes in a folktale must be shown functionally rather than be given descriptively. That is to say, the hero is shown to act nobly and can thus be recognised as the candidate for the role of hero. On the other hand, his qualification for that role is overdetermined by other features – or symptoms – in the narrative, for instance by the fact that he is the third and youngest son, or the last in a row of suitors. Similarly, the hero is finally given the King's daughter in marriage, as a reward for his good deeds. However, these narrative developments go over into the structure of expectations on the audience's part, which allows the folktale to be schematic rather than expansive in its demonstration of attributes. This means that the listener can pick out the clues from the 'symptoms' in the structure of the tale, no longer relying exclusively on a convincing demonstration of attributes. In this overdetermination we can see the folktale's embodiment of its own diachronic development, as it is integrated in the synchrony of its structure as the simultaneous representation of a didactic moral purpose and the confirmation of expectations formed precisely under the tutelage of this didacticism.

One might say that the folktale is a primitive prototype of the notion of genre, if genre is the abstract ideal – never attained – of the 'grammatical' capture of a form. But while the folktale complies diachronically, reconfirming its definition, the diachronic development of a genre continually negates provisional definition, as each work generically redefines itself, thus undermining the very concept of genre. The fact, then, that folklore is so strikingly uniform, reducible to a small number of plots if not indeed to one archetype,[5] is directly related to this self-conservative double structure, where formal features are symptomatic of actional content. This leads to the almost paradoxical observation that the permanence of the written medium in fact helps literary works to shed the formal permanence which the oral medium preserves.[6] The affinity of writing to a kind of exorcism has of course been noted as a phenomenon of writing as the activity of an individual; but it seems to have this curious parallel in the history of writing and the evolution of genres.

The fact that in folklore there does not exist a proper communicative relationship between an author and an audience, because the audience community exercises direct censorship on the product and thus virtually assumes the function of authorship itself, has far-reaching repercussions on the semiotics of the text. The folktale dissembles the fact that there is mediation between reality and representation. That is to say, there is no room for doubt encoded in the structure of the text that what the folktale says, 'is', and is as it says. It presumes a one-to-one relationship between the narrative and the fictional world it creates. Hence the folktale speaks the truth, can only speak the truth: it is *bona fide*. There is consequently no need to distinguish between narrative and narrated content, as there can be no disparity, no arbitrary selection or omission from a putative continuous reality beyond the narrated content. One might say that the folktale is the unselfconscious text *par excellence*, which in turn means that it achieves, or simulates, a complete suppression of the (textual) subject.

It might be well to pause at this point to consider that inevitably our approach to folklore is coloured by our own experience of narrative. To say that the folktale is unselfconscious betrays that our own narrative has turned selfconscious; to point out the virtual identity of narrative and fictional reality is to have noted disparity between *récit* and *histoire* in later fiction. To be puzzled by the naiveté and the uniformity of folklore is to know suspicion and diversity; to find the subject suppressed is to have made the acquaintance of that subject. Almost inevitably, also, the terms applied to folklore seem pejorative or at least implying superiority of another standpoint, thus tacitly enforcing the view of folklore as a 'primitive' ancestor of our 'mature' literature. In a comparison like the present one, where modern fiction is indeed the point of reference, and the aim to show the disparity of the two modes, such bias of the language of analysis is hard to avoid. However, to gain a real understanding of the nature of folklore, or even early literate narrative, a continuous attempt to bracket off our own peculiar historical and literary perspective is imperative.

I would like briefly to discuss a little known study by Clemens Lugowski, *Die Form der Individualität im Roman*,[7] which is not only exemplary in just this respect, but is also highly relevant to the present argument. Lugowski sets himself the task of tracing the emergence of individuality and the development of its form in the novel. His initial point of reference is the relationship of the Greek to tragic myth, namely their *unmediated* engagement with the poetic or fictional world (p. 12). In this Lugowski sees a fundamental definition of community:

> Attic tragedy over and over again shows the old themes which are deeply rooted in the folk consciousness. Those who were not familiar with the heroic subject-matter had no access to Attic tragedy, could not be Greeks, but only barbarians; they did not belong to the people (*Volk*), for the people here means still the circle of spectators before the stage (*skene*). As it was only this communal look to myth which created the communality of the Greek people, so in particular it is in the heroic subject-matter of Attic tragedy, rather than poetic fiction, that the Greek finds his home with the Greek and the Greek communality is truly founded. Later, this relation changes, the circle of the heroic myth, which created the communality, loses its closure and dissolves; partly it extends, partly it is forgotten or no longer taken seriously.   (p. 10; *my translation*)

No occidental nation after the middle ages of course possesses a mythology as comprehensive as the Hellenic. Yet, Lugowski claims, 'the relation of man to poetic fiction – and not only to poetic fiction – shows a peculiar analogy to the attitude of the Hellenic Greek towards the mythic "subject-matter" of tragedy' (p. 10).

> One's attitude towards a work of art is different from one's attitude to an event in real life, different towards a work of fiction than it is towards a sculpture, different again to drama than it is to a novel. Within literature every one of the great genres has a peculiar character of artifice. . . . As literature as such means a (generally) determined artificiality, and as within this sphere of artifice particular modes are differentiated in the great genres, so within a genre a variety of forms of artifice can be distinguished. Certainly, a single poetic work always stands under the sign of a special kind of artifice, and further within a whole hierarchy of artifice. Here, too, people find each other in the understanding of these modes of artifice and in their acceptance of them as a matter of course; and here too a communality originates which defines itself by the recognition of those outside it as the uncomprehending, the 'barbarians', the uninitiated, to whom literature at large, or this specific work, remains a closed world.[14] The mutual relationship between artifice and community presents an analogy to the relationship of Greek communality and tragic myth.   (pp. 10–11; *my translation*)

A further factor is emphasised, following Dilthey, namely that the 'immediate relationship of man with reality, of being in and with reality without objectifying it (in a theoretical sense), equally holds for his relationship to the handed-down forms of the artificial reality which appears in the poetic work' (p. 11). These forms are history, that is, a living reality; 'they do not even appear as artifice to one to whom the work speaks: in contemplation of a poetic work he enters its world without deliberation and without reflection: only then can this world speak to him. Reflection destroys this world, as the "spirit of enlightenment" destroys the mythic coherence of the real world' (p. 11).

Lugowski points towards a distinction between the initiated and the 'barbarians', and adds in a note:

> Or turned the other way: the maid reads her backstairs romance with immediate (unmediated) abandon. One who is aesthetically

and critically competent can no longer do this. He is incredulous *vis-à-vis* the world of this novelette; he cannot, like the maid, enter it without reserve. He has become conscious of its 'artifice' and hence is disqualified from the communality. (p. 189, note 14; *my translation*)

This is a most revealing addition, for it draws on a context in which the 'mythic analogon' must virtually have disappeared. In the German prose works of the sixteenth century which Lugowski studies, in the *Decameron* and in *Don Quixote*, he traces the first signs of the dissolution of the 'mythic analogon', and the emergence of the, no longer mythic, 'forms of individuality'. As we have differently inflected terms to distinguish the 'literary' from 'the trashy', 'highbrow' from 'popular', so we can see a change of inflection in Lugowski's example. In the text it is community and barbarians who are opposed, in the note it is the maid and the artistically critical in a scenario of 'Upstairs, Downstairs'. But now it is the cultured reader who is in the role of the 'barbarian', excluded from the communality of the maid and her type of readership. It is of course to be expected that the cast-out critic will in turn have found his community of like-minded readers: the 'educated', 'literati', the 'cultured', the readers of works which precisely trained his and their critical competence. We will have reason to remember this particular community when discussing Henry James's short stories in Part II. Meanwhile, we can begin to sketch developments and bifurcations from the premises given so far.

What Lugowski's pointer to the maid's reading matter means, of course, is precisely the continued existence of a 'folklore' – a mythic analogon – within a highly developed literary tradition, as we claimed that there would be above. He thus gives an initial position from which to develop a concept of *Trivialliteratur* which is not simply defined negatively with reference to the avant-gardist tendency, that is, as lacking in innovation and shortcoming in originality, but in terms of a 'folkloristic attitude' which is required for reading it.

The starting point, then, is the evolving community of the Greek spectators of tragedy, united in a common mythology. Outsiders are not specified as having any communality of their own, or some other folklore which they do comprehend; they serve merely to define the other side of the boundaries of community. The 'folk' of folklore, of the shared cultural heritage, give rise to the people of Hellene. With the decline of the mythos and the supersession of the 'mythic analogon' the community develops into a reading public – which in turn gradually divides into the individualists and sophisticates of the literati community on the one hand, and the *populus* of popular fiction on the other.

In his remark about reflection Lugowski draws a parallel between reflection as an individual's approach to a work of literature, which destroys his immediate access to the work's 'world', and the 'spirit of enlightenment' as a cultural–historical phenomenon which destroys the possibility of an unmediated perception of, and being in, the world. This parallel is akin and related to the one we drew above between writing as the exorcism of an individual and writing as the exorcism of the timelessness (a-temporality) and the uniformity of folklore. Once more we can correlate these factors – of writing and of reflection – within the developments already mapped.

It would appear that the period of the 'mythic analogon' identified by Lugowski represents a crucial stage of transition between the Folkloristic and the Individualistic, manifesting characteristics of both. Taking oral folklore as the purest form of the Folkloristic, we can say, schematically: it does not write, it preserves; it does not exorcise and hence not develop form in terms of the genre's everchanging evolution. It does not reflect, that is, it has an immediate relationship both with its world and its fictional world. It represents community.

The Individualistic, evolving from the literate culture: writes, exorcises, develops forms which in the writing are themselves exorcised; it reflects and destroys, it must move on, innovate.

We may well ask what 'it' is. Its use betrays the problem of the subject which it substitutes. In the Folkloristic 'it' is one: it comprises the 'author' as well as the audience, the collective authorship of a text produced for collective reception: the community. With writing, there must occur a split; there emerges an author, at first and under the sign of the 'mythic analogon' he is very close to the community, a delegate, and his writing conforms largely to the conventions of his community's folklore, its understanding of artifice and reality. Yet this author develops, sins against the 'mythic analogon' and experiments with first forms of individuality in his written fiction. At the same time the community must be developing, for it does not censor the experiments of the writer. It assumes its own function, namely that of the readership.

The 'one' of folklore's collective author-audience has split into two, writer and reader. He, the reader, reflects in his approach to the text, he is losing his immediacy, and his reflection destroys the poetic world within it. Thus reader and writer push each other in a dialectic of destruction and innovation. The writer's reflection makes him selfconscious of his role as subject, and his discourse becomes 'selfconscious'. The word of fiction is no longer *bona fide*, as the reader reflects on it, and suspicion arises concerning the subject, concerning the representation of reality. The 'spirit of enlightenment', not in a literary but in an epistemological sense, is also destroying the immediacy of the perception of reality. Fictional reality is contrasted with the, no longer immediately accessible, reality of the world, which itself needs representation, in perception or in words. All that once was unity – word and world, fictional world and reality, author and audience – splits up, and splits up further, in a proliferation of bifurcations. Hence it does not make sense to take the tip of one branch, say a modern literary narrative, and assume that a linear development can be traced back to an origin in folklore.

We have already determined that we are on the particular branch of individualistic innovatory literature. There is the pressure of originality and novelty that the dialectic race between connoisseur readers and writers exerts. Another branch pursues the problem of representing reality, and representing it verisimilar in narrative. Where the representability of reality is less the problem, it is the suspicion of the word and the ambiguity of the subject. Indeed, our schema is simplistic, while those branches do not grow organically, forward from bifurcation to bifurcation. For, any one work may participate in the problems, developments and exorcisms of many different 'branches'; and the schema had better be abandoned, together, of course, with the linearity of ancestry. We followed it so far only so as to demonstrate the complexity of 'parentage' of modern narrative, and to prove wrong the assumption that folktale analysis could be grafted on to the analysis of modern literary narrative.

Having spent so much effort to discredit the alleged kinship between modern narrative and folklore, we must now ask what it means if we do find a modern literary fiction which corresponds to the structure of the folktale, as I will show that *The Aspern Papers* seems to do. The terms of reference for the structure of the folktale have been taken from a study by Alex Olrik, 'Epische Gesetze der

Volksdichtung',[8] in which he develops a series of 'laws' for the products of folk literature. But since I hold that these are wholly unexpected in this context, I will have to find an explanation of their presence beyond the obvious fallacy that they are universal. *The Aspern Papers* is an exception for exhibiting them, and examples of fictions which fail to conform to them are the rule.

2 Epic laws and *The Aspern Papers*: A first analysis

Olrik's 'law of three',[1] the most important characteristic of folk literature, can be seen to govern *The Aspern Papers* generally. There are always only three major parties in evidence at any one time, though the constitution of the set may change, and in fact does so three times.[2] In the opening chapters the three are the narrator, Mrs Prest, and the Misses Bordereau lumped together as yet into a single unit. The first and the last party are in opposition, while Mrs Prest acts as their mediator, apparently more or less neutral, as she has no vested interest of her own. She stands between the two in matters of knowledge, which in these opening chapters plays an important role: she is the only one who knows both parties; and if she is not intimately acquainted with the Misses Bordereau, nor indeed with the narrator, she has at least a thorough knowledge of Venice, which the narrator lacks, and is informed of the latter's designs, which the Bordereaus are not. She is also in touch with Venice society and especially the American colony, which presents another advantage over both the others.

With the beginning of Chapter Four Mrs Prest fades out of the narrative, owing to her 'annual migration'[3] which takes her out of Venice for the summer. She has also completed her task of mediation, since the narrator has become a lodger at the Misses Bordereau's villa and now 'knows' as much as she does. At the same time, however, Miss Tina is beginning to be individualised and the collective identity of the Misses Bordereau to be dissolved. She, too, now acts largely as a mediator between her aunt and the narrator, neutral in so far as her allegiance is as yet ambiguous. The narrator consequently works on her in order to win her over to his side and tip the balance of contending interests in his favour. Yet this turns out not to be as easy as he thought, being a matter not solely of emotions, since Miss Tina, for whose benefit such a high rent is charged, can be said to be tied to another interest. At first this financial interest is represented by the aunt, and seems imposed only on her niece, who professes to be disinterested. Were it only for emotions, it would at a certain point seem conceivable that poor Tina, swayed by the narrator's deceitful courtship and oppressed by her aunt's domination, might side with the former. Yet even then her feelings remain anchored through fear on the side of her aunt, and the balance is maintained.

Even when there is talk of conspiracy, the 'law of three' is carefully observed, and underlined moreover by an allusion made to it by the narrator. After confessing to Tina that he had given her a false name and also 'been a party' to the letter John Cumnor sent them some months ago, Miss Tina exclaims:

> 'So it was a regular plot – a kind of conspiracy?'
> 'Oh a conspiracy – we were only two,' I replied, leaving out of course Mrs Prest. (p. 112)

At that time, he claims, it was another trio, and a trio only: John Cumnor, himself and the Misses Bordereau, again combined to the single addressee of their letter. Mrs Prest, at that early stage, should be counted out.

Taking the Misses Bordereau sometimes as a collective and sometimes as two separate individuals is not a mere move of convenience on the analyst's part in an attempt to force the facts into his theory. The two ways of counting reflect an attitude in the narrator's mind, for whom the two ladies become differentiated only later in the plot. Moreover, Olrik reports a minor law which accounts exactly for such a case: the 'law of twins'.[4] This law concerns the event of two different characters appearing in the same role, mostly one of subordinate agents, as for instance child victims in Greek and Roman myths, for which Romulus and Remus may serve as paradigm; or else the duplication of an agent without a complication of the plot, as with the two Walkyries. Yet such minor twin agents may become major actors during the development of the drama, and if they do, will be polarised into mutual opponents, each striving to eliminate the other. This polarisation is itself a result of 'the great law of antithesis',[5] which divides characters into antagonists to make dramatic action possible.

In *The Aspern Papers* we have an illustration of the 'law of twins'

and its development into a new antithesis. But there is a drawn-out
intermediary stage when Miss Tina has already become an agent in
her own right, completing a trio after Mrs Prest's departure,
without as yet turning into a clear opponent to her former twin. In
her mediating role she is 'neutral', which after a twinship, however,
is already a step towards antagonism.

With the death of her aunt the place of an opponent to the
narrator has become vacant, and the niece is now slowly shifting her
position so as to fill it. Thus she is on the one hand fulfilling the
characteristic of the twin who appears in the same role as another
agent, but this time a main actor, as on the other hand she conforms
to the pattern of antagonism and usurpation predicted for twins
rising in status. The death of her former twin is a precondition of her
own autonomy as an agent in the role of chief antagonist to the
narrator.

The resulting set of three includes as its third term the titular
papers, of whose existence we are for the first time positively
assured. And they emerge, in a more than ironic form, to be
mediating between the two characters and their respective interests.
That they are objects rather than persons need not worry us, since
the material of Olrik's study provides many instances of dragons or
magic objects in the role of agents. At the same time we should
remember that women, in so far as they are brides or wives to the
heroes, do not usually count as agents.[6] Hence a further distinction
in this last trio would recognise two 'independent' aspects of Miss
Tina: Tina, the guardian of the papers, and Tina, the potential
bride. If the latter were to marry the narrator, the guardian of the
papers would be 'overcome' and the antagonism be dissolved. If on
the other hand she were to be rejected and forced to merge with the
warden of the papers, the narrator's case would be lost for good. We
shall see later what roles these alternatives play.

Another of Olrik's laws is the 'law of two to a scene',[7] which, since
we discussed the 'law of three' in the context of a trio of
actors, is singularly relevant. It certainly confirms our observation
that Miss Tina does not always 'count', depending on whether she is
a twin or an agent, for there are indeed scenes where three are
present. It further implies that a person does not qualify as an agent
unless implicated in the action.[8] In the scene where the little
portrait of Aspern is brought out, Tina is present as that insignificant third person. The narrator and the old lady seem to agree
on who are the main actors in this drama, for the aunt never misses a

chance to stress her niece's insignificance and to prevent her from participating. They have been discussing the little painting, and following a silence during which Juliana is being wheeled towards her bedroom, the narrator announces that he 'should bring her an opinion about the little picture'.

'The little picture?' Miss Tina asked in surprise.
'What do *you* know about it, my dear?' the old woman demanded.
'You needn't mind. I've fixed my price.'   (p. 100)

As long as the old Miss Bordereau is alive, she is the protagonist and does not tolerate her niece's interference.

It looks rather as if both the protagonists needed to assert their roles by positive emphasis, and both at the cost of Miss Tina who is present against the 'law', as it were, of 'two to a scene'. Although she is reduced almost to the menial status of the narrator's 'man' or the servant Olimpia, a gesture of reinforced aggression towards her seems to suit the two main agents. Just when their talk about the portrait has seemingly come to an end, the following apparently unimportant incident takes place – unimportant for the main action and according to the narrator's presentation: 'Miss Tina laid her hands on the back of the wheeled chair and began to push, but I begged her to let me take her place' (p. 99).

The little dialogue is not even worth reporting in direct speech, not forming part of the main plot evolving between the narrator and the old woman. But the incident complements, for symmetry, the latter's gesture of putting down Tina and of keeping her out of the action. Any other action that might be said to go on between the narrator and Tina during this scene – an exchange of significant looks, his at the furniture in search of the papers' possible hiding place, hers at his glances – occurs only when Juliana has finished and is, at least in the narrative, no longer present although still in the room. But since, as we are told in the next chapter, she cannot see, she is thus automatically excluded from this action composed of looks.

Later on the narrator and Tina, now properly 'two to a scene', are conversing and he has asked her an important question about the papers. 'She was going to answer, but at that moment the doctor came in . . .' (p. 106). It is as if by common decency she had to stop the conversation once a more important agent entered, an agent of the main plot. The narrator seems to accept and even endorse this convention, however much he may be vexed to forfeit his answer. For when his own servant peeps over the doctor's shoulder at the sick *padrona*, the narrator 'motioned him away the more instantly that the sight of his prying face reminded me how little I myself had to do there' (p. 106). In turn he is reinforced in his belief by the attitude of the doctor himself: 'the sharp way the little doctor eyed me, his air of taking me for a rival who had the field before him' (p. 106). Whatever the conventions of common politeness in the face of grief, the 'field' is reserved for protagonists; and the one main part being filled by the ailing Juliana, others must take it in turns for the second.

We see this pattern repeated in the same chapter, again with the narrator yielding his place to another. He has revealed his true identity to Tina, and has just assured her that it does not much matter whether she promises or not to deceive her aunt.

> Nothing is more possible than that she wouldn't have contested this even hadn't she been diverted by our seeing the doctor's gondola shoot into the little canal and approach the house. . . . We looked down at him while he disembarked and then went back into the sala to meet him. When he came up, however, I naturally left Miss Tina to go off with him alone . . . (p. 114)

He might simply have interpreted her silence in terms of their colloquy, as a deliberate and meaningful refusal to answer, as indeed he infers anyway. But he is at the same time a keen observer of the 'field' and never loses sight of the main drama which features Juliana, besides taking the conventions of such action for granted. Again it can hardly be put down to simple respect of the sick, since he does not, as might befit a lodger, sit quietly at the back of the sickroom, ready to help if he were needed. Both times he leaves the scene properly, once to go down to the garden, the other to take a walk on the Piazza. It is not given to our narrator to assume the role of a mere walker-on on any stage, nor indeed to take a real part in any drama other than his own obsession, the Aspern papers. The pending life of Juliana is important only in as much as it reflects on this concern of his own, since in the event of her death he would have to face a new opponent, the inheritor of the papers.

In the climactic scene of his prowling in Juliana's drawingroom while she is supposed to be on her deathbed, his shameful discovery again takes place only between the two of them. It is this time mainly a matter of extraordinary glances, memorable all the more for hers who is said to be blind; and the only spoken line is her exclamation: 'Ah you publishing scoundrel!' (p. 118). Their intermezzo has already ended by the time she collapses into the arms of Tina, who is there ready to catch her. Although the latter is not seen (or said) to have been present during the preceding scene, it is afterwards a source of anxiety for the narrator that she might have been witness to his shame. The gravity, perhaps, would lie in the violation of the 'law of two to a scene' more than in his intrinsic regret, for which Tina's presence would not·be essential.

Another law is illustrated by this crucial act in the drama: the 'law of the plasticity of main situations'.[9] The epic drama is said by Olrik to culminate in one or more main situations which stand out for their plastic quality. This climax, in *The Aspern Papers*, is special for its visual character and the almost total absence of dialogue.[10] Hence the dramatic intensity is enhanced, for both reader and narrator, through the presupposition of Juliana's blindness. For the first and only time she reveals her eyes, and the shock makes the narrator paint her fearful picture rather than narrate her action:

> . . . her hands were raised, she had lifted the everlasting curtain that covered half her face, and for the first, the last, the only time I beheld her extraordinary eyes. They glared at me; they were like the sudden drench, for a caught burglar, of a flood of gaslight; they made me horribly ashamed. (p. 118)

Through the repeated use of the past participle our view is arrested in the final state of a completed movement; and the verbs in indicative form are, semantically if not syntactically, 'stative' rather than 'active' and imply a certain duration.[11] And the emphasis is on the impression which engraves itself in the narrator's memory:

> I never shall forget her strange little bent white tottering figure, with its lifted head, her attitude, her expression; neither shall I forget the tone in which as I turned, looking at her, she hissed out passionately, furiously:
> 'Ah you publishing scoundrel!' (p. 118)

While the usual incidents of this story register themselves through the narrator's rational consciousness and thus are easy to translate into an epic dimension and to paraphrase in terms of content, these crucial moments are direct imprints on his senses, producing what Freud calls eidetic and acoustic memories.[12] They present themselves like a sequence of stills (visual and aural), with the narrative continuity missing: '. . . . the next thing I knew she had fallen back with a quick spasm, as if death had descended on her, into Miss Tina's arms' (p. 118). Miss Tina had not come in, so far as he was aware; she was simply there for this last dramatic portrait. It is the 'impression I made upon her' (p. 120) that haunts him as his humiliation, as well as the acoustic verdict which lingers in his ear on his subsequent journey. The entire scene is a 'midnight monstrosity' (p. 120) – a nominal entity rather than a sequence of dramatic events.

The 'law of beginning and end'[13] lets us expect a continuation after this climax, an ebbing out after the storm. The pace of Chapter Nine has changed, partly of course owing to the narrator's temporary meekness and his stalling of the main plot by his brief absence from Venice. The final scenes with Miss Tina, however, although crucial with regard to the Aspern papers, never again achieve the dramatic intensity of the previous acts with Juliana still in the lead.

The question of main parts, as well as those relating to the 'law of topweight and sternweight'[14] and the 'law of epic single strand',[15] begin to pose problems for our interpretation. The former of these laws recognises two different hierarchies, with the 'top-weight' attaching to the person of highest rank who would be found in the first place, say, at a dinner-table or in a sequence of repeated events (the eldest son, for example). The last place, which goes to the person of least rank in the former hierarchy, designates, however, epic precedence and marks the hero (the youngest son, for example). I shall leave the discussion of the hero of *The Aspern Papers* till later, when the whole status of its epic character will be assessed. The 'law of epic single strand' also begs the question, since we pointed more than once to subsidiary plots, mostly involving the minor of the twins, Miss Tina. But about the 'highest law of folk literature',[16] which rules the concentration on a protagonist, there is no doubt: our narrator is always at the centre of (narrative) events.

I shall conclude this chapter by adding the last of Olrik's observations about folktales, namely that attributes and character qualities have value only if they are expressed as action.[17] Thus

Cinderella would not be described as good, pretty and unhappy, but be shown to scrub the floor, to be given but scraps of food and to be kind to other creatures. This law we see frequently transgressed by the narrator of *The Aspern Papers*.

3 The narrative

This last observation in Chapter 2 leads us straight to the main point, namely that we have been discussing the tale of the narrator rather than the novel by Henry James. It is to his story that Olrik's laws make an interesting contribution, and my contention is that it is the narrator himself who has a vested interest in presenting his story in the true form of a folktale. That is to say, the conformity does not demonstrate the possibility of generalising these laws from the anonymous and collective production of folk literature to the writing of an author pertaining to our literary tradition.

In so far as the narrator thinks he is constructing a single-stranded plot it does correspond to the basic plot of the folktale.[1] This may be summarised as the tale of a hero who sets out to liberate a princess captured by a dragon, or locked up by a villainous father who submits all her suitors to a series of monstrous tests. As a reward for his noble motives he may at the end of his troubles expect, according to the tradition, to marry the princess and inherit her father's throne. The fact of marriage is important, for its implication is that the jealous father has kept the beauty hidden without making 'proper' use of her, since beautiful princesses are there to be given away in marriage – and literary documents to editors and critics who will make the consummation fruitful.

The narrator starts out with noble intentions – or so he would have us believe:

> It isn't for myself, or that I should want them at any cost to any one else. It's simply that they would be of such immense interest to the public, such immeasurable importance as a contribution to Jeffrey Aspern's history.   (p. 82)

The dragon, needless to say, is exemplified by the Misses Bordereau, more than once referred to as 'witches' (for example, p. 10). In particular, Juliana is the principal adversary, not only keeping the papers locked away, but giving the world reason to believe that she

22

might burn them. The fact that she even tries to pass off the 'ugly sister', the niece, to the narrator for marriage in order to distract him from the real prize, corresponds perfectly to a variant of the basic plot.[2] Swan Lake and Cinderella come to mind at once, where the hero is tempted into forgetting the disinterested part of his mission and taking his reward without having accomplished heroic deeds. Our hero is briefly tempted, not because he loses sight of his real purpose, but because he considers that marriage to the 'ugly' one would give him better access to her sister—an incestuous proposition for which he seems duly punished when the ugly sister kills the beauty.

What we have done with the help of Olrik's laws is to isolate as much as possible the facts of the plot, or what is commonly understood as the actional content. It is what Barthes rightly says is translatable or is reducible,[3] and which of course has made it possible for folklorists to reconstruct the 'basic' plot of a given cultural tradition, if not indeed of 'all' tales. But while the narration plays a minimal role in folk literature and thus makes the folklorists' reductive analysis fruitful, this is less true of the written literature of our culture and decreasingly so with its growing modernity. Thus there are clearly two scenes of action in the narrator's story, the one represented in the narrative and the one it supposedly refers to but which is not congruent with its representation. This is why Barthes's 'Introduction à l'analyse structurale des récits' leaves us with the feeling of a great gap in the middle, trying as it does to 'encompass the whole range of written narrative'[4] from folktale to Philippe Sollers.

The motivated form of narration of the narrator has its own share in the plot as we, the readers, see it, since he is our sole informant, standing between us and 'the author' or 'the truth'. We happen to know that we are not in front of a simple tale which, if there were no more to it, the author might have given us 'straight'. Which is to say that we approach *The Aspern Papers* with certain expectations and the presupposition of a literary history. This is why I call this first level of plot the story which is truly the narrator's, and it is this only which happens to fall almost perfectly within Olrik's scheme. For us, readers of Henry James, it is only the beginning.

The existing convention of the 'basic plot' contains a distribution of values which is taken for granted, namely that the hero is good, the dragon bad, and the prize worth having and legitimately to be had by the hero. These values are originally based, of course, on the demonstration of these attributes through 'action', as Olrik points out; but with the diachrony of a tradition they have also become part of the structure of expectations. With the help of this archetypal plot the narrator hopes to lure the reader into accepting just these values for his own story and make him sympathise with his quest and his misfortune. Since he is in fact an unsuccessful hero, overpowered by the cunning of witches, we ought to regard his tale as tragic: the 'goody' beaten, the 'baddies' triumphant and the precious beauty mercilessly killed.

The detective-reader's[5] work begins precisely here; so far he has let himself be carried along effortlessly, but now he starts to question the readymade values that were slipped in from the beginning. Is our hero indeed good? Is his enterprise noble? Are the two ladies really villainous or do they perhaps have a right to privacy and to their insistence on withholding the papers? But how, since there is no authorial voice, no voice of truth other than the 'hermeneutic',[6] are we to arrive at a different 'truth'? We may say that the story is only the narrator's and that there is also a novel by James, but where are his voice and his word? Though the two 'authors' are not, their two texts are absolutely identical.

Henry James's commentary on the narrator's tale resides in the wide space between the narrator's first-person voice and the title and authorship of the novel. There is the space of irony, constituted by James's verbatim quotation of the narrator's account, out of which we read his novel.

I shall proceed to do so before I comment further on this second *lecture* which, for the sake of exposition, I have thus separated from the primary reading of the plot, of the narrator's pseudo-folktale.

We quoted above the narrator's advertisement of his noble ends, yet he is clearly not as disinterested as he claims in that passage to Miss Tina (and the reader), for he is guided largely by personal ambition. If he is to discover yet some other documents about Aspern, it is as much a feather in his cap of literary editor and historian as a tribute to the poet, particularly since he suspects that these papers may reveal some 'dark spots' (p. 7) in Aspern's character, his 'bad treatment' (p. 7) of his mistress.

> The world, as I say, had recognised Jeffrey Aspern, but Cumnor and I had recognised him most. The multitude to-day flocked to his temple, but of that temple he and I regarded ourselves as the appointed ministers. (p. 6)

His aim can no longer be to promote the poet's esteem, but only to establish more clearly the priesthood of himself and Cumnor. His friend, Mrs Prest, appropriately calls his interest in his 'possible spoils a fine case of monomania' (p. 5). We believe in this 'attribute', however, owing to the narrator's constant demonstration of it, rather than because of her simple naming; and his expression here, of comparative recognition, may serve as just one example of his mania.

That he is historian or biographer rather than literary critic he proves beyond question and despite his repeated profession of literary interest. He leaves no doubt about his priorities: 'There was a profession in the poem – I hope not just for the phrase – that he had come back for her [Juliana's] sake' (p. 47). The possibility that a reference in the poem might be 'just for the phrase', that is to say, might be there 'just' for poetic reasons and not because it is 'true', fills him with dread; for the poem serves him as a document of the poet's life. What if you could not rely on the poem's speaking the truth?

Yet he has no doubt that his quest is a virtuous one, so much so, in fact, that he is not even selfconscious about the means he is prepared to use. The noble end apparently justifies 'ingratiating diplomatic arts', such as 'hypocrisy' and 'duplicity'; and 'there's no baseness I wouldn't commit for Jeffrey Aspern's sake' (p. 12). Juliana's prodigious age gives him positive hope: 'She would die next week, she would die to-morrow – then I could pounce on her possessions and ransack her drawers' (p. 24). If his hope became true, it would hardly make for great heroic deeds in the liberation of the precious papers, but thanks to the suffering yet in store for him he succeeds in upholding residual notions of trial and heroism.

These are also positively reinforced by the villainous character he projects of the Misses Bordereau, which we may scrutinise more closely. Our first introduction to the two ladies is through Mrs Prest's impression of them, which incidentally reflects as much on her own character as on theirs:

> She herself had been established in Venice some fifteen years and had done a great deal of good there; but the circle of her benevolence had never embraced the two shy, mysterious and, as was somehow supposed, scarcely respectable Americans – they were believed to have lost in their long exile all national quality, besides being as their name implied of some remoter French

affiliation – who asked no favours and desired no attention. (pp. 3–4)

Since the narrator is a virtual stranger in Venice we take this praise of Mrs Prest's charitable activity to be her own, repeated here by the narrator. As regards the Misses Bordereau, both Mrs Prest and the narrator take shelter behind what is 'somehow supposed' and is 'believed'. For Mrs Prest had once 'made an attempt to see them', but had only got as far as meeting the niece, and hence knows nothing about Juliana. 'She had heard Miss Bordereau was ill and had a suspicion she was in want . . . ' (p. 4). The channels of such information are not described in more detail and must be the prevalent opinions, prejudices and rumours among the American contingent in Venice, and for the rest the rationalisation of Mrs Prest's curiosity in want of a pretext for a visit. Yet the allegations expressed are serious, considering that our minds are 'blank' and unbiased, as must have been the narrator's when first confronted with them. Of him we have to admit, however, that he had ample opportunity to revise this information in the light of subsequent experience, since his narrative is a retrospective account. But he makes no attempt to correct any of these generally held ideas, and on the contrary uses them to back up his own and as an authorisation for subjecting the unwitting reader to the same bias.

The underlying presupposition of the general belief is that the loss of national – that is, American – quality is the loss of quality *tout court* since it implies 'scarce respectability'. And 'besides', that is, disregarding even this decline in quality, they have 'some remoter French affiliation' which their name betrays. The lack of an American name is the lack of American national quality, and what little they have left since they are nevertheless Americans they have squandered in too long an absence from the mother soil. Although they are only 'somehow supposed' and 'believed', it is to all intents and purposes enough to make them so, since the narrator refuses to intervene on their behalf. We gather that he subscribes to this popular truth (popular no doubt amongst the Americans in Venice), and we later have it confirmed in a different context, the prime reason for the narrator's admiration of the poet Aspern: 'His own country after all had had most of his life, and his muse, as they said at that time, was essentially American. That was originally what I had prized him for . . .' (p. 50). Patriotism – or national chauvinism – is obviously a virtue in the narrator's system of values.

It helps at any rate to supply in wondrous ways the missing links for the final assessment of the Misses Bordereau. The *palazzo* they inhabit is deemed, by Mrs Prest, 'more Dutch than Italian', and 'as negative – considering *where* it is – as a Protestant Sunday' (p. 10). So bad is it indeed that people, although they might easily pass there on foot, scarcely ever do so; and she arrives magnificently at her conclusion: 'Perhaps the people are afraid of the Misses Bordereau. I dare say they have the reputation of witches' (p. 10). Again the narrator fails to intervene, 'given up' as he is to 'two other reflections' (p. 10). The second of these turns out to be of major importance and will concern us again.

All that remains to be said of this episode is that this is what serves as the basis for our tale of a self-appointed hero and his enemies, but that we have statements rather than dramatic actions expressing their attributes. The narrator is to take up the suggestion of witches later, spontaneously and unprompted, and it is likely that the 'docile reader',[7] prepared here for a subliminally effective symbolic, will follow his narrating mentor along the same undercurrent of thought. This is the vested interest of the narrator, to present his story as an archetypal folktale of heroes and villains, and hence he spends the first few pages establishing his categories accordingly.

Besides the references to witches we find complementary features designed to endear the narrator to his reader and assure the fact that he is the hero. Thus in his opening sentences he pays a handsome tribute to his friend Mrs Prest, claiming that 'it was she who found the short cut and loosed the Gordian knot': ' . . . without her in truth I should have made but little advance, for the fruitful idea in the whole business dropped from her friendly lips' (p. 3). Of himself he bashfully says: 'I was beating about the bush, trying to be ingenious . . .' (p. 3). This surely is charming, and together with the acknowledgement of his debt is bound to create an impression of honesty and truth which invites the trust of the reader. Furthermore, we are soon presented with 'some definite facts' (p. 3) brought from England and concerning the Misses Bordereau, which also cannot but inspire confidence. That these 'facts' are later reclaimed as mere hopes, and indeed suspended until Miss Tina confirms them again, little concerns him now, for his real purpose is to secure the reader's abandonment to his tale.

It is only the docile reader, however, who will oblige him, while the obstreperous one finds ample ground for suspicion. The compliment to Mrs Prest, for instance, is mere lip-service, embedded as it is in a soft and engulfing prejudice disguised as a general truth: 'It is not supposed easy for women to rise to the large free view of anything, anything to be done' (p. 3). Again he does not contradict the generalisation, citing only an exception which is surprising and hence confirms the rule to which he subscribes. Besides not rising to a large free view – *the* large free view – of anything, positive action is not a female strength. Activity is a male prerogative, while the passive typifies the female, so that it is only in character that the fruitful idea 'drops' from Mrs Prest's lips, is '[thrown] off . . . with singular serenity' (p. 3) which practically implies how unaware she must be of its importance, having chanced upon it rather than actively discovered it.

The reader with hindsight might further suspect that the tribute to Mrs Prest is also an elaborate ploy on the narrator's part to unload responsibility on to her in anticipation of a 'final reckoning': it was she, after all, who sowed the seed of his undoing. Adam had done it before, blaming Eve for the bright idea of eating an apple from the tree of knowledge; and if we wonder who, if not the Lord, would take the narrator to task, the reader might not be the last to do so. (One might of course also suggest that the narrator's account was prompted by his conscience, acquired after the event and necessitating a self-justification. But this argument leads us far out of the text and into the domain of Lady Macbeth's children.[8])

Whatever Mrs Prest's share in the matter, the narrator adds his own substantial contribution and transforms her idea according to his own mode of operation. He has been searching for a 'combination of arts' (p. 3) through which to become acquainted with the Misses Bordereau, and her less than bold proposal, 'simply make them take you in on the footing of a lodger' (p. 3), becomes in his own words: ' . . . that the way to become an acquaintance was first to become an intimate' (p. 3). This, in the common order of things, is the wrong way round, since to be an 'intimate' involves a higher degree of intimacy than to be an acquaintance and only follows the latter, if at all, after some time. This may simply seem odd at first, and a peculiar lapse from 'inmate', which is after all the core of Mrs Prest's suggestion and one which he successfully, that is, without slipping, repeats elsewhere (p. 11). But the slip has true Freudian significance, since on second reading we discover that his involuntary prophecy is absolutely accurate. Thoughts of a mock courtship of the not-yet-known niece indeed form his original plan.

To phrase it then as a recession from such intimacy to acquaintance foreshadows the dire progression of their relations.

His prejudice against women is important enough, seeing that his business is largely with them. He thus takes it for granted with due contempt that Juliana did not appreciate the poetic genius of Aspern but fell for his handsome face. Aspern himself was 'not a woman's poet' (p. 7), the narrator claims for whatever reasons, and his conspicuous success with them can only have been due to the beguiling charm of his voice, to which they were spellbound like the Maenads to Orpheus's (p. 7). Yet while these women earn the narrator's contempt for their lack of artistic appreciation, he seems unaware of exhibiting precisely the same. While they, according to him, needed the handsome incarnation to 'fling' themselves at, required 'the man's own voice [to be] mingled with his song' (p. 7) which otherwise they could not hear, he, the appointed minister, regrets that 'we had not been able to look into a single pair of eyes into which his had looked or to feel a transmitted contact in any aged hand that his had touched' (p. 8). He is, in other words, after the pressure of the hand and the impressions of the eyes of the great man, while all the traces of his literary genius are before him in the collected works. This hero-worship reaches its peak once the narrator knows himself in the actual footsteps of the adored master. He trembles at the sight of the aged Juliana, not for any sympathy with her person (his wish for Juliana's death follows immediately), but for the profit accruing to him in his mimicry of Aspern:

> They come back to me now almost with the palpitation they caused, the successive states marking my consciousness that as the door of the room closed behind me I was really face to face with the Juliana of some of Aspern's most exquisite and most renowned lyrics . . . as she sat there before me my heart beat as fast as if the miracle of resurrection had taken place for my benefit. Her presence seemed somehow to contain and express his own, and I felt nearer to him at that first moment of seeing her than I ever had been before or ever have been since.   (p. 23)

Never on reading his divine lyrics had he ever felt so close to the poet as when he stood face to face with his aged mistress. Proud of his adoration he calls his associate Cumnor a 'fellow worshipper' (p. 6), and as one of the first two disciples embarks on a holy pilgrimage. He likes to imagine himself in the master's place and to re-experience parts of his life: '. . . it struck me that [Aspern] had been kinder and more considerate than in his place – if I could imagine myself in any such box – I should have found the trick of' (p. 7). Modest disclaimer aside, he obviously *can* imagine, and it makes his heart beat as he 'had known it to do in dentists' parlours' (p. 16). 'The old lady's voice was very thin and weak, but it had an agreeable, cultivated murmur and there was wonder in the thought that that individual note had been in Jeffrey Aspern's ear' (p. 25). Rather than identify with her who had known Aspern as he would have liked to, he identifies with the poet and tries to derive the latter's emotions from his former mistress. Despite her age 'I felt an irresistible desire to hold in my own for a moment the hand Jeffrey Aspern had pressed' (p. 30).

The culmination of this self-aggrandisement is reached no doubt in his diabolical plan to emulate the Aspern–Juliana affair by a fake courtship of Juliana's niece.[9] Very probably he is not fully aware of the neat pattern of his idea, since consciously he employs it as a stratagem for obtaining the papers. But in the light of his secret re-enactment of Aspern's life it assumes a special significance. The plan to court Miss Tina is conceived in cold blood, before he has even set eyes on her. Nor has he any illusion that it might be an affair of the heart, since Mrs Prest has already given him a most unflattering description of her: 'The niece . . . was of minor antiquity, and the conjecture was risked that she was only a grand-niece' (p. 6). If she is 'only' a grand-niece her value as a direct 'descendant' of Aspern obviously goes down, although it would make her a younger and more suitable candidate for courtship. But this latter advantage is callously played down, and instead of being presented as younger she is simply 'of minor antiquity'. The presupposition of her unattractiveness is so strong that the narrator consistently applies this negative way of presentation to her. It is as if from the expected worst she falls ever so slightly short:

> Her face was not young, but it was candid; it was not fresh, but it was clear. She had large eyes which were not bright, and a great deal of hair which was not 'dressed', and long fine hands which were – possibly – not clean.   (p. 17)

The negative foregrounding of all the niece does not have, emphasised by the repetition of 'not', prevents even her positive qualities from having a redeeming effect, and the impression of absences (of merits) prevails. 'Large eyes' and 'a great deal of hair' would usually be terms of the highest praise of a woman, but here the largeness of her eyes only increases their fault of not being bright, just as the great deal of 'undressed' hair seems worse than a lesser amount of it. Again the information is carried by the negative predicates 'not bright' and 'not dressed' (there is no comma after 'eyes' nor after 'hair'), while the positive qualities are only nominalised. That this form of portraying her verges on malice is obvious with the last remark where, carried away by his rhetorical pattern of negatives and antitheses, he invents a gratuitous and purely hypothetical derogatory attribute for want of a real one concerning her 'long fine hands': 'which were – possibly – not clean'.

Yet despite his cynical view of Tina he musters enough poetic rhetoric to create the impression of a real infatuation for the reader, while maintaining towards her a carefully studied ambivalence which suffices to mislead her into hope. 'I used to look out for her hopefully as I crossed the sala in my comings and goings, but I was not rewarded with a glimpse of the tail of her dress' (p. 40). We might indeed expect a shy but ardent lover to have spoken those words, had we not been briefed. But the following highly romantic passage, superficially provoked by 'the fragrant darkness' and 'the breath of the garden', also gives us a deeper clue to his scheme:

> It was delicious – just such an air as must have trembled with Romeo's vows when he stood among the thick flowers and raised his arms to his mistress's balcony. I looked at the windows of the palace to see if by chance the example of Verona – Verona being not far off – had been followed; but everything was dim, as usual, and everything was still.   (p. 52)

The invocation of the most classic romantic lover is not due to the geographical proximity of Verona, which at most adds to a mood already conjured. It is the poetic father of Romeo, however, who provides the next associative link to Aspern – the two having already been compared, and Shakespeare's sonnets been found 'scarcely more divine' (p. 48) than Aspern's 'less ambiguous' ones. Hence it comes naturally that the latter's Juliet appears – in the narrative if not at the window: 'Juliana might on the summer nights of her youth have murmured down from open windows at Jeffrey Aspern . . . ' (p. 53). Then another link, on the rhetorical surface

incongruous, completes his thought: 'but Miss Tina was not a poet's
mistress any more than I was a poet' (p. 53). He and Tina are joined
as a pair of common lovers only by contiguity, Tina being Juliana's
niece, the narrator the master's first disciple. Aspern is the strongest
and most complex link in this little matrix, linked both to
Shakespeare, divine poet, and to Romeo, romantic lover. The
rhetorical matrix leaves only one possibility of fitting in the
narrator, namely as a lover. Miss Tina, once again, is accommodated on the basis of a negative definition, as not being a poet's
mistress, and hence becomes the partner to the only non-poet.

What this pattern betrays, once we recognise the association of
lovers as spurious, is again the hero-identification of the narrator
and his desire to align himself with Aspern. Elsewhere he takes
solace from

> the revived immortal face – in which all his genius shone – of the
> great poet who was my prompter. I had invoked him and he had
> come; he hovered before me half the time; it was as if his bright
> ghost had returned to earth to assure me he regarded the affair as
> his own no less than as mine and that we should see it fraternally
> and fondly to a conclusion.   (p. 42)

This 'mystic companionship' (p. 43) sounds like some literary
spiritualism, although the epithet is of the narrator's choosing, who
warms his 'literary heart' (p. 42) by it. He continues to deceive
himself about his own activity and its literary status:

> My eccentric private errand became a part of the general
> romance and the general glory – I felt even a mystic compan-
> ionship, a moral fraternity with all those who in the past had been
> in the service of art. They had worked for beauty, for a devotion;
> and what else was I doing?   (p. 43)

What indeed. His eccentric errand is certainly in the service of
romance and glory – the personal glory he strives after, but hardly
in the service of art and beauty. His devotion to parallel patterns,
however, is still not exhausted, for, as he and Tina are to mirror the
great couple, so their servants on yet another platform are to do the
same:

> I should have been glad if [my servant] had fallen in love with

Miss Bordereau's maid or, failing this, had taken her in aversion: either event might have brought about some catastrophe, and a catastrophe might have led to some parley . . . . But . . . I afterwards learned that Pasquale's affections were fixed upon an object that made him heedless of other women.   (p. 41)

This last romance was designed for the satisfaction of the manipulator rather than for those involved, and a catastrophe might serve as well as a success. And as he thinks that love affairs – one's own as well as others' – are there to be fitted into schemes and matrices, so he betrays his conviction that women are paradigmatic alternatives to objects. A parallel unasked for by the narrator begins to emerge: Pasquale's affections are 'fixed upon an object that [makes] him heedless of other women', just as the narrator's are fixed upon the papers and make him have no scruples about virtually trampling over an old lady and her unfortunate niece. The fact that Pasquale's 'object' of affection turns out to be a woman in the flesh reflects the more ironically on the narrator's underlying design on the papers instead of Miss Tina, and its degree of obsession which makes him project it into others and into his rhetoric.

This mode of displaced object choice characterises the narrator throughout, both on the level of dramatic action and that of his narrative expression. We promised above to return to one of the narrator's reflections. It occurred to him at that moment that the garden of the Misses Bordereau might serve him as a pretext for becoming their lodger. His eyes simply happen to fall on it, while his mind is preoccupied with finding a feasible strategy for gaining a footing in their house, where he believes the papers to be hidden. In a psychological sense a pattern of associations is thus established, which connects the papers, the house and especially the garden. It is transformed into a metaphorical relation, since the papers can never be mentioned to the Misses Bordereau as the real reason, and the pretext of the lodgings is substituted. At least this is what the narrator holds necessary: 'The old woman won't have her relics and tokens so much as spoken of . . .' (p. 11). But in order to bury the unnameable signified still more securely, the focus is displaced from the house on to the garden which, as an 'objective correlative' to his intention, is appropriately attached to the house – linked, that is, through physical contiguity. How much conscious awareness may be attributed to the narrator again is uncertain; but while the two levels of intention and 'correlative' are part of the dramatic content, the metonymic displacement feeds into his narrative account of it, which we assume to be marked also by the expression of unconscious elements. His tale concentrates, as we have said, on the primary 'single-stranded' plot, while the discourse appears unselfconscious. Reference henceforth is made only to the 'objective correlative': 'The place was a garden and apparently attached to the house. I suddenly felt that so attached it gave me my pretext' (p. 11). He 'suddenly felt' the suitability of the garden rather than constructing the complex of metaphoric relations.

The displaced object thus fixed, it becomes endowed with the obsession due to the papers: 'I must work the garden – I must work the garden . . .' (p. 15). For the reader, who conversely substitutes the papers again for the pretext inserted by the narrator, the ensuing dialogues become more telling. The narrator's first plea is addressed to Miss Tina:

> 'The garden, the garden – do me the pleasure to tell me if it's yours!'
> She stopped short, looking at me with wonder; and then, 'Nothing here is mine,' she answered . . . coldly and sadly. (p. 17)

The narrator wants to ascertain, here from Miss Tina, that they do possess the treasured papers, while she evades the question by stating roundly that she, certainly, calls nothing her own.

> 'But surely the garden belongs to the house?'
> 'Yes, but the house doesn't belong to me.' . . .
> 'Well then, would you kindly tell me to whom I must address myself? I'm afraid you'll think me horribly intrusive, but you know I *must* have a garden – upon my honour I must!'   (p. 17)

And with a 'confused alarmed look' she breaks out: 'Oh don't take it away from us; we like it ourselves!' (p. 18). It is interesting that she should feel threatened at this point, since he could hardly pick up the garden and carry it off, as he could (and would) the papers. But it is as if she responded unconsciously to his tacit intention, while she may suspect, at least, that he would be capable of evicting them from their home should he find it necessary. But all he wants at the moment is to set eyes on their precious possession: 'Now can't I look at yours?' (p. 18). He then assures her that they need a man to work their garden, that they must not let it go to waste. He would be just the man, and he promises them an abundance of flowers – so confident is he of his own fertility as a literary critic, if only he is given a chance. His literary enthusiasm spills over on to the subject of flowers: 'It's absurd if you like, for a man, but I can't live without flowers' (p. 18). We later see the same wonder and confusion in Miss Tina when she is confronted with her lodger's real purpose, his quest for the papers: 'She listened with great attention, almost in fact gaping for wonder . . . and she remarked after a moment, as in candid impartial contemplation: "How much you must want them!"' (pp. 111–12).

In his interview with Juliana the next day he continues the crusade of the garden, prefixed by an interesting Freudian signal. His own remarks are reported indirectly: 'Perhaps the other lady, the one I had had the honour of seeing the day before, would have explained to her about the garden. That was literally what had given me courage to take a step so unconventional' (p. 25). There is a sense, of course, in which this is 'literally' so, in that the garden constitutes the first concrete strategy which prompts him to action. Yet he does not lack the courage for unconventional steps either, prepared as he is to commit any 'baseness' for Aspern's sake. In another sense, then, his courage derives not literally but metaphorically from the garden – that is to say, from the bundle of papers the garden has come to stand for. While pleading frankness by confessing the 'literal' he succeeds in rooting the complicated metaphoric deception more firmly. Just so his 'word of honour' that he is a 'most respectable inoffensive person' (p. 25) is a vacuous guarantee and literal bluff, since it is worth anything only if he is, tautologically, a most honest, respectable man.

But let us continue to read the 'tenor' of the narrator's metaphoric discourse on gardens, and pay special attention to Juliana's reply to his promise:

> I would conform to any regulations, any restrictions, if they would only let me enjoy the garden . . .
> She was silent a little after I had ceased speaking; then she began: 'If you're so fond of a garden why don't you go to *terra firma*, where there are so many far better than this?'
> 'Oh it's the combination!' I answered, smiling; and then with rather a flight of fancy: 'It's the idea of a garden in the middle of the sea.'

'This isn't the middle of the sea; you can't so much as see the water.'

I stared a moment, wondering if she wished to convict me of fraud. 'Can't see the water? Why, dear madam, I can come up to the very gate in my boat.'   (p. 26)

It appears that two different conceptions of the propriety of the literary enterprise are here at odds. The dialogue quoted suggests that Juliana – a poet's mistress after all – does not find it proper, or at least needs yet to be convinced that it could be, to try to grow flowers – literary exploits – from a garden so peculiar as hers. If literary critic he be, he had far better go to *terra firma* – literature proper – which is the real soil from which such flowers come forth. What is special about her garden is its location in the middle of the sea, surrounded by abundant water and based on very little soil. The peculiarity of the literary material she owns derives from the fact that it pertains to life rather than to art and concerns Aspern as man and lover rather than the poetic voice of his poems.

The experience of life, of personal life, is inevitably what the poet draws on in order to nourish his art; but the measure is limited since the flowers cannot take root in that element alone. Even though the Aspern papers are now in an environment of sea, namely in the possession of people who value them for purely personal reasons, that water which once vitalised them can no longer be seen. The life of Aspern and the young Juliana is long gone and out of reach. For a moment he is perplexed by Juliana's shrewdness and wonders if she means to uncover his metaphoric deception – were they only talking of gardens his fear would be unfounded. With a 'flight of fancy' he hopes to win the point, arguing that he can come up to the very gate in his boat. He is unable conceptually to grasp the distinction between the garden and the sea, since the continuity of life permits him to touch the 'gate' to the past. Since he can meet a live contemporary of his adored hero, he thinks he can make contact across the past. Hence also his great attachment to 'relics', a class of objects in which he obviously also places Juliana: 'After all [the sacred relics] were under my hand – they had not escaped me yet; and they made my life continuous, in a fashion, with the illustrious life they had touched at the other end' (p. 43). As he thinks the aged Juliana to be the same as the poet's lover, so he thinks that the waters surrounding the garden are still the same as those which once irrigated it. He equates the 'cultivated murmur' of her voice with the 'individual note [that] had been in Jeffrey Aspern's ear', the hand he wants to hold in his own with 'the hand Jeffrey Aspern had pressed'. The only time a doubt arises in his mind it is deflected on to an 'objective correlative', is accommodated on the literal level of what could be metaphorical. Having just revelled in the thought of being face to face with 'the Juliana of some of Aspern's most exquisite and renowned lyrics', he continues: 'Then came a check from the perception that we weren't really face to face' – a hope for the reader that the perception might have been acute, yet only to find the narrator once more fixate on a displaced object – 'inasmuch as she had over her eyes a horrible green shade which served for her almost as a mask' (p. 23). He hovers about the real understanding, yet without ever hitting upon it properly: 'it created a presumption of some ghastly death's-head lurking behind it. The divine Juliana as a grinning skull – the vision hung there until it passed. Then it came to me that she *was* tremendously old' (pp. 23–4). But he is only distracted into relating this to his present task, and then to the hope that she might soon die and leave the papers accessible.

He is deluded in two ways: not only does he believe Aspern, the man, to incarnate the elusive singer of the poems so as to make him palpable, and the live Juliana to be identical with the inspiration of the lyrics, but he also thinks that personal identity and the permanence of 'relics' can span the lapse of time and build a bridge through which the past can be touched.

Another hint that the narrator's literary work is improper if not dangerous is reflected at the level of discourse, and we may take it as an unconscious expression since it has not been edited out: 'If I should sound that note first I should certainly spoil the game. I can arrive at my spoils only by putting her off her guard . . .' (pp. 11–12). The close association through proximity of the two senses of 'spoil' cannot be without significance and is certainly not without effect on the reader, for whom they are called to mind at the same time. It confirms the suspicion that the booty of the narrator's strife, at the very moment he can call it his 'spoils', must also be spoilt and destroyed. The same play on the double sense of this word is of course familiar from another novel by Henry James, *The Spoils of Poynton*.

But while this involuntary pun takes place on the special level of rhetoric as a part of the action (as part of a speech addressed to Mrs Prest), and thus naturally invites an analysis of discourse, the 'metaphor' of the garden has a different status. Calling it a metaphor at all is speaking metaphorically, for it is constituted, so to speak, on the level of action and events. In a figure of rhetoric a signifier is substituted for another, yet without eliminating the signified of the replaced sign which on the contrary is evoked mediately with its figuratively enriched meaning. Referring to a man as a 'lion' does not let one forget the man. But the narrator of *The Aspern Papers* substitutes one thing, the garden, for another object, the papers, in his strategy for obtaining the latter. The strategy itself appears like an actional syntagm in which the appropriate noun phrases have been exchanged. His intention, moreover, is precisely to suppress the meaning of the replaced objects rather than to confer metaphorical meaning on them. The metonymy is properly constituted on the level of such an actional syntax, in that the garden and the narrator's plan are linked by perceptional contiguity; his thoughts concentrate on the plan while his eyes happen to fall on the garden.

> The . . . idea that had come into my head was connected with a high blank wall which appeared to confine an expanse of ground on one side of the house. . . . The place was a garden and apparently attached to the house. I suddenly felt that so attached it gave me my pretext. (pp. 10–11)

Only if we regard his consciousness, at the time of action, as a 'primary historisation',[10] as a narrative structure or a discourse of perception, can an idea and a wall (the perception or 'appearance' of a wall) be 'connected'. They are drawn on to a common metonymic dimension in the sense Jakobson gives this term[11] – an axis of combination – and are contiguous only on this plane. They are brought together, of course, also on the narrative level, but at that point the account is a 'representation of events' – here the narrator's perception *then.*

However, when we as readers interpret the dialogues concerning the garden in the way we have done above, we are reactivating the suppressed signified, the papers. Unlike the addressees of the conversation, who must be ignorant of the garden's deeper significance, we as addressees of the narrator's account are reminded of the double layer of meaning. After asking Tina if she would let him rooms in their house the narrator goes on, to himself and the reader: 'I had now struck the note that translated my purpose, and I needn't reproduce the whole of the tune I played' (p. 20). We are thus quite entitled to keep the secret meaning in mind and to carry out a simultaneous translation.

Considering the preliminary dialogues about the garden as action we must of course take the Misses Bordereau's ignorance of the garden's deeper meaning into account, so that their answers could only be read literally. We cannot therefore assert that Juliana actually engages in a discourse on poetics as I suggested above. But of course we read the dialogues not only as direct speech proper, but also as speeches reported by the narrator, albeit in 'direct speech'. They are filtered through his first perception as well as his later account of them, and are embedded in the same consciousness which also holds the secret continually present. Thus the meta-phoric reading of his first interview with Juliana is a synthesis in his perception of his first historisation of the actual dialogue with the mental translation of the tune he played. It is his mental image of Juliana which can give pertinent answers in the aesthetic dispute, while the real Juliana talks only of gardens. The struggle between his imaginary perception and a rational construction of reality is evident: his suspicion that Juliana might be accusing him of fraud pertains to the imaginary, while he goes on to cover up for it realistically, that is, in terms of real gardens and the particular location of Juliana's. We do not know whether his concentrated attention allows him also to follow up his translation, and hence cannot attribute a full consciousness of this escalating aesthetic discourse to the narrator. Nor, seeing how the metaphoric complex is extended according to external and pragmatic needs (that is, in the realm of the real) can we infer that it is intended as metaphoric in this expansion. Rather, we realise that his pretext involves a temporary substitution, with no guarantee that it will 'extend'. I shall return to the problem of our reading of the dialogues in Chapter 5, which deals specifically with the narrational dimension.

It remains to show up a last grave misconception on the narrator's part, to explain his failure with his story. Certain problems were seen to arise in the context of the 'law of epic single strand', as well as with regard to determining the last set of actors and the dramatic culmination of the plot. These confusions are due to the narrator's one great blind spot, since we must not forget that it is he who moulds his story into the pre-existent form of the folktale. It is he who makes a third character disappear from the narrative when they are still on the scene and he who elects the hero and the antagonists, as it is his preoccupation which determines the polarisation. It is on that score, however, that his single-mindedness lets him down and spoils the simple tale. His purpose is so fixed, and pursued with such obsession that an emerging rival plot escapes him altogether. This second strand of drama is conceived by the Misses Bordereau, though sparked off by his own appearance on their stage.

Seeing that Juliana accepts, as it were, the role of antagonist to himself, the narrator assumes her sole purpose to be the withholding of the Aspern papers. The fact that she succumbs to the 'bribe' of his high rent he considers a triumph on his part, as it brings him a (physical) step nearer the papers. Tina's candid admission that the money is for her fails to alert him to the possibility that a different interest might be at stake for the Misses Bordereau, while he is only too glad that Tina responds to his wooing. While trying to lure the Misses Bordereau into handing over the papers by ingratiating himself with money, they in turn seem to lure him into marriage by dangling the papers in front of his nose.

Juliana dead, her interest remains unprotected, so that the division of Tina into Juliana's successor and into the 'bride', object of exchange, is instituted. Miss Tina is bound to the 'last will' of her aunt, although its formulation and interpretation are of her own making. The dying Juliana 'could only make signs' (p. 129) after her midnight shock, but had tried apparently to communicate something to Tina. In desperation on seeing the narrator ready to leave Venice, Tina once more tries to hold him with the papers, though referring herself as always to her aunt:

> 'She wanted to say something to me – the last day – something very particular. But she couldn't.'
> 'Something very particular?'
> 'Something more about the papers.'
> 'And did you guess – have you any idea?'
> 'No, I've tried to think – but I don't know. I've thought all kinds of things.'
> 'As for instance?'
> 'Well, that if you were a relation it would be different.' (pp. 132–3)

It is thus a matter of whose plot we consider, whether Tina is first and foremost a 'bride' or the guardian of the papers. In her plot the narrator is the antagonist to her marriage interest, and the papers serve as a mediating object, while he is contending with the heiress of the papers, considering the bride as a mediator who could pacify the former.

One may even say that there are three interests, one for each protagonist, though Juliana's affects both the others' more directly and in fact interlocks them. She 'lives' on the papers (p. 132), hence cannot give them away until after her death, at which point her responsibility for her niece must also be handed on. The niece, having her own emotional interest, which coincides with her aunt's responsibility, seems to have sufficiently grasped the usefulness of the papers to tie them closely to her own aim even after her aunt's death, so that the narrator will either take both her and the papers or get neither. It thus transpires that if anyone is a certain winner it is Juliana, who cannot lose either way. Her drama ends with her death, through which she is freed of all responsibility; for the narrator it ends with the destruction of the coveted papers and for Tina with the loss of a husband. Neither can be a hero in the sense of the folktale, nor can there be a single dramatic climax when more plots than one are going on at the same time, that is, when the tale is multiple-stranded.

There is 'plasticity' in the main scene of both Tina's and the narrator's respective plots, though naturally the latter's receives fuller description. Tina's realisation of her defeat is accompanied by tears, as is her last long look at the narrator in the final scene. But the narrator has to undergo a more memorable sequence of impressions and of intense embarrassment. Having had a night to think Tina's proposal over, of which he gives no explicit account, he is then 'startled' by an unforeseen observation, and he tries again to 'paint' rather than narrate:

Poor Miss Tina's sense of her failure had produced a rare alteration in her, but I had been too full of stratagems and spoils to think of that. Now I took it in; I can scarcely tell how it startled me. She stood in the middle of the room with a face of mildness bent upon me, and her look of forgiveness, of absolution, made her angelic. It beautified her; she was younger; she was not a ridiculous old woman. This trick of her expression, this magic of her spirit, transfigured her, and while I still noted it I heard a

> whisper somewhere in the depths of my conscience: 'Why not,
> after all – why not?' It seemed to me I *could* pay the price.   (pp.
> 141–2)

There is deception even in this apparently candid admission of his
corruptible mind, and it is due to a trick of *his* expression. For the
disposition to accept the 'price' of the bargain is clearly a result of
having considered it overnight, or at least having mulled it over
subconsciously. One by one he answers the objections we have
heard him raise before: that Tina is ugly, old and pathetic – 'a piece
of middle-aged female helplessness' (p. 126). It is as a consequence
of these reflections that his perception is changed, of his attempt to
make the marriage more palatable and convince himself of its
feasibility. For he has realised it as inevitable if he wants to gain
possession of the papers. Conversely, we see the magic work
backwards as soon as the papers are pronounced lost. Tina describes
their destruction, sheet by sheet:

> 'It took a long time – there were so many.' The room seemed to go
> round me as she said this and a real darkness for a moment
> descended on my eyes. When it passed Miss Tina was there still,
> but the transfiguration was over and she had changed back to a
> plain dingy elderly person.   (p. 143)

Such transformations must have abundant plasticity for the
narrator – and his painting them for the reader – as does his last view
of Tina which reminds him unpleasantly of his own so much less
dignified exit the day before:

> . . . at a venture I made a wild vague movement in consequence
> of which I found myself at the door.   (p. 135) . . . she did what
> I hadn't done when I quitted her – she paused long enough to
> give me one look. I have never forgotten it and I sometimes still
> suffer from it . . .   (p. 143)

She clearly takes the nobler part this time, apparently beyond
resentment and revenge, as she seems to accept without false pride
the sum of money he later sends her for the picture. He has not sold
the picture and sends the money perhaps pricked by his conscience.
It is hanging over his desk to remind him: 'When I look at it I can
scarcely bear my loss – I mean of the precious papers' (p. 143). The

fact that he feels it necessary to specify leads one to suspect that some other loss is also rankling in his mind – however vaguely – and that it is not the sum of money for the picture. Yet he still does not allow himself to articulate it clearly, so that it only lurks behind the signifier. To the last, and including the momentous occasion of her proposal, he insists on missing the plot of the Misses Bordereau and fails to recognise its denouement. Instead, he continues to direct his own play and to interpret Tina's part as he would have designed it:

> It was a proof of how little she supposed the idea would come to me that she should have decided to suggest it herself in that practical argumentative heroic way – with the timidity, however, so much more striking than the boldness, that her reasons appeared to come first and her feelings afterward. (p. 137)

She certainly does not put her reasons afterwards, but keeps them firmly employed in the interest of her emotions. However, he cannot see beyond his own characterisation of her, which makes her innocent, timid, and none too clever. Thus we end up with a hero not dead, but vanquished and, very possibly, without the redeeming peripeteia his tragedy might have induced.

4 Folklorists and detectives

We have seen in the preceding chapters how folkloristic analysis is concerned with a 'primary plot', constructed according to a strict grammar. But this method helped us only on the primary level of 'plot' or story with *The Aspern Papers*, the level which in Barthes's terminology articulates the hermeneutic code or invites the hermeneutic decoding by the reader; yet even this plot has been accessible only through the narrative of the narrator.

It has been pointed out that the detective story offers a singularly apt example of the hermeneutic code at its purest, of the hermeneutic in dominance.[1] Yet, the detective story itself is but a special case of the Realist convention, and before we turn to it we should consider briefly the folkloristic plot and the Realist plot in comparison.

The suspense plot, calling forth the hermeneutic of the plot, is itself a relatively recent invention, a result of Realism in fiction and the particular understanding of reality in general epistemological terms that goes with it. It requires the strong sense, so familiar to us, of time as a forward-moving vector, and the concept of causality as operating on this axis. The surface linearity of the linguistic medium can most suitably mirror the temporal sequence of events; or, it can set up a narrative linearity which deviates from that of the plot, creating the tension between *histoire* and *récit*.

The folkloristic plot, however, shows a quite different relationship to temporal sequence, reflects another experience of time. We mentioned above the role expectation plays, not only in one performance of telling and listening, but in the self-preserving structure of its actional grammar. From the structure of the grammar we infer the expectations of the audience, who do not want to be told a new anecdote but hear an old story fulfil itself once again in a satisfactory performance, to see a well-known pattern repeat itself in a new variant. The expectation, or the anticipation of a known and expected ending necessarily alters the significance of the narrative linearity of the plot. Lugowski[2] singles out what he terms, idiosyncratically, 'motivation from the back' (*Motivation von hinten*), retroactive motivation, which of course contrasts markedly with our own narrative expectation of forward or preparatory motivation (*vorbereitende Motivation*). 'It is a matter of a suspense, a torment, which itself already contains its own alleviation, and which is there in order to be alleviated' (p. 74; *my translation*). As this is true of the whole story and its known ending, so it applies to intermittent sections or events of the action. 'It is not the outcome which is determined by the premise of the action, but the individual features of the action which are determined by the outcome and its only demand: to be revealed' (p. 75; *my translation*). Evidently, this concept of retroactive motivation jars with our sense of causality and with our experience of the logic of dramatic development. And indeed it is necessary to qualify the status of this 'motivation' for us, to whom it is inextricably bound up with causality, and because we do not wish to impute to the 'folks' of folklore the actual belief that results and events motivated or caused the preceding developments which led up to them. What Lugowski is discussing, and we are concerned with, is *narrative* motivation, which however seems singularly autonomous *vis-à-vis* an experiential concept of causality.

> All individual features of the action which seem motivated in terms of 'retroactive motivation', are justified in their existence only in the light of their outcome; they are not causally grounded, as with preparatory motivation, but still justified. (p. 75; *my translation*)

Of course, internally the folk narrative is also subjected to a rudimentary recognition of temporality and logical consequence, binding its actional elements in a loosely verisimilar fashion. Yet the overall dramatic stringency derives from the outcome and the fulfilment: 'Strict "retroactive motivation" knows no direct connection between concrete elements of the narrative fiction; the connection always goes via the outcome' (p. 79; *my translation*). And, Lugowski goes on, 'in so far as today we have preparatory motivation in our blood, we can only perceive disconnectedness' (p. 79; *my translation*).

It is worth stopping at this point to compare Lugowski's findings with Propp's morphology of the folktale. Lugowski obviously goes beyond Propp's descriptive, 'scientific' morphological structuralism to interpret the forms he identifies, and to let this in turn influence how he sees them and what he sees in them. This is strictly beyond the aim stated by Propp, and which is representative of a particular kind of 'scientifically objective' structuralism, the kind which wants to establish a scientificity for the humanities, but which leaves the status of the structures found undiscussed, or identified with 'fact':[3]

> Naturally, it is not our business to interpret this phenomenon; our job is only to state the fact itself . . .
> The morphologist does not have the right to answer this question. At this point he hands over his conclusions . . :

All one needs to say here is that Lugowski's practice of interpretative structuralism (which is of course a label I give it) is more stimulating and inspiring, as it makes sense of its own description.

In Propp's exposition of the thirty-one narrative functions of the magic folktale we find no mention of any 'retroactive motivation'. On the contrary, it is obvious that Propp operates with our customary expectation of forward motivation, although this seems not as strict as the logical necessity of causality. He states, for instance, that the first two functions after the 'initial situation' (p. 25) have an inverted narrative sequence to the 'factual' one. Function I is defined as the temporary 'absentation' of a family member from the house; function II defines an 'interdiction' made, usually, by the same member who absented himself in function I: 'The tale generally mentions an absentation at first, and then an interdiction. The sequence of events, of course, actually runs in the reverse' (p. 26). One could say, for instance, that the temporary absence of the authority who makes the interdiction is necessary for the drama of prohibition and transgression to take place. The emphasis is on the *result* of the 'absentation', namely on the house which is left without its protector (the variant β^2 of this function is the death of the parents). That is to say, our interest does not follow the traveller on his journey, which of course would be a reasonable interest for a modern reader to show. This is borne out in the third case of 'absentation' (β^3), of the children absenting themselves from the house, away from the centre of protection. In conclusion Propp summarises the sequentiality of the functions as follows:

> if we read through all of the functions, one after another, we observe that one function develops out of another with logical

and artistic necessity. We see that not a single function excludes another.   (p. 64)

And the German translation specifies: 'we see that not a single function excludes the *following* one'.[4] 'They all belong to a single axis and not, as has already been mentioned, to a number of axes' (p. 64). This looks at first sight like logical stringency ('logical and artistic necessity'), but this is not quite the case. It is not the case that one function follows necessarily from the preceding one, or inversely, that function I must lead to function II; but that II is allowed to be preceded by I, which is a different matter. Propp himself shows that the first function may be absent and the tale begin with function II, the prohibition. It cannot, then, be said that function II is determined by function I. It is only *compatible* with the narrative sequence for it to be *preceded* by function I. This means nothing else than that the functions are motivated backwards; a function allows a sequence of functions to lead up to it, but is not necessarily and sufficiently determined by them.

Having based the grammar of complex combinations of functions on the premise that 'the sequence of functions is always identical' (p. 22), and having noted a prevalent order for complex sequences, Propp discusses a few exceptions which might be thought to be counterexamples. But, he argues, these are mere variants, and the ungrammatical sequence is always an inversion.

The assertion concerning absolute stability would seem uncon-firmed by the fact that the sequence of functions is not always the same as that shown in the total scheme. A careful examination of the schemes will show certain deviations. . . . Does this not break the rule? No, for this is not a new, but rather an *inverted* (*obraščënnyj*) sequence. The usual tale presents, for example, a misfortune at first and then the receipt of a helper who liquidates it. An inverted sequence gives the receipt of a helper at first and then the misfortune which is liquidated by him . . .   (p. 107)

Again this seems to confirm Lugowski's observation that the tale is result-orientated, making sure that an initial situation – misfortune, lack – and a means for overcoming it are provided, with no great attention to the order in which they appear – in the fictional fact or in its presentation. What needs to be said from our point of view is that these elements are precisely logically unordered: they constitute a coincidence, of which the order of the coinciding elements, since they must be given one after the other, is arbitrary. Our realist fiction has become selfconscious to a degree about such coincidence, of the helper appearing *ex machina* just when he is needed. But this seems of no concern to the folktale. Its concern lies with the fulfilment, the victory of the hero and the liquidation of the misfortune, which determine both the elements (initial lack, and means) which are necessary for any fulfilment to take place. It may be an intermediary result only, one victory on the hero's path to final victory, but its dramatic development is characterised by the result-orientation noted by Lugowski.

Propp further observes that a number of functions appear in pairs throughout: 'prohibition–violation, reconnaissance–delivery, struggle–victory, pursuit–deliverance, etc.' (p. 64). These are sequences of a logical order rather than an artificial narrative ordering of a coincidence, and correspond to the concession to verisimilitude and realism we mentioned above, constituting a temporary linearity and temporality in an overall a-temporal design.

This elemental recognition of temporality, together with the global a-temporality of a fulfilment already inherent at and in the beginning, creates a 'double-reality' (p. 80), or a double standard of realism in folk fiction. The elemental temporality is really a 'temporarity', a sequentiality necessarily transient and finally subsumed under the 'pure being' (p. 79) revealed in the eternal outcome.

> From the 'physical' side timeless being can only be conceived of as fulfilment/result; from the 'metaphysical' side the 'physical' in its temporary character is the action of man, who strives for the full realisation of his participation in the timeless order.   (p. 80; *my translation*)

In so far as there is intermittent temporality of the narrative we have of course also the creation of, temporary, suspense. It is, however, fundamentally different from the suspense we know, derived from a result which cannot be anticipated, a plot which can go anywhere, whose options for an ending are all open. Again, this temporary suspense is contained in the larger certainty which is devoid of suspense:

To arouse the participation of the reader, to move him to sympathy, is but to strengthen in him the notion of the power of the outcome, in that he is consolingly led to the temporary approbation of what he sees and to the certain promise of the happy outcome which he has already been given.   (p. 77; *my translation*)

As Lugowski points out, one could ascribe the motto 'not yet' to this form of suspense, a suspense which does not consist of the question *whether* a fulfilment will at all occur, but of a knowledge that it is only 'not yet' achieved.

Even with the disintegration of the 'mythic analogon' fictions and their readers have held on, in some form, to this 'promise' of a happy ending. Lugowski notes how the *Decameron* deliberately pre-empts suspense, in that individual stories are placed in the category of each day's programme and moreover provided with a brief summary at the outset. This is a tradition going back to Greek fiction, where the initial prophesy of the oracle anticipated the histories to be told.[5] Thus the suspense of a potential 'whether at all' is deflected into the suspense of 'how', a suspense essentially a-temporal. I dwell on this here because we will have occasion later to consider the suspense of 'how' again, where it plays a new role in Henry James as a reaction to the realist plot's suspense. With regard to suspense plots, where we should have no knowledge of the outcome, our expectation is still not neutral, counting on a happy ending unless warned in advance. It is largely with the modern age and its advanced disillusionment with reality that such expectation is fading.

Given that in a general way anticipation of outcome is still at work, in however vague terms, it is the detective story which has specialised in creating a more total suspense, demanding the full spectrum of options of 'whodunnit' as opposed to the binary 'whether or not'. Of course, our natural expectation of a happy outcome is again in some fashion guaranteed: it will be a happy outcome in that we will know 'whodunnit', and will have had a satisfactory reading. This particular combination of openness as to outcome and yet certainty that the genre is happy-ended, derives from the special form of the detective story as investigation. The thriller in general may describe evolving events with an open outcome, but the detective story conducts an analysis of events already fulfilled; it takes its unhappy ending, the murder, at the beginning and promises a happy outcome of the truth that will win, and the officer of truth, the detective, who will have achieved its victory. Thus the detective story is not only a prime example for hermeneutic decoding because of its well-structured plot, but it also dramatises hermeneutic interpretation thematically.

If we now return to the conventions of Realism in general, we understand to what extent the fundamental premises of plot differ from those of the structure of folklore. We no longer operate within a mythology, or a 'mythic analogon' which provides the knowledge of an order to be fulfilled, and which will be fulfilled again by every narrative. The emphasis is now on the beginning, on the initial situation, the premises from which dramatic action is spurred onward, to a destination unknown. The order of the world of fiction is that of our own, in which 'anything can happen', will happen along the axis of time and according to the principles of only the vaguest verisimilitude. It is symptomatic of the Realist attitude to fiction that the boundaries between fiction and reality are blurred, that distinctions are not sharply drawn between the plausibility of happenings in the real and the requirements of verisimilitude in fiction. The cliché, on the contrary, asserts that an unfair burden falls on fiction, where some of the implausibilities of life would be censored as unrealistic or novelistic (hence the problem of coincidence). This simply as a remainder of the 'mythic analogon' of Realism, its ignorance of its own artifices and its lack of definition of such concepts as verisimilitude. However, the world of the Realist fiction is of course given by its author, who thinks himself a faithful deputy of the order of reality. In order to qualify he needs to be omniscient, at least to the extent of his own province of reality, the world of his fiction. He is not only omniscient with respect to everything that is going on, at the same time and in different places of his world, including the thoughts of his characters, but he also always knows how it is all going to end.

Thus for the reader the axis of suspense coincides with the temporality of events and of the narrative, and if he faithfully proceeds along it he cannot fail to traverse the 'gap' and consume the enigma in the final attainment of knowledge. The detective story, as we have said, constitutes a loop in this linear scheme; the narrative, and the detective's investigation, casting backwards into a mystery of the past, to recuperate the linear causal development which was missing at the outset of the narrative, where the outcome of the 'story' was presented. But it is again the omniscient author who provides both the maze and the guiding hand of the detective by which the reader is led through it. As the God of his created universe his voice holds, and eventually gives, the truth. A truth which is, needless to say, determined fictionally or authorially. Around the figure of the detective the author designates a place for the reader: a locus for identification, which is at the same time the source of (narrative) information, where the reader is defined narratee, a position which requires some elucidation.

It is not at all clear what roles the narrative discourse assigns. We speak of narrators and narratees, in analogy to the speaker and the addressee in linguistics. Thus the voice of the Realist author understands itself as the subject of its discourse, assuming that it addresses a listener in confidence. It is an unselfconscious subject, to the extent that it seems unaware of the problematics of narrative. For the reader is not a simple listener; he becomes himself an imaginary subject of his reading, traversing the narrative space along the traces and clues provided. It is the assumption of Realism that proper guidance can, and is, supplied by the author, that he has full control over the subject of reading. Thus in the detective story the reader is virtually dramatised: the detective becomes his Virgil for his journey through the Lord's universe, from the Hell of the initial crime which is to be solved, through the Purgatory of its investigation, to the Heaven of the final Truth.

Anti-Realist though it is, the French *nouveau roman* sees itself as a direct development from the detective story.[6] The main difference lies in the fact that there is no longer any pretence of a fixed and certain reality which is to be revealed as the Truth, that no promise is given of a 'well-made' narrative which ties up all loose ends and explains all clues. The mystery of the puzzle and the overwhelming confusion of the clues are, if anything, the reality, thus putting the interpreter, whether hero or reader, in the position of a paranoiac. This theme, however, of the individual in the face of a reality not 'well-made' is a general preoccupation of twentieth-century literature, from Kafka to Thomas Pynchon.

Butor as a representative of the *nouveau roman* formulates the relationship between author and reader in terms of detective story characters. Now the writer is like the detective, searching for a new and uncertain truth and working, if necessary, against the police who stand for the old and established order. He is that artist who challenges rather than represents the accepted, who 'makes strange' what seems normal and who dares the unconventional. The reader, no longer the detective's apprentice, is assumed to side with the

police and the familiar order, so that he receives enlightenment
from the detective's novel perception, finding his expectations
frustrated and his preconceptions refuted. The polemic of the
writers of the *nouveau roman* explicitly concerns the reader's attitude
and its need for reform, to which their new techniques will
minister.[7] The reader is once more cast in the role of listener.

Henry James belongs neither to the tradition of the classical
detective story nor to the more sophisticated one of its proclaimed
successors. The *bona fide* confidence between writer and reader of
the Realist novel is a contract which James refuses to sign. With the
introduction of 'point of view' and the renouncement of om-
niscience the Realist guarantee of Truth is not granted, and the
relation of reader and writer is built on a different basis. James has
spoken out as the writer who wants to trick (not guide) his readers,
and especially those who think themselves expert at interpretation,
as his remarks on *The Turn of the Screw* announce clearly:[8] 'it is a
piece of ingenuity pure and simple, of cold artistic calculation, an
amusette to catch those not easily caught (the "fun" of the capture of
the merely witless being ever but small) . . .'. He does not dispense
that final authorial word of truth to praise him who has found out
and ridicule him who has not. James's *amusette* has

> the immense merit of allowing the imagination absolute freedom
> of hand, of inviting it to act on a perfectly clear field, with no
> 'outside' control involved, no pattern of the usual or the
> true . . . [It is] an exercise of the imagination unassisted,
> unassociated – playing the game, making the score, in the phrase
> of our sporting day, off its own bat.   (pp. 170–1)

The contract of confidence and listening has been replaced through
the constitution of the game, which implies a symmetry which the
telling of the truth could certainly never have. Writer and reader
are partners on equal terms, and it is significant that the passage just
cited describes as accurately the reader's part as it does the writer's.
Neither the one nor the other player ever gives himself quite away,
just as the poker player triumphs not in showing his superior hand,
but in never revealing it at all.

The result, as said, is an attitude to the reader very different from
the quasi-priesthood of the writers of the *nouveau roman*, who preach
a new order, a transformation of reality, to those who know no
better. For these writers the reader is in need of an educational

programme; with Henry James he is invited to join the game – he is honoured by the challenge.

It may appear paradoxical to find such a disposition in a writer whom we know to be an élitist at heart and a close associate of the aestheticists whose motto is *l'art pour l'art* if not *l'art pour les artistes*. It is paradoxical on the surface only, or if we focus more sharply on the biography of the writer than on the effect of his writing. It is thought élitist to choose to speak but to one's equals, yet it is only patronising, of course, to speak down to one's inferiors as does the didacticist. The effect of the aestheticist's decision to abstain from a consciousness-raising for the masses and to presuppose an audience only of fellow artists and equally cultivated sensibilities necessarily turns out more flattering for the reader. Henry James has a vision of those supersubtle critics (though most of them pertaining to the Paradise of art and very few only living in this world),[9] a vision of readers with a sensibility as refined as a writer's. The reproach of élitism is the result of a confusion over the classification of the élite and of who does the classifying: it is entirely up to the reader to join the illustrious audience and take on the reader's share, while the élitist artists have no power whatever to exclude anyone. The reader of books (in the plural), whatever his education, is bound to learn the ways of their authors and to acquire, especially, the tricks of the hermeneutic. The 'ontogenetic' development towards a reading sophistication reflects the 'phylogenetic' literary history and the evolution of genres.

It becomes obvious, then, that with a basis so different from the contract of the detective story the aim of the game in a Henry James tale cannot simply be the hermeneutic of the plot. We may say that plot hermeneutics form a primary basis for the reading, but that a second hermeneutic, which James would probably call 'artistic', takes place on another level. If we follow the 'voice of truth' which leads to the denouement of the plot, we let ourselves be carried along a comfortable *lisibilité*;[10] and there is not so much a puzzle to be solved retrospectively, as time to be bided for events to take their course. In *The Aspern Papers*, for example, it is not difficult to see the relativity of this (voice of) truth, since it is only that of the narrator and not of an author, that is, of a mere 'human' and a participant in the events. In other words, it is a mere point of view. As such, however, it turns into a sort of 'voice of experience',[11] with the narrator naming units of significance which he recognises among the disparate data of observation.

If we look at *Sarrasine*, object of Barthes's code analysis, we find there too a first-person narrator with whose viewpoint we ought to have reckoned. But seeing that for him there exists a fixed and true reality outside viewpoint, an objectivity outside subjectivity, his own voice, if not directly that of truth, is at least amenable to it after a little research and some biding of time, and can become the carrier of truth eventually. Rather than having a relative perception, a stubborn point of view as does the narrator of *The Aspern Papers*, he is simply not in the possession of the full truth at the beginning of the plot. He is, like the good reader, faced with an enigma, a gap in the truth, but one which is gradually filled in the course of events; the truth is being revealed for him to narrate. James's narrator, however, seems locked forever in his chosen subjective view and bad faith, open only to such empirical facts as the death of Juliana, but not, say, to a changed perception of Tina or indeed of his own motives. For these possibilities we have to listen to his *parole pleine*.[12]

The recognition that there is something else to be sought, some further puzzle to be solved, amounts to saying that there must be a second level of hermeneutics involved. If the reader again plays detective, it is no longer on the scene of the crime where he is misled by falsely planted clues. The narrator is now his principal suspect whose narrative is a cunning attempt to disguise his traces like a murderer.[13] But the reader engaged in a detective reading, that is, in a carefully interpretative scanning of all possible clues, wants to know more after the principal witness's defence. His work properly begins after the hearing, if he is to arrive at a verdict of his own and does not just wish to accept the attribution of guilt presented by the defendant. But the important point is that his investigation is directed at the witness's presentation of his defence rather than at the 'facts' and clues underlying it. For just as the reality of the crime is inaccessible to the detective since it belongs to the past, so the plane of reference of the narrative is beyond the reader's reach.

Professor Kermode demonstrates by his example of E. C. Bentley's *Trent's Last Case* how the reader, if not docile, processes information 'independently of the intention or instruction of the author'[14] and, one might add, of the narrator or the detective. We could say that the author of literary fiction has drawn his conclusions from the behaviour of the reader in the hermeneutic game; he is aware, and trusts his reader to be aware, that 'the hermeneutic spawns the cultural and . . . also spawns the symbolic'.[15] Hence his game selfconsciously provides for greater reading expertise, for greater skills in detective intelligence, psychoanalysis and above all the interpretation of discourse.

In the modern first-person narrative we have a paradigm of the 'court case'. Discourse is under suspicion, and with proliferating consequences. For while we recognise the possibility of lies and deceit on the narrator's part, including anybody else's testimony he may cite, we are obliged to extend our suspicion to the word altogether, having lost faith in its *bona fide* status as representing reality. In *The Aspern Papers* we have considered a rival plot, a dramaturgy and motivations different from those offered by the narrator-witness; we have a plurality of possibilities. We may prefix different premises with an 'if' of hypothesis and then read the text accordingly. 'If' Tina is innocent – which we do not know – then Juliana is a bully and uses her shamelessly. 'If' Tina is not so innocent, she may be conspiring with her aunt, working for a common interest. It is possible to suspect that Tina reports everything the narrator confides in her to her aunt, which could explain Juliana's introduction of Aspern's portrait shortly after the narrator admitted his interest in Aspern to Tina. When she summons him to her aunt, he question's the latter's sociability, but 'Miss Tina was not embarrassed by my question; she had as many little unexpected serenities, plausibilities almost, as if she told fibs . . .' (p. 67). But unlike the reader, the narrator never changes his firm presupposition of Tina's truthfulness. His direct question, whether she has repeated to Juliana that he is looking for 'materials', she evades by another, rhetorical, question: 'If I had told her do you think she'd have sent for you?' (p. 68). She then assures him that Juliana 'won't speak of [Aspern]', before asserting that she told her aunt 'nothing'. Of course, Juliana later does speak of him, which admits the possibility that Tina might indeed tell 'fibs'.

With respect to the literary text we have to assume a total relativism, a scepticism towards any reconstruction of the plane of reference, be it the narrator's interpretation or our own variants.

It is thus also understandable that Henry James recounts the genesis of a tale as if it were itself an adventure story. The protagonist is his tale, which has to pass the test of many adventures and must overcome numerous dangers, before it can emerge successful and victorious like a hero. Over and again in his prefaces we come across formulations like the following:

this perfectly independent and irresponsible little fiction rejoices, beyond any rival on a like ground, in a conscious provision of prompt retort to the sharpest question that may be addressed to it. For it has the small strength – if I shouldn't say rather the unattackable ease – of a perfect homogeneity, of being, to the very last grain of its virtue, all of a kind; the very kind, as happens, least apt to be baited by earnest criticism . . .   (p. 169)

Or else: '. . . the side by which this fiction appeals most to consideration: its choice of its way of meeting its gravest difficulty' (p. 174). The victorious tale proudly manifests the heroic qualities of old: perfect independence and irresponsibility,[16] though coupled with the greatest integrity, quick wit, ease, courage to fight dangers and elegance in the fighting. And the tale clearly knows its opponent, the detective reader who addresses 'the sharpest question', since it gives 'consciously' 'prompt retort', presenting an altogether watertight case – 'the unattackable ease . . . of a perfect homogeneity'.

Of *The Spoils of Poynton*, a tale of the most daring kind owing to its choice of mere objects – furniture – as protagonists and as the centres of 'consciousness', James writes:

> The real centre, as I say, the citadel of the interest, with the fight waged round it, would have been the felt beauty and value of the prize of battle, the Things, always the splendid Things, placed in the middle light, figured and constituted, with each identity made vivid, each character discriminated, and their common consciousness of their great dramatic part established.   (p. 126)

The prize of the tale's heroic deeds, of the battle won and the dangers overcome is, typically, the beauty in the citadel, the princess held captured in the castle. She is the one who draws the interest towards herself, the interest of her liberator as well as of those listening to the tale.

Thus we find the prototype of the folktale once more underlying the fiction of Henry James, but not quite in the manner envisaged by those who wish to marry folkloristics and literary criticism.

5 Analysis of narration, or *la parole pleine*

We have already begun to read 'through' the narrator's discourse and to form a view of the events which differs from the one intended and 'represented' by him. That is, we have tried to abstract 'real events' from the personal inflection of values and to judge them, so far as possible, independently of the narrator's guidance – an analysis which the *bona fide* (and impersonal) representation of a real folktale does not require. But from the precarious events we move to the narrator's presentation itself, in which we distinguish his *parole pleine* and his illocutionary act of story-telling.[1] We recognise the construction of the narrative as directed at a listener or reader (hence the courtroom analogy above), directed at another which moreover is also the self. Telling his tale is therefore another adventure on which the narrator embarks, of precisely the kind James has described.

We have already translated the peculiar form of the narrator's story into motivation aimed at the reader, who is meant to accept the values implied in the traditional folktale. Just as the narrator was practising elaborate deception towards the Misses Bordereau in 'action', so he once more, on another level, attempts to cover his tracks and deceive the reader, if not first and foremost himself. That this deceit is not always and not fully conscious is obvious from the fact that he has not more carefully edited out anything that to us precisely gives him away. We are in fact directing our analysis at that unconscious level to which we attribute knowledge of the truth, without which there could be no talk of self-deception.

It is impossible to adduce the evidence I want to discuss in a linear order, since it constitutes evidence precisely in combination; it is thus arbitrary with which I begin. We have noted the narrator's tendency to classify, both formally and thematically, the Aspern papers and women in the same paradigmatic group, in that he assigns to the documents the role of the beautiful princess in the structure of his would-be folktale, and chooses to pretend an interest in Tina as a cover, and as a means for obtaining the papers. The link between these two levels is the 'metaphor' of the garden, whose multilevel function we have already pointed out. A link first of all in his own scheme, it further connects these meanings in a way not anticipated by the narrator, and reveals in turn the subconscious motivation for all the elements in the matrix. For we may indeed ask ourselves whether the 'princess' and Tina are substitutes, metaphors and pretexts for the papers, or if we cannot rather read his excessive desire for the papers as a sublimation of some other desire. As a virtual aside we learn that as a 'man' the narrator 'had not the tradition of personal conquest' (p. 22). The obsessionality with which he pursues the literary documents has all the characteristics of sexual desire, which we suspect in the narrator to be starved and repressed. Similarly, we discover his professed quest for beauty and poetry to be really a search for 'Life', though life in a secondary and sublimated form too. Through Aspern's history he hopes to experience a small share of the life he does not permit himself to live through at first hand. It is above all – in the episode we witness – Aspern's love affairs that exercise an irresistible attraction on the narrator; but only following this great model does he dare to conceive of its pale imitation featuring himself and Tina.

His quest for the lost hero itself shows the duality of identification and desire; on the one hand he steps into Aspern's footsteps, identifying with him when confronting his mistress, on the other he pursues the poet's ghost as if it too were a lover. He invokes a 'spiritual fraternity' and imagines a 'mystic companionship' which would naturally be stronger than any bond between the poet and his mistress.

> It was as if he had said: 'Poor dear, be easy with her; she has some natural prejudices; only give her time. Strange as it may appear to you she was very attractive in 1820. Meanwhile aren't we in Venice together, and what better place is there for the meeting of dear friends? . . .' (pp. 42–3)

In this light the choice of the garden as a cover for the papers which themselves incur the displaced desire for (secondary) life and love, seems singularly appropriate. The balcony, for instance, which he notices and mentions (p. 9) might have served his superficial pretext just as well, since it too is so attached' to the house. But the garden is already one of the richest complexes of metaphor, invested with the associations of centuries. It is his recognition of the metaphor's potential that determines his choice: he knows what 'lilies' and 'roses' and a 'mound of fragrance' (p. 45) can achieve, especially with ladies, and is aware of the conventions that attach to the sending of flowers. Even if at the point of utterance his meaning is entirely metaphorical, it bespeaks the cultural code: 'I think it was the flowers that won my suit . . .' (p. 20). Similarly, standing in the garden he is reminded most strongly of the lovemaking of Romeo and Aspern to their lovers on the balcony. But it is no less significant that personally, beneath the show of his passion for flowers, he prefers the garden arid, 'with its weeds and its wild rich tangle' (p. 45).

It is a feature of the narrator's style to use metaphor dissociatively, that is, with an intention of emphasising the disparity of the elements under comparison rather than their similitude. Thus he thinks it safe, for instance, to invoke the image of the 'caught burglar' to describe his sensation on being discovered prowling by Juliana, with the 'as if' of association holding equation at a distance. Just so he assumes that the obviously formal analogy between the papers and the role of the princess, through its very openness, asserts the sheer figurative value of the construction. But instead, we as readers examine the motivation for the choice of these figures and images.

In his strategy, however, the garden is no mere rhetorical figure, as pointed out above. It is the concrete garden of the Misses Bordereau that enters into the dramatic development, and not just the mention of the concept that adorns the narrator's speeches or later his narrative account. The advantage of a real metaphor is that it can be dropped when it has served its purpose; but the garden of the Misses Bordereau, once 'acquired', remains a permanent feature in the drama. The narrator must cultivate it according to his promise and against his own preference, in order to uphold his original deceit. For the same reason, and for his 'fond fancy that by flowers [he] should make [his] way' (p. 45), he must send the flowers of his labour in the garden – significantly he has a deputy for his 'horticultural passion' (p. 44) – to the Misses Bordereau. 'His way' is the agglomeration of all his desires and purposes, ultimately of course the papers, but intermediately ingratiation with the ladies and assuring his continued sojourn in their house. But he makes his way most successfully, supported as it is by a general stratagem of wooing, with Tina. As the real soil which his gardener works, the garden yields an abundance of flowers, and these in turn win his suit with Tina. Our metaphoric reading, it appears, must come to a halt, for the pretext no longer covers its text. While the narrator has possessed himself, in a way, of the garden, he has not yet even set eyes on the alleged documents, let alone worked on them. The flowers as an extension of the garden metaphor, invoked with respect to future literary exploits, have no complement in the 'tenor' as fact. Similarly, those flowers entail consequences in the real world which are beyond the narrator's rhetorical design. The metaphor, taken literally and enacted, has got out of hand and out of the narrator's control.

Yet, where such a reading suggested and manipulated by the narrator ends, our independent interpretation continues. We recognise that the multiple layers of pretexts and metaphors, each designed to dissociate the connected elements, neutralise each other to the extent that the garden is precisely well chosen. It fails to work as an image for the papers, but it fits perfectly what these in turn substitute: the narrator's quest for love. The displacement from one level to another, from one quest to its pretext, makes it possible for the narrator to enact his real desire openly, screened as it is, for him, by dissociations and disavowals on all sides: he can pretend to himself that he is only pretending when courting Tina.

The awareness of pretence, of figurativeness of meaning, which permeates all his actions is so strong that he fails to imagine properly the effect on those who are expected to fall for it. Hence his oversensitive response to Juliana's scrutiny of his passion for strange gardens, which he cannot take on the simple literal level which he intends her to understand. Just so he never seems to have reckoned with a 'personal conquest' as a consequence of his impersonated suit. But the traumatic quality of his encounter with that possibility must be attributed to the 'blowing of his cover' and the open presentation of his most deeply and complexly repressed desire, rather than simply to modesty surprised. For a displaced choice of a displaced object choice Tina as bride was perfectly acceptable, thanks to his heightened sense of covering up what really matters.

The narrator is not only unfortunate in these displaced ('metaphoric') choices, but he also confuses intermediate and long-term goals in his strategies. While the papers are only one step in his quest for Aspern's life, he presents them to himself and us as his ultimate end, their literary exploits being a natural consequence of the consummation of his desire, just as the marriage between hero and princess is the real ending of the folktale, with the many little princes and princesses only its implication. The courting of Tina is meant only as a means to this end, just as the garden serves only to gain access to the house. But thus the cart is several times put before the horse, as it were, always one step closer to his real ultimate goal. Tina is won before the papers are even in sight, and the garden, which should help to win his pursuit of the papers alongside, blooms too soon and wins him Tina instead. The degree of repression of his desire has lengthened the line of dissociations to the point of its most abstract presentation as love of poetry, which seems to furnish the same desire with the corresponding energy to manifest itself ever more urgently and to accelerate its fulfilment by the steps indicated. Indeed, it springs out before he even properly begins his sublimated quest; in front of the house, with his plan not yet fully formed and before his first contact with the Misses Bordereau, he proposes spontaneously and rather unconnectedly 'to make love to the niece' (p. 14).

Generally we find his narrative discourse adorned by metaphoric sexual language which, once its basis is established, we interpret accordingly. Discussing stratagems with Mrs Prest, he hesitates to use any one of them for fear 'to meet failure, for it would leave me, as I remarked to my companion, without another arrow for my bow' (p. 11). Considering the power of flowers he muses: 'I would bombard their citadel with roses. Their door would have to yield to the pressure when a mound of fragrance should be heaped against it' (p. 45). Money seems to play a particularly important role as a weapon,[2] yet one from which he is not wholly detached and which leaves him with a feeling of personal loss. He likes to pretend that he is a man capable of spending whatever is asked, and though his means are positively limited, is carried away into a little boasting for the benefit solely of himself and the reader. When Juliana puts it to him that he may have the rooms if he will pay 'a good deal of money' (p. 28), he patronisingly assumes that 'her idea of a large sum would probably not correspond to my own' (p. 28). But when she quotes a figure he is truly amazed and continues:

> The figure, as they say, was startling and my logic had been at fault . . . . But so far as my resources allowed I was prepared to spend money, and my decision was quickly taken. I would pay her with a smiling face what she asked, but in that case I would

make it up by getting hold of my 'spoils' for nothing. Moreover if she had asked five times as much I should have risen to the occasion . . . (p. 28)

His own man-of-the-world manner with money aside, he thinks it very improper indeed that 'the pecuniary question' (p. 34) should be touched upon by the ladies and without the least bit of shame or coyness. The money, of course, is for Tina, as she conscientiously points out several times. But this lady in turn admits a certain shyness of the subject, though after directions are given by her aunt. When she articulates her relief that the sum mentioned concerns francs rather than dollars, her aunt sharply asks:

'What do *you* know? You're ignorant' . . .
'Yes, of money – certainly of money!' Miss Tina hastened to concede. (p. 29)

One may again examine this passage in view of the possibility that the Misses Bordereau are acting in perfect agreement, with Tina posing as the innocent Cinderella who is bullied by her aunt. Juliana is then seen almost as giving Tina the cue for stressing her unworldliness. But we will return to the narrator's struggle with money. How he can think he would have got hold of his 'spoils' for 'nothing' after spending so much and with such effort is a puzzle. But he insists on being above worrying, though not without frequent lapses: 'My experiment was turning out costly, yet now that I had all but taken possession I ceased to allow this to trouble me' (p. 33). He is also extremely annoyed when Juliana fails to acknowledge his rent with a receipt and worries about this for several days (pp. 41–2). Indeed, spending carries over its irksome condition into other areas:

I made a point of spending as much time as possible in the garden, to justify the picture I had originally given of my horticultural passion. And I not only spent time, but (hang it! as I said) spent precious money. (p. 44)

When Juliana takes things into her own hands and brusquely asks the narrator to stay and pay for another six months, their conversation is again all about money. He is satisfied with explaining her sudden conversion to lodgers, and nosey ones at that, by her greed, failing to catch the significance of the money as a metaphoric link. The money is for Tina, and he must spend it, but since his 'suit' seems not to advance speedily enough the point needs to be made more directly.

We also remember of course the final passage of the novel, where the narrator admits to having sent Tina, 'as the price of the portrait of Jeffrey Aspern, a larger sum of money than I had hoped to be able to gather for her. . .' (p. 143). But he has not sold the picture, and once more spends out of his own pocket. And when he contemplates his loss – 'I mean of the precious papers' – it is again the sum of money that might be implied, which makes the connection to a loss even graver.

This analysis may look more like a psychoanalysis of the narrator than an interpretation of the narrational dimension. But as readers we take the role of the addressee (or 'narratee') in which we also find the narrator's ego – the image he prefers to have of himself and to which he owes explanations. It is the ego which 'knows' nothing of the deeply buried deceit and which censors what is not acceptable to itself. But as non-docile readers we also articulate the voice of the narrator's unconscious, which manifests itself where it can in his discourse by circumventing the censorship. Hence those features which to us 'give the narrator away' are only indirectly telling, since only thus could they escape the censor. Thus our study is not so much an analysis of the narrator's character, which would extend beyond narrated time and narrating time, but a scanning of his discourse which reveals repressed desires and emotional meanings in and through it.

The adventure of the narrator's tale, just as his adventure in the tale, leads to a doubtful ending; it has struggled not wholly 'successfully with its dangers', presenting a case not altogether watertight, since it has not met its gravest difficulty and has let its closely kept secret out. Which is to say, of course, that Henry James's novel has passed the test of *its* adventure and shows 'the unattackable ease . . . of a perfect homogeneity'. The fight has waged round the citadel of interest, and that princess has been liberated.

II The Guild of Artists and Men of Letters

6 A linguistic fallacy

Another attempt at literary exogamy envisages a union of literary criticism and linguistics, with the latter as the dominant partner and the master model for conduct. The appropriateness of such a relationship, at least in a more egalitarian form, is in fact implied by the crucial distinction the folklorists draw attention to between oral and literate culture, suggesting a linguistic, not excluding socio-linguistic, study. But we have also stressed the importance of locating the difference between individualistic and collective, or folk, art in order to show that the shift in interest from plot to medium is not simply an historical development, as it might appear when we describe the detective story as a predecessor of the *nouveau roman* or even of the Jamesian game, while of course the species is not extinct. As Barthes explains this shift in the context of poetry, the content of all lyrical poetry could be crudely paraphrased as 'Love' and 'Death',[1] which in turn means that with the 'signified' determined by the genre, the only possibility of originality lies with the 'signifier'. With these terms we are, however, already in the domain of linguistics.

Yet the terms of signifier and signified should be applied with caution to such constructs as lyrical poems. Saussure, who in-troduced the terms, also devoted a good part of his work to the theory of 'values' of the signs in a syntagm, implying what Lacan then calls the 'sliding of the signified under the signifier' when signs are linked in a 'signifying chain'.[2] What is also implied is that one cannot generalise from the simple sign to the complex without taking into account the dynamics of the latter's constitution, and hence that the semiology of word-signs is not sufficient for the analysis of sentences. This should warn us also against the direct application of linguistic methods to units larger than the sentence.

While the relationship between signifier and signified in the word is strictly arbitrary, that is, one of symbolic attribution, it is not entirely arbitrary in the sentence, whose syntactical structure reflects to some degree the logical structure of its content. The work of art is at the other extreme from the simple sign, with a maximum share of meaning lodged in form: form reflects content and content reflects form in a dialectic which renders the common distinction between them virtually futile.

Another reason which makes linguistics a poor ally for literary studies is its bias in favour of *langue* at the expense of *parole*. The practical critic is eminently disposed towards the specificity of the individual instance of literary *parole*, towards the uniqueness of the work of art, although the theory of literary *langue* – the theory of genres, of historical development, of text grammar – has its own prominent place in literary studies. But in textual analysis greater interest attaches to the freedom of individual creativity and to the flexibility of the *langue*, than to the constraints it imposes on *parole*. This freedom is well known to be greater at this level than at the level of linguistics.[3]

I shall cite one example of the grave misconceptions which can arise from too close an allegiance paid to the linguistic master model; and I have chosen this particular one, first because the author's intentions and aims coincide in principle with those expressed here, while it is his practice which breaks down, and secondly because this leads us to a position diametrically opposed to that of James.

In his book, *Semiotics and Literary Criticism*, Cesare Segre defends a literary intentionalism directly extrapolated from linguistics:[4]

> A sign is emitted with the precise intention of its meaning something, and the receiver decodes it on the basis of the premise that such an intention exists. A sender–receiver relationship is based on the mutual acceptance of a convention, what Saussure calls a 'social contract' . . .

As a matter of course Segre shares the bias of linguistics and philosophical semantics toward the sender aspect of language, the preoccupation with the repertoire of denotational symbols and the intentional coding of deep-structure. In terms of Peirce's triadic sign relation, the focus of linguistics and language philosophy is on the object relation, which ideally is singular and unambiguous, while the relation to the interpretant is plural.[5] It is in the interpretant relation that the sign achieves (or suffers) its optimal flexibility, its highest degree of freedom and hence its scope for creativity. Bense expands on Peirce's semiology:[6]

Meaning is in the one case given as *code*, in the other as *context* [object relation and interpretant relation respectively]. As code, meaning is a word, as context it is a connex of words. Through the single word meaning is limited to *denotation*, more or less unambiguous. Through a connex of words meaning becomes polysemic and plural, and essentially A PROCESS OF INTERPRETATION. (*my translation and emphasis; Bense's italics*)

And as regards the sender or author's 'intentional semantemes', which in Bense's system must be considered 'semiotic objects', in other words, *denotata*, he states:

It is certain that they function as interpretant relations . . . The proper process of semantisation consists in a semiotic transition from object relation to interpretant relation, from designation to sense [*Bedeutung*]. (pp. 101–2; *my translation*)

It seems obvious that a semiotic literary criticism would concentrate more on the receiving end of the artistic communication, a position already implicit in the notion of literary criticism. While the main goal of everyday communication is clearly optimal accuracy of denotation and minimal ambiguity, and hence involves disambiguation processes on the part of the listener, the literary emphasis is on sense and polysemy. But Segre's polemic is directed exactly against the tendency to 'eliminate the sender' (p. 57), which is of course what the focus on sense and polysemy means. He sees the root of this tendency in a confusion of sign and symptom, or the elimination of the distinction between them, which in turn 'is a logical consequence of absorbing semiotics into linguistics' (p. 56). Warning against this he writes:

It seems to me that the only signs which ought to be taken into consideration are intentional ones – when a direct connection exists between what happens in the mind and its expression. It seems dangerous to me to confuse these signs with symptoms or indexes, such as are found for instance in clothing or cuisine, where they correspond to social categories, regional differences, and so on. In other words, they are part of the category of customs, and, until they contain an *individual desire to express something*, they cannot be considered meaningful in a linguistic sense . . . (pp. 27–8; *Segre's italics*)

If this is not 'absorbing semiotics into linguistics', it is certainly a subjugation of semiotics to the stringency of grammar. For Segre, linguistic meaning is strictly limited to conscious expression of intention, which may be an acceptable way of defining a certain scope of linguistics. Yet since he fails to produce a non-linguistic methodology for the interpretation of other categories of sign, his contention amounts to refuting the presence of meaning in those signs altogether, or at least the desirability of their interpretation. The notion of unconscious meaning or unintended sense is for him a contradiction in terms, just as many critics of Freud cannot accept his concept of unconscious thought. Segre thus denies implicitly that such social categories as the codes of clothing or cooking help to articulate social 'knowledge' of which the 'speaker' or sender is by definition not usually aware. Ridiculing what to his mind is misguided interpretation of uninterpretable manifestations, he says:

> On the one hand we have Something (Being?) which speaks through nature, things; and on the other we have semioticians who, as they know the language of this Something – for them it is all either codified or capable of codification – use linguistic techniques to interpret it . . . . As it happens *no dialogue is established* between this Something (Being?) and man; *there is no chance of replying or of checking.* Indeed, man is seen as engaged in a desperate decoding of things; he is an interpreter who is *condemned never to know with any certainty whether his interpretations are exact.* (p. 56; *my italics*)

The passage speaks of his conviction that interpretable signs must derive from a language, and more likely, a grammar, that they must be codified *by someone*, that is, with a sender intention, as well as of his assumption that linguistic techniques alone lead directly to this intention. In fact, for Segre, interpretation *is* linguistic decoding, and it is either correct or incorrect, since potentially it can achieve perfect congruence with the sending intention. Only if sender and receiver can compare notes can this correctness be verified.

I have quoted this passage and underlined some of its phrases because they seem to me to describe with perfection, despite the irony, the peculiar nature of literary communication and the predicament of the reader–interpreter. In the literary 'dialogue' (*if* a 'dialogue is established'*) the author speaks but once and then leaves his critical interlocutor to spin out his answer as endlessly as he pleases (and, James would say, 'off [his] own bat'), without offering any further assistance, correction or confirmation. The reader certainly is 'condemned never to know with any certainty whether his interpretations are exact', and some critics are involved in debates over true and false analyses; but as is clear from Segre's argument itself, the quest for correctness is misplaced in a context where verification is impossible.

The literary critic cannot agree with Segre. If he wants to read his text differently from a historical document or a newspaper, he must start out from an axiomatic assumption that everything in the work of art matters, 'signifies' or is functional, and that nothing can be accidental or unnecessary. Aware that he is not in a position to verify the author's 'individual desire to express something', he will refrain from limiting intention, or meaningfulness, to the deliberate, the rational and the conscious – to 'what happens in the mind'.

Just as our everyday command of language issues from 'beneath' our rational consciousness, the literary writer can never achieve full control over his writing. The question of intention or purposefulness is usually raised with respect to such sophisticated patterns as Jakobson and Lévi-Strauss extract from Baudelaire's *Les Chats*,[7] which tend to stretch the plausibility of conscious design. Moreover, doubts are reinforced by the fact that the phonetic is a constraint imposed by language which should be hard for the poet to manipulate at will. The point is that all lingual or stylistic elements have an *effect* in and on the work, while it matters little whether they derive from the author's scheming reason, his aesthetic intuition or his repressed psychology. I stress 'effects' because they also play an important part in James's view of the literary.

Segre has thus pushed himself into the awkward position of an old form and content dichotomy, since he grants the connotation of Hjelmslev's linguistics. But for him formal or connotative phenomena are without meaning, since they do not embody intention, although they may be 'intentional', that is, deliberate. Again this testifies to his equation of intention with content; hence he must postulate separate systems for formal features:

> Language is the system whose status is clearest. It is made up of signs, with the double aspect of signified and signifier. It is the characteristic of other systems that they are realized (as if by a sort of symbiosis or parasitism) by means of linguistic signs themselves which already have a semantic content of their own.

For this very reason connotative systems are preeminently formal; they are realized by a special use or by a special selection of linguistic signs, and these then give rise, not to other signs, but to symbols and icons, and as a result linguistic meanings are clarified, more fully realized, even perhaps turned upside down, but not annulled. There is little to be gained in lingering over the obvious, the symbolic nature of the metaphor, the simile, etc., but it is worth emphasizing the iconic nature of many 'figures of words'. (p. 60)

He goes on to argue that rhetorical figures 'imitate in visual terms . . . mental procedures', in a sort of syntactical onomato-poeia, and that metre and rhythm, 'tripping or solemn, heavy or smooth-flowing, may have a vaguely iconic function' (p. 61). This seems, if not naive, singularly unsatisfactory as an account of what goes on in a literary work. Segre wishes to relegate these formal phenomena securely to secondary importance, with the primary linguistic level dominant with content and modified at best by the formal. First and foremost, that is, we read literature as ordinary verbal communication, and then admire the icons of its embel-lishment separately. Rather than imitate structures of thought, rhetorical figures create those structures and help produce meaning. The relatively small number of formal – visually distinct – struc-tures would severely limit the mental structures represented, and the notion is as naive as that phonetics is onomatopoetic. Anaphora ('repetition of the same word at the beginning of successive clauses or verses')[8] and geminatio (for example, 'O horror, horror, horror')[9] would perhaps express iconically a stuttering chain of thought? And by saying that a metaphor or simile is symbolic, we are perhaps saying less than if we stated that a metaphor is a metaphor. Moreover, Segre uses 'symbol' in a confused way, on a par with icon and symptom and in juxtaposition with sign. In traditional semiology based on Peirce, 'sign' is the generic term for a subordinate set whose members are distinguished according to their object relation: the 'symbol', which is arbitrarily connected to the signified; the 'index', where a causal relation exists between the object and its representation; and the 'icon', which shares at least one quality with its object.[10] But above all, it is not the privilege of the (linguistic) sign to have 'the double aspect of signified and signifier', but a characteristic of all signs. Presumably Segre is misled here by a tacit equation of signifier with phonetic form and signified with semantic content. Yet in fact Segre uses 'symbolic' here as meaning 'non-literal', which is true enough of the metaphor, but not of the simile which says, literally, 'as if'.

Furthermore, there is no causal relation between the fact that semiotic systems are parasitic on linguistic signs and its imputed consequence that they be pre-eminently formal. Words and sentences are typically parasitic on phonological and semantic systems, and they are not therefore formal but pre-eminently full of content. As communicational language is a system of double articulation, so the literary text may be said to articulate on a third level, but one which carries full weight and is not merely contingent on the other two. We must abandon the notion for good of the work of art as a single layer of meaning decorated by a top of baroque icing which, moreover, is supposed to mimic iconically the contents of the cake.

The communicative function of art and literature has often been disputed, as a result of the feeling that their function is not the same as that of ordinary language. A sentence of ordinary communication is assumed to contain some given and some new information, which the message indicates structurally.[11] These two categories depend directly on the concrete speech situation and the identity (the respective 'knowledge') of the speakers. A literary text lacks that context, since reader and writer do not share a *hic et nunc*, nor can the reader be said to 'know' more in this sense after reading the text than before. Which amounts to saying that the realm of discourse is fiction, that is, indeterminate, and not reality.

It is from such considerations of 'knowledge' and information that one defines the literary communicative act more specifically as a game, in which linguistic communication plays a different, and essentially subordinate role. The notion of subordination in turn leads to the postulated level of 'literary articulation', built upon the second level of 'content' in the linguistic sense of meaning. In our analysis of *The Aspern Papers* we singled out this secondary level, which constitutes the hermeneutic of the plot. In the Jamesian game this hermeneutic is about as essential as winning is to the game; it is a constitutive factor, yet serves mainly as a pretext and an incentive for playing. Winning cannot be the sole aim of the game, and the pleasure lies in the playing, which is a matter of skill and technique, both of one's own and one's partner. This is what is meant by 'competence' of reading: a deeper understanding of the techniques of the text and the structure of its game.[12] And as sentential meaning

directs attention away from its phonological and phonetic composition, so the 'third articulation' diverts attention from content or
plot towards itself.

Barthes, who does not want to say 'competent' or 'experienced'
reader, simply defines him negatively as one who does not just read
for the story, who is no longer a consumer but a producer of his
text.[13] To space out this complexity of reading it is described
temporally and termed *la deuxième lecture*: reading the text as if it had
already been read (p. 22). In actual fact, the 'skipped' first reading
of the story is coexistent with this second reading, just as in our
everyday use of language we subconsciously decode phonetically
while our attention is concentrated on the meaning of the sentence
heard.

By the time of *S/Z* Barthes states that 'all connotation is the
departure of a code' (p. 15), just as we would say that the codes,
'symbolic' or 'cultural', 'semic' or 'proairetic,' are articulated at the
third level. Concerned now primarily with the *texte intégralement
pluriel* (p. 13), Barthes denies it the level of narrative structure which
was the object of his earlier study, 'An Introduction'. While the
folktale seemingly can be analysed in terms of pure plot and without
special attention to the use of the medium through which it presents
itself, Barthes's 'classical' text is analysed on the level of narration.
The distinction between *histoire* and *récit* suggests itself, since the
presentation of events does not necessarily follow the structure of the
events themselves. Enigmas are posed by the narrative, and solved
in the denouement of a *récit* which has at last joined the voice of
truth. In terms of our triple articulation, plot hermeneutics
simulates an intact secondary articulation, following the principles
of a linguistics so far formulated up to the level of the sentence, but
which could extend to units beyond it. But with the Jamesian game,
'the events' do not furnish a singular level of reference and are
suspended in the structural ambiguity of their presentation. Levels
of perception, of 'primary' and 'secondary historisations' are
intercalated, defying the notion of narrative as representation.
Since plot hermeneutics fails to solve a mystery of plot, the necessity
of another hermeneutics, exploring this enigma of form, becomes
imperative. Thus it is true in a different sense that the hermeneutic
'spawns' the other codes – spawns, that is, a secondary reading even
at our first perusal.

7 A literary taboo

Having raised the problem of the nature of the literary game in theoretical terms, and in particular for the benefit of the Jamesian game, we shall now turn to James's own fictional treatment of it. A number of his tales feature characters of literary and artistic vocation, as well as editors, critics, journalists and readers of all shades. From their behaviour and their fates we can gain insight not only into James's vision of the artist, but also into his conception of the reader's share[1] in the game and of what constitutes fair play.

From our analysis of *The Aspern Papers* it has already emerged that the reader's reading beyond the story and for the pleasure of seeing how it is made is absolutely taken for granted. In *The Figure in the Carpet* (1896) this quest for readerly pleasure is reified into an 'object' – a quest perforce implying one – and guised in many metaphors: a gem, a treasure, the figure in the carpet. This reification could not have been thematised if it had not been clear at the outset that there is more to a story than its story, and that readers are accustomed to an extended 'dialogue' conducted in solitude.

The play on this theme in *The Figure in the Carpet* turns of course precisely on the critic's having lost sight of the nature of his search[2] and of the solitary asymmetry of the literary dialogue, so that he resorts to 'checking' with the author. Even the latter is tempted in a weak moment to right this congenital default of the 'literary condition', being a partner equally frustrated by the dialogue at cross-purposes. Yet he collects himself in time, realising the futility of his attempted remedy.

It is left up to us whether to draw a dire moral from the fact that the critic, who has eventually found out for himself but proceeds nevertheless to the impermissible course of checking with the author, dies in a tragic accident. He either takes his illegitimately confirmed secret with him to the grave, or leaves it locked in the breast of his solemn bride who, if she perceives its shame, has the strength to live with it, even live off it. I would certainly not wish to attribute this moral to James, since it is uncertain in the tale what exactly passed between Corvick and the writer and subsequently between Corvick and his bride. However, it is potentially there, and I shall expand on it.

The delicate topic of checking back, of live communion with the author, is treated like a literary taboo, comparable to the taboo of incest which prohibits what constitutes the greatest threat to the continuity of society. It appears that the literary community has a social contract like any other,[3] whose central statute demands the strict separation of the two parts of the literary dialogue. This is not just a warning against the pitfalls of an 'Intentional Fallacy';[4] it is a constitutional injunction. No literary 'intimacy' must exist between the writer and his reader, and the text, the 'message', must stand between them as their only contact. This is to say, it must be a *literary* message; for it is in normal language use only that other means of communication are allowed to supplement the purely lingual message: facial expression, gesture, situational context and meta-linguistic discourse, that is, further messages about the first as a means for checking its meaning. Hence the 'communicational gap' in the literary dialogue cannot be a shortcoming: it is a fundamental necessity.

The letter of this law obviously reaches only a small number of the literary players, namely those who have contemporaneous partners for their game. But it is not difficult to see that it must be extended to cover also the cases where time would appear already to have successfully separated the partners of the dialogue. For even if the author is dead, there is his biography (his 'Life'[5]) or some descendant whom the reader might want to consult. Such removed incest is better known by the name of bardolatry or idolatry; yet critics are by no means agreed on the boundary where crime ceases and legitimate biographical scholarship begins.

The Aspern Papers has already presented us with a case in point, but with the literary dispute carefully embedded in the metaphor of the garden. In *The Birthplace* (1903) and *The Real Right Thing* (1899) we have two more explicit examples. The former exposes the shakiness of literary legend and its 'Facts', in which the public trust as firmly as does the narrator of *The Aspern Papers* in the 'definite facts' he brought from England. Above all, their attitude to the interpretation of facts is that 'there can only be *one* way, and . . . I'm sure it's quite enough!'[6] In the case of the great poet of *The Birthplace* the facts and relics are minimal, and hence the irony is all the sharper that they should be the object of a public cult while the monument of the poet's unparalleled work remains untouched by their enthusiasm.

The Real Right Thing shows the temptations of a critic who, after the death of his writer friend, is invited to write his 'Life'. Although acquainted with one of his late friend's opinions which could not be more explicit, he fails to let it govern him in his own case. The writer Doyne, while granting the high value of certain biographies – of men with interesting lives – seems to have held that 'the artist was what he *did* – he was nothing else' (p. 475). In other words, let his work be his sole representation to posterity. But his friend and prospective biographer is seduced by the abundance of private material – 'diaries, letters, memoranda, notes, documents of many sorts' (p. 471) – which open up 'the possibility of an intercourse closer than that of life' (p. 475). There were natural limits to their intimacy when Doyne was alive, not least, one suspects, owing to their integrity as members of the literary community. But while the danger of 'checking back' has passed with the death of the author, the privacy of his personal affairs has been laid bare without a defence – at least of a natural order.

Having shifted his focus from Doyne's work to his life, his biographer has left the domain of literature; but gradually he even gives up his claim of disinterestedness. He drops his original aim of writing the biography for the public, which alone put him in his present position, and decides to pursue his studies henceforth for his personal benefit alone: to enter 'an intimacy so rich' (p. 475) with 'the spirit . . . of his master' (p. 474). He is 'looking forward all day' to his hours in 'Doyne's personal presence', and 'waiting for the evening very much as one of a pair of lovers might wait for the hour of their appointment' (p. 477). Like a man blinded by love he mistakes the felt presence of Doyne's spirit for an inevitably favourable response to his advances, until he must finally recognise it as a warning: such intimacy, in literary terms, is prohibited.

The prohibition of literary incest appears to be supported by further 'kinship' regulations, which are darkly hinted at in *The Figure in the Carpet*. The young couple's marriage is strangely dependent on Corvick's progress in his studies on Vereker's work; and then, having found its 'solution', he will not communicate it to Gwendolen until they are married. The young widow in turn finds it impossible to impart her new knowledge to her literary friend, the narrator. The latter does not fail to notice this peculiar link, speculating even if he 'should have to marry Mrs Corvick to get what [he] wanted'.[7] But he has miscalculated when he assumes that her second husband shares her secret. Indeed, that gentleman may have been preferred to the narrator for a husband on the grounds of his ignorance of the incestuous content of her first marriage. In *The Aspern Papers*, too, the possession of the titular documents is linked to the condition of marriage. It is as if marriage in a literary critic might be a safeguard against literary incest; yet it is also obvious that it cannot be a sufficient deterrent. Vereker gives an indication that he has faith in the first proposition, for he seems to attach particular importance to the marital status of his ardent student and his fiancée, of whom he first hears from the narrator:

> 'Do you mean they're to be married?'
> 'I daresay that's what it will come to.'
> 'That may help them,' he conceded, 'but we must give them time!' (p. 289)

Yet we know that his planned marriage did not prevent Corvick at least from attempting literary incest, although he may have been aware of its possible preventive effect and thus have purposely postponed it till he found the 'solution'.

While the social intimacy of marriage may help to deflect the critic's desire for literary intimacy of the wrong kind, a different law exists for the writer. The 'lesson of the master', in the story of this title (1888), consists in his warning to a young writer that the union with the Muse must be monogamous, that marriage to another woman slowly kills off the literary mistress. He, the master, is a living example of a polygamist on his way down, so that he may as well make a sacrifice of himself and marry the potential bride of the young writer, thus forcing him to be faithful to his Muse. That the good faith of this sacrifice, as well as the implied self-justification, must be regarded with scepticism is plain enough from the tale and has been discussed by other critics. But the motive matters little for our purposes – as it does perhaps ultimately to the young writer himself; what regards us here is the application of the 'law'. Of course we are not told if the trick worked: 'it is too soon to say',[8] the narrator apologises. Yet his apparently non-committal phrases at the end of the story sufficiently indicate a direction; they accentuate the promise shown by the young writer and the sinking back into comfortable matrimony of Henry St George. 'Mr and Mrs St George', inevitably coupled, are now in the position of critics and admirers, while the young man has brought out a book and 'is doing his best' (p. 284). It is a proof of this that he keeps as his haunting standard St George's 'early quality – something of the type of *Shadowmere* and finer than his finest' (p. 284).

Another master, the Lion of *The Death of the Lion* (1894), divorced his mundane wife in order to live with his art alone; and his devoted disciple, who narrates the story, effectively staves off another woman and potential lover, to prevent her from disturbing the domestic harmony of the master and his Muse. This time the sacrifice is the young man's, and by choosing to marry the girl himself he is destined to become (only) a literary critic or editor, and like Henry St George a detector and promoter of talent.

There are apparent exceptions to this literary kinship system, for as we have seen, it works more as a recommendation than as a preventive. Gwendolen of *The Figure in the Carpet*, who is herself a novelist, marries twice, first Corvick and later Dayton Deane, the journalist. However, her books are actually conceived either when she is still a young girl, or else between her two marriages, when she is a widow. Of a third novel she publishes during her marriage with Deane, our narrator is convinced that it is 'inferior to its immediate predecessor', and he asks the pertinent question: 'Was it worse because she had been keeping worse company?' (p. 311). Yet he has not fathomed the real depth of the marital law. It is not because she is married to a mediocre journalist who he deems inferior to Corvick (and to himself): it is because she is married at all.

Another notable exception is Vereker himself: he is married at the same time as being a great artist. However, his wife is hardly in evidence in the story, and Vereker appears everywhere by himself. The first thing we learn about her is that Vereker had to leave England 'for motives connected with the health of his wife, which had long kept her in retirement' (p. 293). And 'that poor lady' (p. 310) in fact dies within a year of her husband's death. If she is ailing, there is little chance of her interfering with a strong and healthy Muse, at the level at which competition counts. But the fact that she is 'in retirement' indicates perhaps even better that she has yielded her place to the new 'wife'. That she does indeed make no claim to 'understand' her husband's lover can be inferred from Vereker's own remark that nobody has ever understood the point of his work – an indication that the author at least does not maintain incestuous literary relations with his wife. The narrator too suspects as much, although in his confusion and despair he would have tried, against better judgement, to approach the widow, had she lived. But 'it was much to be presumed that for more reasons than one she would have nothing to say' (p. 310).

From these exceptions to the 'marriage law', that is, from the cases of artists who are married, we can gain some insight into the reasons for that law and its recommendation of artistic monogamy or social celibacy. The marriages of Vereker and the Lion hardly count as counterexamples, since the latter's was dissolved and the former's turned into the care of an invalid. The real threat seems to consist of the women who, rather than compete with the Muse, condone, and even perversely delight in a polygamous *ménage à trois*. St George's wife instals a study in the house, built with her own money which she brought into her marriage, where the master and his Muse are to be locked up 'in peace'. It is not quite certain, however, that the wife's devotion is to the Muse and not rather to the augmentation of the family fortune which her union with the master, if fruitful, is liable to cause. Yet it is precisely the wife's 'understanding', her excessive sanction of the lovers' affair, which renders her husband impotent with his mistress.

The Real Right Thing presents another true artist who was also married, but 'Doyne's relations with his wife had been . . . a very special chapter – which would present itself, by the way, as a delicate one for the biographer' (p. 471). Though we never get to read that particular chapter on the wife, we receive an excellent portrait of the widow. It is she who pushes the idea of a 'Life' – 'she talked of "volumes"' (p. 472) – and who 'offered the temptation' (p. 474) of absolute freedom, of complete access to the entire literary and private estate of her husband to the young critic. And she shows that remarkable understanding to him which we noticed in St George's wife:

> Mrs Doyne had for the most part let him expressively alone, but she had on two or three occasions looked in to see if his needs had been met, and he had had the opportunity of thanking her on the spot for the judgment and zeal with which she had smoothed his way. (p. 475)

To leave him 'expressively' alone and to smooth his way with such zeal, shows an officiousness that is enough to drive any Muse away. Moreover, she hovers just behind the corner so as not to miss any possible development:

Though she was full of consideration, she was at the same time perceptibly *there*: he felt her, through a supersubtle sixth sense . . . hover, in the still hours, at the top of landings and on the other side of doors, gathered from the soundless brush of her skirts the hint of her watchings and waitings. (p. 476)

She is a nightmare of consideration and understanding, and we can only say in her defence that, since she had no comparable stake in her late husband's projects, her forbearance as a wife probably never quite rose to such heights. Even the biographer is eventually disconcerted, though he does not himself have a tryst with the Muse; but he is not yet aware that she is advocating, and he is committing, literary incest. James may have toned Mrs Doyne down into a widow, yet she stands for the worst a wife can be to the artist; and since both she and the biographer prevent Doyne from finding his final peace, she is even, a little, still his (spiritual) wife. For when, after all, is a man dead if not when his spirit has followed his body to eternal rest?

A more intricate case for the literary anthropologist is presented in *The Next Time* (1895). In Ray Limbert we have perhaps the only successful writer of quality who seems also reasonably happily married, though both his literary and his marital status must be qualified. His marriage bears the seal of sacrifice, and one cannot help feeling that its domestic squalor – rather than his wife's personality – is a perpetual torture to him. And Maud, unfortunately, is interested in Limbert's art, which we have come to recognise as a signal of danger. Yet their constrained domesticity prevents her from exerting her devotion in any other way than the bearing of his children, thus increasing their material difficulties. The function of the 'evil wife' is displaced into the figure of the mother-in-law, who stands both for the inevitable consequences of marriage and for the destructive female who smothers the Muse with her keen interest. Like the master's wife in *The Lesson*, she has a vested interest in Limbert's vocation, as well as pretensions of prestige – interest in the fullest sense not excluding dividends.

More strangely, however, we discover that this personal masochistic streak in Limbert – after all he has knowingly married Maud 'and her mother' – is complemented by a sadistic tendency in his art. Instead of compensating the Muse for having degraded her to the status of concubine, he now even takes to the whip. His perverse ambition is to suppress her wholly and instead produce commercial successes like his sister-in-law, Mrs Highmore. The entire story is structured on an inversion – or perversion – of values, which rests on the tension between the artistic and the popular. What the narrator, Limbert when in his right senses, and a few other literati consider literary merit virtually guarantees commercial failure, owing to the public's poor, or different, taste. To be praised by one of them in a literary review means certain disaster for one's career.

Thanks to this clear polarisation it can occur to Mrs Highmore, celebrated author of numerous novels, to set her heart on producing a commercial failure and expect it to be, automatically, of artistic value. In order to achieve it she asks the narrator to write her a rave review. In this world of *The Next Time*, 'tit for tat' becomes 'tat for tit',[9] a favour turns into injury, praise into libel, and trying every time to do one's best means trying to do one's worst. Consequences seem so inevitably linked to their causes that it seems possible to inverse the relation and achieve the causes through their effects.

Hence Limbert conversely tries hard to write something popular, carefully avoiding the esteem of his literary friends, and hoping for commercial success. But the most disconcerting factor in the story is the Muse's unfailing loyalty; despite consistent torture she remains constant, turning Limbert's efforts into rare artistic achievements, as if she too found a certain perverse pleasure in the relationship. In complementary fashion, Mrs Highmore's novels continue to turn out true to type.

The mistake of both writers is that they ignore the real causes, their respective Muses, and analyse two different sets of effects with regard to causality: a good review 'causes' literary merit, which 'causes' commercial failure, while contempt of the literati is thought invariably to entail popular success. One set of effects occurs in the literary circle, the other in the public at large, and the mistaken causality is simply the fact that one and the same 'cause' – a book – can simultaneously be welcomed by the one and ill-received by the other community.

The prohibition of incest and the recommendations of marriage or celibacy concern the organisation of the literary community, while the possibility of 'exogamy', the critic's marriage, already makes a link to its larger context. The confusion of *The Next Time* highlights the relationship of the 'guild of artists and men of letters'[10] to the society around it, and the problems which commerce between the two creates for the members of either. We shall now examine this relation more closely.

8 The literary community in the context of society

While the writer is the central figure in the literary community and fully contained by it through the endogamy with the Muse, the literary critic is more of a hybrid with one foot in each camp. The writer's intimacy must be fully devoted to the artistic, whereas the critic is allowed both social marriage and the pursuit of literature. The degree of his literary competence distinguishes him from the public at large and defines his membership of the circle of initiates who share the values of aesthetic quality with the writer. His borderline position qualifies him for the task of mediator between the two communities, in his role as reviewer, editor or journalist.

But this neat division into communities appears only under the special perspective of the productive artist, who does not, in that capacity, consider himself a social being. But for the public he always is one; he can be celebrated, and shown off as an asset at fashionable country houses and dinner parties. The knowledge of the initiated literati, on the other hand, consists precisely in understanding that the author ought to be a literary subject who had best remain socially anonymous.

In the eyes of society the strange social reticence of the artist appears as a minor pathology, possible to overlook if he has independent credentials such as fame and economic success. Society even meets him half way, when a copy of his 'latest' is put on display to be handed round by the guests, who try to remember the titles of his works and to weave them into conversation. The situation is perfectly described by the narrator of *The Death of the Lion*:[1]

> The house is full of people who like him, as they mention, awfully, and with whom his talent for talking nonsense has prodigious success . . . . There is supposed to be a copy of his last book in the house, and in the hall I come upon ladies, in attitudes, bending gracefully over the first volume. I discreetly avert my eyes, and

when I next look round the precarious joy has been superseded by the book of life . . . and the relinquished volume lies open on its face, as if it had been dropped under extreme coercion. Somebody else presently finds it and transfers it, with its air of momentary desolation, to another piece of furniture. Every one is asking every one about it all day, and every one is telling every one where they put it last.

Later the manuscript of Paraday's latest, and to his mind greatest, book suffers the same and worse treatment, is packed away by some thoughtless guest and then left behind in a railway carriage and lost for good. But when the great man, despite his talent for talking nonsense, blunders in his social conduct and falls ill at the same country house, society drops him at once. They were willing to overlook his pathological infirmity so long as he concealed it; but once it breaks into the open society must think of saving itself. The Princess 'departed as promptly as if a revolution had broken out' (p. 116), and the hostess 'was fundamentally disappointed in him' (p. 117). He has failed her by falling ill and spoiling the charming reading she promised her guests. Luckily for the hostess, two other celebrities are present, the woman novelist of 'trash', Guy Walsingham, and her male counterpart, Dora Forbes, with whom she can enjoy a deeper intimacy than Paraday ever allowed her and with whom a couple of days later 'she went up to town . . . in great publicity' (p. 116).

The unfortunate aspect of the two communities' relations is that each side is tempted to dabble in the sphere of the other. But while society has an instinct for self-preservation, for avoiding threats like epidemics and revolutions, the writer, though possibly aware of his danger, is often unable to withstand it. The 'Lion' agrees with his disciple that the sooner he should terminate his stay at the country house the better, yet he feels the terror of social misbehaviour: 'I'm afraid, I'm afraid! Don't inquire too closely . . . only believe that I feel a sort of terror. It's strange, when she's so kind!' (p. 109). And here, too, we can detect a slight perversity, a trace of masochism in the great writer:

It sounds dreadfully weak, but he has some reason, and he pays for his imagination, which puts him (I should hate it) in the place of others and makes him feel, even against himself, their feelings, their appetites, their motives. It's indeed inveterately against himself that he makes his imagination act.   (pp. 109–10)

To understand why the novelist allows himself this straying of the imagination, we have to go back to an earlier passage which explains his decision to '[force] open . . . . a new period':

His old programme, his old ideal even had to be changed. Say what one would, success was a complication and recognition had to be reciprocal. The monastic life, the pious illumination of the missal in the convent cell were things of the gathered past.   (p. 95)

The complication is indeed success. If the simple kinship system aims at the seclusion of artists from the hubbub of society, this does not mean that there is no exchange between the clans. There is interaction on two planes; the first regards the material for the writer's books, which treat more or less directly of society and its members, so that he must, despite his position of outsider, know it, so to speak, intimately. Secondly, there must be a distribution of his product and an audience to his work, since he is not writing for himself alone. Hence the eminent need for a mediating class, the group of critics who are both members of society and members of the literary community. But they are fighting a paradoxical battle for success for their writers, advocating their merits, yet protecting them from social welcome as celebrated personalities. The tensions arise from the ambiguity of authorship, since what the critics really champion is the work rather than its creator; while society, if it celebrates, wants to gather in its midst real people.

In addition there is the economic level to consider, unless the artist happens to be a man of leisure. But Ray Limbert 'belonged to nobody and had done nothing' (p. 190), the Master is living off his laurels and his wife's money, and none of the others seems to enjoy the benefits of a private income. This is why 'recognition had to be reciprocal', why the writer, if society is willing to support and celebrate – not quite his work, but at least himself as a Famous Writer – must give them in return what they desire rather than what he would prefer to give. If their communication is at cross-purposes, yet they both dodge to the same side, they can nevertheless meet – or bump into each other – for a compromise. The critic as mediator may minister in both directions, as the narrator in *The Death of the*

Lion testifies, whose champion no longer needs advertising: 'Let whoever would represent the interest in his presence . . . I should represent the interest in his work – in other words in his absence' (p. 95).

The narrator of *The Next Time*, on the other hand, seeks to recommend to the public an as yet unknown but first-class writer. The image of monks is recalled in this story too, with an allusion to Flaubert's hatred of society. But *The Next Time* is a study in pragmatism and cynicism, with a writer who chooses the real rather than the ideal, and who tries to make the step aside, the 'dodge', his deliberate route from the start instead of awaiting a compromise. His analysis leads him to the conclusion:

> I have been butting my skull against a wall . . . and, to be as sublime a blockhead, if you'll allow me the word, you, my dear fellow, have kept sounding the charge. We've sat prating here of 'success', heaven help us, like chanting monks in a cloister, hugging the sweet delusion that it lies somewhere in the work itself, in the expression, as you said, of one's subject or the intensification, as somebody else somewhere says, of one's note. One has been going on in short as if the only thing to do were to accept the law of one's talent and thinking that if certain consequences didn't follow it was only because one wasn't logical enough. (pp. 207–8)

This, and the narrator's remarks which introduce it, invite a new analysis:

> Some ingenious theory was required at any rate to account for the inexorable limits of his circulation. It wasn't a thing for five people to live on; therefore either the objects circulated must change their nature or the organisms to be nourished must. The former change was perhaps the easier to consider first. Limbert considered it with extraordinary ingenuity . . . (p. 207)

The 'ingenious theory' looks like a Marxian economic analysis, into whose terms I shall briefly translate it.

Limbert and his friends are on the verge of grasping the full complexity of the literary work as commodity, as 'an object undergoing market exchange'.[2] The young literary idealists have been convinced that art is pure use-value, the power to satisfy a rare but wonderful desire which the literary circle experience. The 'success' of a use-value is of course intrinsic to it, since use-value is defined as giving, successfully, satisfaction; so that the object which has use-value, *is* use-value. The question in literature is, then, to select the works which truly have, or are, use-value, to find the real rather than the pretentious works of literature. This is the task the literati undertake, and they sort the Paraday works from the Highmore novels.

Yet the spectre of 'circulation' destroys this innocent satisfaction, since exchange must take place between those who produce use-value and those who have a desire to be satisfied. And here the extraordinary quality of literary works, their 'immortality', comes to light and creates a particular difficulty. Unlike other objects of consumption which satisfy human needs, they have the paradoxical property of not being consumed in the consuming, of not transforming fully into satisfaction. The one product can satisfy again and again, and many different people. The literary community, as said, is an idealistic one, and its members

> appeared to have a mortal objection to acquiring [the books] by subscription or by purchase: they begged or borrowed or stole, they delegated one of the party perhaps to commit the volumes to memory and repeat them, like the bards of old, to listening multitudes. (p. 207)

They refuse, in other words, to enter the sordid market of exchanging material objects and draw exclusively from the works' inexhaustible use-value, for which they pay the author with their appreciation and understanding. That the circulation 'wasn't a thing for five people to live on' marks the writer's quandary – that he expects the physical multitude of copies from his work to earn him a living besides fame. For him the work must have exchange-value as well; but for it to have exchange-value it must be desired by a feasible market, and the market so far encountered and in which use-value counts, is the literary circle with its strange abhorrence of market and exchange. What is more, in the socioeconomic world of the tales this market is extremely limited and of poor resources. Hence it must be expanded to attract society at large, which has the wealth to give the writer what he needs, a living.

The simple sale of books to that society is obviously not viable if there is no demand for them, and a second commodity must come in. We remember that the narrator saw but two ways, to change 'either the organisms to be nourished', that is, adjust desire to the object in supply, or else modify the object to meet the demand. The critics' advertising may be a step in the first direction, but as we have seen in *The Next Time*, one which remains ineffectual. Hence Limbert opts for accommodating his product.

There is in fact a desire on society's part which the writer could fulfil, and this is its appetite for celebrities. In a multiple exchange society is willing to bestow 'success' and fame on the writer so as to turn him into this new commodity, the celebrity. A celebrity has use-value and exchange-value, though of a very special kind. In the hands of a society patron he becomes in fact capital for the latter, namely 'exchange-value used as a means of increasing the amount of exchange-value possessed by its owner'. For Mrs Weeks Wimbush, who has monopoly use of Paraday, his residence at her country estate increases her own social prestige – her exchange-value – allowing her, for instance, to secure the presence of the Princess at the same party, herself an additional exchange-value. The creation of success for the writer is a subtle investment achieved through the purchase of books and the organisation of readings. The cost is small, but by virtue of it the writer becomes that eminently more precious and useful commodity, the celebrity, since success is at least partly measured by financial status. The writer perforce accepts the first level of exchange, unable to prevent the consequences which turn him into capital. If he is a realist, he knows that the first exchange is made largely for the benefit of the second, which is the insight Limbert has just acquired, but of which his family have long been aware. But this enterprise can of course take place regardless of the use-value of the books, which is borne out by the fact that society markets both the truly literary works of a Paraday or Limbert, and the 'trash' of Mrs Highmore or Dora Forbes. This makes for unwanted competition, particularly as the latter class of writers are more readily turned into second-order commodities. Limbert's 'vision of his remedy' (p. 206) is precisely to break into the circle at the second stage and with more effect. He is to sell himself in another capacity, as editor of a 'high-class monthly' with a salary and pretensions that are both 'rather high' (p. 205). Although Bousefield, the proprietor of the journal, 'wants literature', he is not such an incompetent businessman as to suggest that they deal in unwanted goods. When the narrator asks Limbert: ' "Where will you get literature?" ' . . . he replied with a laugh that

what he had to get was not literature but only what Bousefield
would take for it' (pp. 206–7). And the narrator continues: 'In that
single phrase without more ado I discovered his famous remedy.
What was before him for the future was not to do his work but to do
what somebody else would take for it' (p. 207). In other words,
Limbert's production is now governed by a goal set no longer in
terms of use-value but in terms of exchange-value. As it is the
capitalist manufacturer's business to make money rather than
products, so it is Limbert's to promote the journal and himself
rather than literature.

There are other assets that make the artist more marketable as a
celebrity, and the right kind of wife may prove to be capital. Thus
the shrewd mother of Harold Staines, in *The Sweetheart of M. Briseux*
(1873), says of her son, the would-be painter:[3] 'he must depend
upon a clever wife to float him into success; he would never prosper
on his own merits'. Both Limbert and the Master of *The Lesson* have
invested in this particular line. The narrator of *The Next Time* gives
a picture of 'pretty pink Maud' (p. 190):

> It struck me all the more that Mrs Limbert was flying her flag. As
> vivid as a page of her husband's prose, she had one of those
> flickers of freshness that are the miracle of her sex and one of those
> expensive dresses that are the miracle of ours. She had also a neat
> brougham . . .   (p. 205)

And Maud's mother is 'the second cousin of a hundred earls' (p.
190) – not a great use-value, but a good deal of capital which should
help her daughter tread the 'paths of gentility' (p. 190). St George's
wife is not without a position in society, and has 'a high smartness of
aspect' (p. 217) that makes her look 'as if her prosperity had deeper
foundations than an ink-spotted study-table littered with proof-
sheets' (p. 218).

It is for pecuniary reasons, which in literary terms have nothing
to do with his art, that the writer may be led to accept more than
simply 'the law of [his] talent' and to doubt the logic of its necessary
consequences. Vereker, piquéd that the 'point' of his work has been
consistently missed, is tempted to drop hints in promising quarters
and to allow critics, against his better judgement, to check their
findings with him. To no avail, as it turns out: the critic dies, he dies,
and no profit accrues even to his posthumous fame.

All such infelicities are of course a result of the fact that the artist, for all his membership of his own guild, remains always a social being. If we pursue the metaphor of the clans for just a little longer, we come to realise that the artist must at one point have joined the literary community (unless we believe that artists are 'born'), that he has become an artist through marriage and that our impression of his being almost a different species is only a consequence of his preferred allegiance to the clan of his wife. The Muse is really the only full member of that tribe, while the humans who join it are arranged on a descending scale. The artist is closest to the top, followed by the real devotees who defend the interests of the writer and his art; next the mediators with their eyes turned more towards society and the promotion of the arts as well as their own 'artistic' careers, thus joining eventually the ranks of all other members of society determined to make a living in it.

9 Twin demons

The fact remains that an all-too-real conflict arises for the artist from his dual allegiance. Success and admiration are always ambiguous, and he is never free from wondering if they are due to his work or his fame. Although fame counts as a social currency like other social credits, there never accrues from it the same security as does from a name or a fortune or both. The aristocrat carries the conviction of his worth at all times and in every place; he is 'Olympian'.[1] The artist reaches the certainty of his own value only in rare moments, and when he is silent, as artist, is often haunted by doubts and self-criticism that make him 'blush for himself'.[2] Such insecurity in turn affects his life in society, in which he can never move with 'irreflective joy and at the highest thinkable level of prepared security and unconscious insolence'.[3]

The Private Life (1892) can be seen as an allegory of the writer's dilemma, his inner division into an artist and a social persona. The famous author Clare Vawdrey has a social 'self' which he delegates to those fashionable gatherings in which, as an artist, he would find no pleasure; while his artistic 'self' stays behind in his room to get on with his work. He is found out by the narrator, 'a searcher of hearts – that frivolous thing an observer',[4] only because the social double lacks the glamour and wit on which the author's reputation rests.

We have seen, however, that the writer cannot afford to stay at home for ever, and that one reason for his going into society is its richness as a field of inspiration. He is himself 'a searcher of hearts', and if not an ardent participant in, certainly a constant observer of the spectacle offered on the social stage. As the narrator says of Vawdrey's two selves: 'after all they're members of a firm, and one of them couldn't carry on the business without the other' (p. 215). Whether he researches with intent or out of *déformation professionelle*, the 'twin demons of imagination and observation'[5] ride him wherever he goes. The inspiration from life as a transaction between the two business partners may be effected at a profoundly subliminal level, and tracing it in the following examples will reveal its curious connection with the law of artistic monogamy.

In *The Tone of Time* (1900) a middle-aged, somewhat old-fashioned painter and copyist excels herself in the production of a masterpiece. She has been asked to paint a picture of a '*très-bel homme*'[6] and 'to give it . . . the tone of time' (p. 194), that is to say, make him a young man of about thirty years earlier. Mary Tredick finds the perfect model in the memory of her past lover who betrayed and deserted her. So many years later she paints his likeness with a passion, not of love, but of rage, which instils the painting with an exceptional aesthetic quality. It is an act of exorcism, for she is finally freed of her bitterness: '"It took – whatever you will! – to paint it," she said, "but I shall keep it in joy"' (p. 215). This recalls another famous novel of a painting into which the painter has put too much of his life and soul: Oscar Wilde's *The Picture of Dorian Gray* (1890). But its painter, Basil Hallward, holds that 'An artist should create beautiful things, but should put nothing of his own life into them. We live in an age when men treat art as if it were meant to be a form of autobiography.'[7] The age has not yet passed, one might add; but also Hallward sees life and art curiously well divided, considering his own experience.

It is not so much the fact of 'autobiography' that makes the case of *The Tone of Time* interesting to us, as the flow of passion from the artist into her work. If passion of such intensity, be it rage or love, goes into the making of masterpieces, it may explain why the artist must not direct it elsewhere, that is, into 'life'. Mary Tredick's story indeed implies that all this time, with her passionate bitterness cooped up inside her, she never rose to artistic greatness, although she acquired remarkable technical expertise from her copying of great works and 'had at the end of her brush an extraordinary bag of tricks' (p. 197).

The narrator of *The Special Type* (1900), another painter of portraits, is the observer of the complicated triangular affair of his friends who all pour their hearts out to him. His studio seems the nodal point where all the threads of the action intersect, and his own favourite model Alice is taken away from him to play her part in the drama. He is not without emotional stakes in the events, for he is truly fond of his friend Frank and has real affection for his model, besides inevitable keen interest in their extraordinary characters. It is really Mrs Cavenham, a client and sitter, whom he cares least for; yet he remains as impartial as he can and listens to all of them according to their demands. His own wish is, or would be, 'to wash my hands of it':

> I cared only to be out of it. I may as well say at once, however, that I never *was* out of it; for a man habitually ridden by the twin demons of imagination and observation is never – enough for his peace – out of anything.   (p. 179)

But while he seems 'to sit back and observe',[8] to renounce participation in the action and stem back the flow of sympathy and passion, it is only in order to take part all the more actively in the drama on an extended scene. Feeling by no means 'out of it', not, at any rate, 'enough for his peace', he proceeds to create a fourth and no less important character: Frank's full-length portrait. The ladies get almost more heated about the possession of the latter than about betrothal to the original; and in the terms of the story it is distinctly Alice Dundene who emerges victorious. She only ever allows herself to set her heart on the possession of this one, and succeeds in making 'him' hers, while Mrs Cavenham swallows the bitterness of renunciation on the very day of her wedding to the real Frank.

It does not come as a surprise, then, that this portrait of Frank, at the height of the drama, turns into a masterpiece: 'the work remains as yet my high-water mark' (p. 188). Unlike Basil Hallward, this painter sees no blame in Mrs Dundene's praise:

> 'Why, it's of a truth–! It's perfection.'
> 'I think it is.'
> 'It's the whole story. It's life.'
> 'That's what I tried for,' I said . . .   (p. 191)

Indeed, it is so much of 'life', or perhaps life made sublime, that it can 'make up' to Mrs Dundene: '"It will be *him* for me," she meanwhile went on. "I shall *live* with it, keep it all to myself . . ."' (p. 191). Yet for her it will not just be a dummy husband to show off to her visitors, as the *très-bel homme* was to be for Mary Tredick's client. Alice Dundene is 'the special type', with an artistic intuition that makes her the perfect model. She 'never saw him alone' (p. 191) and does not, as her less subtle rival might suspect, have to make up for a lost romance in a sentimental second-best way. Her interlude with Frank had been a fiction, a make-believe in which once more she showed her quality as model – 'the ideal thing'[9] rather than the real. There was a part to be filled, by a 'special type' (p. 177), to create the perfect 'appearance' (p. 176), and Mrs Dundene stepped in. And as it is the painter who arranges her pose for a sitting, so it is Frank who determines her part in the drama: 'It was what *he* wanted' (p. 191).

For all his professed passivity and non-interference the painter-narrator is the dramatist in control, and he makes the play end to his satisfaction. He could have lied on behalf of Mrs Cavenham, when Mrs Dundene requested a portrait of Frank; or he could have agreed to paint a second – even inferior – portrait of him for the sake of contenting both ladies. But he delights in the course things are taking: 'I had no difficulty in replying that my best was my best and that what was done was done' (p. 192). And where life does not quite come up to his envisaged dramaturgy, he helps a little. On seeing the portrait already there, which her rival had commissioned for herself, Mrs Dundene delightedly conjectures:

> 'Then he had himself the beautiful thought of sitting for me?'
> I faltered but an instant. 'Yes.'   (p. 191)

Anything for beauty – even the beauty of a thought.

It is not of course an extraordinary thing to say of the artist that he is a keen observer, and it has been said as often about James himself as about his artistic characters. I have already used an expression from a statement by Leon Edel in his biography of James, which I shall now quote more fully. It concerns James's relationship to Minny Temple:

> A young man naturally shy and tending to hover in the background of any social situation, Henry in reality wanted only to worship Minny from a quiet and discreet – and we might add safe – distance. Henry was as uncompetitive in affairs of the heart as in matters of literary import. . . . To sit back and observe his cousin, to worship her from afar . . . this seems to have been the love stratagem of Henry – as it was of a number of his early young fictional heroes. . . .   (p. 235)

I do not wish to argue here about whether this really was a 'love stratagem', nor whether James was indeed as uncompetitive in matters of literary import. I merely quote for the following views:

Fear of women and worship of women: the love-theme plays itself out in striking fashion throughout Henry James's work. And usually love, in these fictions, as one critic has put it, is 'a deterrent to the full life'. It is more: it is a threat to life itself. (p. 56)

There are two arguments here which I wish to discuss briefly. The first is the emphasis on the passivity of the artist and observer – here James – who sits back to observe from a safe distance and who 'hover[s] in the background of any social situation', not only like so many of his early young fictional heroes, but like so many of his narrators and late heroes. It is the well-known theme of the artist feeling that he must make a choice between Art and Life. From here Edel passes on to a seemingly contradictory contention, namely that love is not only a deterrent to 'the full life' but a real threat to life itself. In terms of our interpretation of the first argument this does not make sense, for what is life if not full of love? The precarious choice between art and life is that between the dedication to a creative vocation or to the pursuit of personal happiness in social life, love, marriage, a career.[10] We might of course specify the 'full life' in Jamesian terms as the artist's fulfilling but socially withdrawn life for the 'one critic's' statement; but in Edel's amendment 'life itself' unquestionably means Life.

This second position of Edel is connected with his theory 'love = death' (p. 331), based on an all-prevailing vampire relation which begins with the mother (p. 55) and ends with the wife. But if all the cited examples from the 'James family annals' prove the strong dependency that grows between couples – one giving fully, the other drawing on the offered strength – these examples prove precisely that these people *live* by it and not that they must die. Leon Edel further cites three works by James where love leads to the death of one partner. In James's work there are many more marriages which do not have such dire consequences. Edel concludes: 'To be led to the marriage bed was to be dead. Henry James accordingly chose the path of safety. He remained celibate' (p. 57). One's impression is rather that if James lives in fear of such dependency, it is because it presents a threat to his work. The theme we have seen play itself out in the tales so far is that of artistic 'monogamy', the choice of the artist to live with his Muse and renounce the full social life of an ordinary man; that is, social celibacy to save himself from Life rather than death. Leon Edel speaks further of 'significant equations of art and love which become also glory and power as well as fear and terror' (p. 77). If we add these to that of 'love = death' we should then logically draw the final conclusion 'art = death', which Edel however leaves undrawn. We shall return to this later with the discussion of *The Sacred Fount.*

Tony Tanner puts the point in more abstract terms:[11] 'The intimate connection between comprehensiveness of vision and renunciation of participation is discernible in James's work almost from the first'. This corroborates the view of Henry James sitting back and observing, of passivity in favour of keener perception. The polarisation is indeed along the axis of active *versus* passive, in Edel's portrait of James the 'stay-at-home' (p. 234), 'a sedentary literary youth . . . all hidden passion without action' (p. 231), as well as in the juxtaposition of active participation and the passivity of vision.

In the social world of the tales discussed these opposites are clearly borne out. In the eyes of society the artist is passive: he does not marry, or get involved in other fashionable intrigues, and fails often enough to appear on the social stage altogether unless lured by a public reading or the performance of a play. And when his presence graces their feasts, it is in the role of a 'hovering' observer who drinks in the spectacle and consumes the show.

We need only to change the perspective and regard the artist from within his own community, for him to appear active, hard at work, struggling, driving himself, but producing and creating. It is under this perspective that in turn the reader and critic shows as passive, a receiver, perceiver, consumer. The critic may of course write his critical articles, but these are not creative productions in the same sense, though they may count in the world of careers. But he has social involvement which the artist lacks, both through its work and the recommended marriage.

In fact we have a complete matrix that distinguishes the artist and the critic along the axis of activity and productivity according to the perspective under which we consider them:

	active/ *productive*	*passive/* *receptive*
social world	critic	artist
artistic world	artist	critic

And it also appears as if the 'twin demons' reflected this same division, keeping company to the twin selves of the artist's personality: the more passive demon of observation going with one to the social world, the creative imagination staying at home with the other to work.

But the division into active and passive is wrong under both perspectives. It is based on the misguided equation of observation, perception, reception with passivity and its separation from the 'creative' twin, imagination. The tales to which we are now turning begin to adjust our perspective once more and to reveal the keener vision as a highly active occupation.

10 Products of observation and imagination

Nona Vincent (1892) presents three different members of the artistic community: Allan Wayworth, a playwright, Miss Violet Grey, an actress, and Mrs Alsager, who is 'an ideal public':[1]

> She loved the perfect work – she had the artistic chord. This chord could vibrate only to the touch of another, so that appreciation, in her spirit, had the added intensity of regret. She could understand the joy of creation, and she thought it scarcely enough to be told that she herself created happiness . . . . She had not the voice – she had only the vision. The only envy she was capable of was directed to those who, as she said, could do something. (p. 155)

She certainly qualifies for 'the guild of artists and men of letters', though she is also quite clearly placed, in her own mind, well below the artist through her lack of productivity, accentuated by the repeated 'only'. Envious though she might feel, she is most generous and 'admirably hospitable to such people [who could do something] as a class' (p. 155). She is a constant partner to the playwright for the discussion of his ideas, until he indeed succeeds in writing his play 'Nona Vincent'. Like a Socratic midwife she has crucially assisted at the birth of a work of art, and she now goes on to help as practically with the production of the play on stage. It is again she who, when the play has succeeded but Miss Grey in the lead 'has failed' (p. 179), comes to the rescue of the young actress. Understanding that she herself was the source of inspiration for the protagonist Nona Vincent, she visits the actress to let her look at her, hear her speak, know her – in short, to make her see Nona Vincent. And indeed, Violet Grey is 'perfection' (p. 186) in her role the same evening. Having performed her duty, Mrs Alsager leaves London at once, while the play continues to run for two hundred nights. Joined in

98

success, the playwright and the actress get married. We are told that 'his plays sometimes succeed', but that 'his wife is not in them now, nor in any others' (p. 187). Married, she ceases to be a performing artist, while the praise of her husband's plays is lukewarm; to say that they are, sometimes, a success is to avoid judging them good or bad. Success on the London stage is not necessarily always a direct consequence of literary merit. It seems almost as if of the three Mrs Alsager were the truest artist, though her product remains intangible.

Curiously, the narrator says as much at the very beginning: 'She was even more literary and more artistic than [Wayworth]' (p. 153), although she remains 'inedited and unpublished' (p. 154), while Wayworth 'had his limitations, his perversities' (p. 157). She possesses the vision, and if she does not have the voice to express it directly, she has her own ways of inspiring the writer and 'lighting up the imagination' of the actress (p. 187). Why, asks the narrator in a question he thinks Wayworth should have put, should 'a woman whose face had so much expression . . . not have felt that she achieved. How in the world could she express better?' (p. 155).

Having expressed herself through two artists she has perhaps done better than if she 'scribbled' herself, and what she has produced is vision grown from her own vision, in the playwright and in the actress.

The Beldonald Holbein (1901) is told by a painter, but he is an artist 'who [has] in him all the splendid egotism of art' which Leon Edel imputes to James,[2] and which lowers a veil of insensibility over his narrative. The self-complacency with which he regards 'our set'[3] leads him to trust in 'the conscious triumph' (p. 297) Mrs Brash-Holbein's promotion will present, as well as to delight in the 'beauty' of his anecdote 'on the whole, and in spite of everything' (p. 301).

It is a French colleague who first discovers Mrs Brash and her extraordinary likeness to a Holbein. Though from France, where 'they do see . . . more than we; and they live extraordinarily, don't you know, *in* that' (p. 292), he, like the narrator, wants to paint her portrait. They are neither of them content to live in the seeing, though the reason may be that they are commercial artists who cannot resist such a certain success and a bargain on top of it. For the Frenchman is well aware of it: 'But, my dear man, she *is* painted – and as neither you nor I can do it . . .' (p. 290). He would nevertheless like to have 'a crack at her' (p. 291), and so would the narrator: 'It was before me with intensity, in the light of Mrs Brash's distant perfection of a little white old face, in which every wrinkle was the touch of a master . . . ' (p. 291). When they are certain never to be allowed to paint her, they nevertheless continue to enjoy her as the 'work' of another, though without any consideration for 'what among us all was now unfailingly in store for her' (p. 296). Both the enjoyment and the lack of concern for her consciousness are expressed in one breath: 'the thing was, for any artist who respected himself, to *feel* it – which I abundantly did; and then not to conceal from *her* that I felt it – which I neglected as little' (p. 297). Forgetting that he claimed earlier 'that time and life were artists who beat us all' (p. 297), he already asserts: 'She was, in short, just what we had made of her, a Holbein for a great museum' (p. 298). His 'making', in fact, is that of a promoter, yet his sense of benefaction is great:

> . . . what I can tell you is why I hold that, as I said just now, we can do most. We can do this: We can give to a harmless and sensitive creature hitherto practically disinherited – and give with an unexpectedness that will immensely add to its price – the pure joy of a deep draught of the very pride of life, of an acclaimed personal triumph in our superior, sophisticated world.　(p. 301)

It might well be true that Mrs Brash feels a rare new pleasure in discovering 'in her fifty-seventh year . . . that she had something that might pass for a face' (p. 296); yet the condescension from 'our superior, sophisticated world' adds a note of discord on the level of the narrative that fills the reader with foreboding. The narrator himself must admit, however, that 'she was really, to do her complete justice, the last to understand; and I am not sure that, to the end – for there was an end – she quite made it all out or knew where she was' (p. 297). It is doubtful, in other words, whether Mrs Brash ever enjoyed her 'conscious triumph' and drank 'the pure joy of a deep draught of the very pride of life'. What she certainly feels is the full force of the effect and the consequence of 'her little wonderful career' (p. 295), when she finds herself 'simply shipped . . . straight back' 'to her original conditions' (pp. 304–5). Thus the narrator's theory of her death, that 'the taste of the tree . . . had been fatal to her' (pp. 305–6), will not stand up, since there is no positive sign Mrs Brash ever attained such 'knowledge'. On the contrary, she seems to retain her original humility and good nature to the end, the qualities which are essential for her qualification as a Holbein. We do not see her wake up to her triumph and transform under our eyes. Rather, the fatality lies in the consciousness stirred up in the Holbein's owner. The Beldonald Holbein is 'banished from its museum', and finding no other collector, accomplishes one last act of complete humility, 'turning . . . its face to the wall' (p. 306).

The juxtaposition of Life and Art is the scaffold for our next example, *The Story in It* (1902). The heroine herself seems beholden to the inevitable antithesis, and it is really the narrator who achieves its transcendence. Yet Maud Blessingbourne intuits the fallacy of the strict opposition, and lives the example of a practical synthesis.

She is a fairly literary lady, well versed in the new French novel of the yellow type. Indeed, she and her hostess together mimic this Art–Life polarisation through the contrast of Maud's aesthetic sensibility with the latter's social vivacity. Maud selfconsciously refers to it when Mrs Dyott asks 'what' D'Annunzio is:[4] '"Oh, you dear thing!" [She] was amused, yet almost showed pity. "I know you don't read," Maud went on; "but why should you? *You* live!"' We would almost suspect a tone of self-defence, were it not for the pity she 'almost showed', and were it not for the fact that between the two contrasts – the one between reading and living, and the one between herself and Mrs Dyott – she prefers to accentuate the latter.

In her discussion of the merits of modern novels with Colonel Voyt the component Life also seems to play the main part. Her preference for French fiction is based on her impression that 'I seem with it to get hold more of the real thing – to get more life for my money' (p. 314). The two agree on the inferiority of 'the novel of British and American manufacture' which 'seems really to show our sense of life as the sense of puppies and kittens' (p. 315). But when the Colonel suggests that perhaps she would claim that the French *had* a subtler and more complex sense of life and certainly more interesting relations – an opinion he would hardly wish to support, considering himself an expert in the field – he has grossly miscalculated her response. He relied on her experience of a tranquil life and her preference for its sublimated French variant, having from the first seized with complacency on the easy division into Life and Art that seems to fill the house. So long as Maud does not 'know' (p. 313) – about his affair with Mrs Dyott – he is more than happy to chat to her a while about books – books which to his mind should be burnt. Mrs Dyott does everything to exacerbate the distinction, and after Maud's confession to 'keep up with three or four authors' (p. 314) she throws in: 'One must keep up with somebody' (p. 315), alluding to Maud's refusal to look for a new husband.

But now Maud surprises them by revealing both a more sophisticated sense of life than they thought her capable of, and a notion of art that they might find difficult to follow. The problem for her – as for us in our reading – stems from the fact that their discourse, although so smooth on the surface, is deeply at cross-purposes, and conducted in two different languages with over-lapping vocabularies. The Colonel and Mrs Dyott – in so far as the latter has any opinion on the matter – assume that the content of art is Life, and in particular 'a relation, say, between a man and a woman – I mean an intimate or a curious or a suggestive one' (p. 315). Thus if Maud is bored by 'the eternal French thing' (p. 315), 'again and again . . . the same couple' (p. 316), she must be looking, the Colonel infers, for a relation more curious. But wise in his experience he can tell her it 'doesn't exist' (p. 316), not in life and, since modern novels express life, not in art either. Art comes to life 'as near as [it] can come', and 'it can only take what life gives it' (p. 317). Maud's protest that she never looks 'for anything but an interest' (p. 316) is overheard, or rather twisted back into an interest in romance. It is clear, though, what she means from her comments on 'subjects' in art: 'I *have* . . . a lovely subject, but it would take an amount of treatment–!' (p. 316). This is a vocabulary with which we are familiar from James's own critical writings, but it is obviously meaningless to Voyt. For he goes on:

> 'Tell us then at least what it is.'
> At this she again met his eyes. 'Oh, to tell it would be to express it, and that's just what I can't do . . . ' (p. 316)

It cannot simply be paraphrased as 'a relation, say, between a man and a woman', nor can its treatment be divorced from it. Retrospectively, we then also reinterpret her remark that with the French novel she gets more life for her money: she does not find another romance there, nicely wrapped up, as it were, in lemon-coloured paper; but her aesthetic adventure in following a 'treat-ment' enriches her life by another experience. In her eyes, art does not come to life to refuel with new stories, but the 'full life' is filled with art. So that, *mutatis mutandis*, she can get more 'art' for her money.

The feeling that it might 'depend a little on what you call' (p. 319) art, and 'depend perhaps on what you mean by' (p. 317) life, is prevalent in this discussion, so that such a reversal of 'life' into 'art' is not entirely out of character. But unfortunately, it is mainly Mrs Dyott's discovery of the conversational phrase as a powerful device for contributing to the discussion of any topic she knows nothing about, rather than semantic sensitivity, that prompts its repeated occurrence. She is practising the social skill of polished conversation, while her lover – who once fought the enemy, is 'fighting Liberalism in the House of Commons' (p. 310), and has just enjoyed 'a struggle with the elements' (p. 310) – is going to grapple with what lies somewhat beneath this stylish surface:

> 'Of course you may call things anything you like – speak of them as one thing and mean quite another. But why should it depend on anything? Behind these words we use – the adventure, the novel, the drama, the romance, the situation, in short, as we most comprehensively say – behind them all stands the same sharp fact that they all, in their different ways, represent.'
> 'Precisely!' Mrs Dyott was full of approval.
> Maud, however, was full of vagueness. 'What great fact?'
> 'The fact of a relation. The adventure's a relation; the relation's an adventure. The romance, the novel, the drama are the picture of one. The subject the novelist treats is the rise, the formation, the development, the climax, and for the most part the decline, of one . . .' (p. 319)

Behind this confusion of language where one thing may mean any other, there is always and reassuringly a 'sharp fact' to get hold of, quite apart from the 'fact' which he takes even more for granted, that 'they all . . . [*do*] represent'. There may be different representations, but at least they all represent the same thing, and if you take off these wrappers you will always find a 'relation' inside.[5]

Once more Maud is obliged to risk: 'Doesn't it depend, again, on what you call a relation?' (p. 320). She is arguing for a greater variety of 'relations' presentable in fiction and asking if, say, a good woman and an innocent relation could also make a good story. For the others have already decided that 'badness' (p. 318) is the basis of a thrilling relation, that a relation is a passion and that moreover it is 'always the same passion' (p. 317). 'Adventures of innocence' (p. 320) simply do not make good fiction, even if examples regretfully exist:

> . . . that's exactly what the bored reader complains of. He has asked for bread and been given a stone. What is it but, with absolute directness, a question of interest, or, as people say, of the story?   (p. 320)

The substitution of story for interest makes it clear how he earlier failed to understand the 'interest' Maud is looking for in a novel; how from 'interest' he got to 'romance' since 'romance', like 'story', stands for a 'relation'. And if she is thus looking for a relation, as the phrase now reads, she is looking for a passion, and since the passion is always the same, will not find any other.

Outside the storm has blown over, and Voyt amiably gets up, while Mrs Dyott sighs: 'We 've spoiled her subject' (p. 321). For the subject, like the 'romance', the 'situation', the 'novel' etc. is but a passion – *the* passion; and Maud has not found, as she thought, her very own and 'a lovely subject'. All that remains to her – and only to her since the others do not think anything is left – is the treatment.

The treatment is just what we are now coming to. Maud already said that she cannot express her subject in words, and her medium remains her own experience. In conversation with Mrs Dyott she admits, by way of proving that she had not been 'so wrong' (p. 322) in her aesthetic contentions, that she has '[her] little drama', but that she also has '[her] little decency' (p. 322). Mrs Dyott asks her all the questions from the aesthetic catechism as laid down by the Colonel, who, 'you know, is right' (p. 322):

> 'An attachment?'
> 'An attachment.'
> 'That you shouldn't have?'
> 'That I shouldn't have.'
> 'A passion?'
> 'A passion.'   (pp. 322–3)

But here Maud's answers fail, for the passion is not shared and the gentleman in question does not even know. But the romance, Maud claims, lies in '[her] not wanting him to' (p. 323), which at the same time upholds her 'decency'. Mrs Dyott cannot see any romance in that, nor how a passion kept to oneself can begin 'to make the sentiment a relation' (p. 323). But it is sufficiently a relation for Maud, with her at the subjective end and the object of her love well in view. It is a relation fully formed, fully played out and fully felt in her own perception, and it does not require anyone else's.

At this Mrs Dyott drops the subject, but she continues to draw her own conclusions which she later relates to the Colonel: Maud is in love with *him*, and he must not know, or else, she conjectures, the flame is doomed. Thus the Colonel does know, but he has the decency not to want to show it to Maud and kill the flame. But in fact, not even his knowing can affect Maud's edifice any more: wholly within, it is sheltered, and even if the Colonel really were the unnamed object of her love, it is not the same man who has just been informed by Mrs Dyott. The impression of the Colonel (if it is the Colonel) which Maud guards in her consciousness has been told nothing, and continues in his beautiful innocence which is essential for her romance.

The real Colonel with his minimal sense of aesthetic matters observes that indeed Maud's consciousness '*was*, in the last analysis, a kind of shy romance' (p. 326). But he thinks it a 'fact' very feeble for representation, say, in a story: 'Not a romance like their own, a thing to make the fortune of any author up to the mark – one who should have the invention or who *could* have the courage . . .' (p. 326). For they are, you know, thoroughly 'bad', and there exists even a 'Mrs Voyt' (p. 324) – stuff which so far only the French have had the courage, and the invention, to handle.

With the next tale, *Flickerbridge* (1902), we have a narrator fully aware of the activity of observation. He gives the following description of Frank Granger, an American painter staying in Paris and who now visits London for the first time:[6]

> The British capital was a strange, grey world to him, where people walked, in more ways than one, by a dim light; but he was happily of such a turn that the impression, just as it came, could nowhere ever fail him, and even the worst of these things was almost as much an occupation – putting it only at that – as the best.

That is to say, Granger is ridden at least by the demon of observation, though we will soon recognise also the presence of the twin imagination.

Granger has a literary lady friend in Paris, his relation to whom is singularly ambiguous: ' . . . the young woman to whom it was publicly both affirmed and denied that he was engaged . . . the last phase of the relation . . . had passed into vagueness' (p. 327). But now that Addie has sent him to a newly discovered relative in England, to whom she must have specified a relation, Granger expects to find it revealed on arrival.

> He was indeed to learn on arrival to what he had been committed; but that was for a while so much a part of his first general impression that the fact took time to detach itself, the first general impression demanding verily all his faculties of response. (pp. 333–4)

Again he is wholly occupied with an 'impression', and this is how his faculties of response are engaged:

> It was a case he would scarce have known how to describe – could doubtless have described best with a full, clean brush, supplemented by a play of gesture; for it was always his habit to see an occasion, of whatever kind, primarily as a picture, so that he might get it, as he was wont to say, so that he might keep it, well together. (p. 334)

This cannot be perception of a passive kind, but is a projection of the imagination that forms a 'picture', that 'gets it together' and 'keeps it together'. When Granger has got it together he shows it to Miss Wenham: 'You fit your frame with a perfection only equalled by the perfection with which your frame fits you' (p. 340). The frame is as important as the picture, and Flickerbridge is an experience so new to him with its quaintness and its expression of tradition and a sense of the past, that it strikes him with unprecedented force. In his first enthusiasm he writes a rave eight-page letter to Addie to share his joy with her, aware of how much she herself would 'rave' (p. 337). But an intuition prevents him from sending the letter, and he gradually recognises the quality he most admires in Miss Wenham and Flickerbridge: her total lack of self-consciousness and of consciousness of the impression she creates with her surroundings. Yet he has not quite fathomed the full significance, the frailty of this flickering quality, and naively trusts:

All the elements, he was sure he should see, would hang together with a charm, presenting his hostess – a strange iridescent fish for the glazed exposure of an aquarium – as floating in her native medium. (pp. 338–9)

And a similar faith underlies his own appreciation of the view she – or anything else – presents: 'I only put things just as they are, and as I've also learned a little, thank heaven, to see them – which isn't, I quite agree with you, at all what anyone does . . .' (p. 341). This recalls the facts of *The Aspern Papers* or *The Birthplace*, the facts 'as they really are'. But as one fact 'took time to detach itself' from 'the first general impression', so another astute observation made earlier takes its time to trickle through into his consciousness: although a picture in a perfect frame, this is one which is harmed by too much looking at and so is hardly for 'the glazed exposure of an aquarium'. 'How one might love it, but how one might spoil it! To look at it too hard was positively to make it conscious, and to make it conscious was positively to wake it up' (p. 337). Thus he arrives at his second image of Miss Wenham of Flickerbridge: 'the Sleeping Beauty in the wood' (p. 340). His own part in it, however, dawns on him at the same time, as well as the fear that with his own raving he may have given her 'the fatal shake' (p. 341) already, may have, like the fairy prince, begun to wake her up. His friend Addie, however, seeing eye to eye with him anyway, will have tools even more dangerous than the gentle kiss of the prince:

He knew just what she would call quaint, just what she would call bland, just what she would call weird, just what she would call wild. She would take it all in with an intelligence much more fitted than his own, in fact, to deal with what he supposed he must regard as its literary relations. (p. 338)

She would know how to 'call' things, how to 'deal' with the impression, in short, how to 'put things just as they are' with a vengeance. And he expresses his fears accordingly to Miss Wenham:

She'll rave about you. She'll write about you. You're Niagara before the first white traveller – and you know, or rather you can't know, what Niagara became *after* that gentleman. Addie will have discovered Niagara. She will understand you in perfection; she will feel you down to the ground; not a delicate

> shade of you will she lose or let anyone else lose. You'll be too
> weird for words, but the words will nevertheless come . . . . You'll
> be in the magazines with illustrations; you'll be in the papers with
> headings; you'll be everywhere with everything . . . (p. 344)

Such a picture of publicity is in itself horrendous, but the real
danger lies in the waking of the Sleeping Beauty. Unlike in the fairy
tale, it would be her undoing, since awake she no longer is what she
was. If he wants to preserve her in her original innocence, he must
save her from any further 'seeing'. With a helpless literalness he
proposes to 'throw dust in [Addie's] eyes' (p. 345) and to surround
Miss Wenham with a hedge of thorns:

> I would tell her that you don't do at all – that you're not, in fact, a
> desirable acquaintance. I'd tell her you're vulgar, improper,
> scandalous; I'd tell her you're mercenary, designing, dangerous;
> I'd tell her the only safe course is immediately to let you drop. I
> would thus surround you with an impenetrable legend of
> conscientious misrepresentation, a circle of pious fraud, and all
> the while privately keep you for myself. (p. 345)

Yet he must know deep down that such a scheme is doomed and that
Addie is not a person so easily blinded. In fact he is already in
possession of a real solution, of which, however, he is barely
conscious and which he yet has to work over to its full realisation:
'privately [to] keep you for myself'. He is still thinking literally
when it first dawns on him:

> There was a preposterous possibility – yes, he held the strings
> quite in his hands – of keeping the treasure for himself. That was
> the art of life – what the real artist would consistently do. He
> would close the door on his impression, treat it as a private
> museum. He would see that he could lounge and linger there, live
> with wonderful things there . . . (p. 343)

He is saying the 'truth' without understanding it properly, but a
truth which we will shortly see him act out. 'Closing the door' is as
unfeasible as throwing dust in Addie's eyes – and they are hardly
strings he is holding in his hands. He falls victim to the confusion,
quite astounding in an artist, of the impression with the original, for
he wants to shut the portals of Flickerbridge and ensconce himself

inside with his easel – 'for himself he was sure that after a little he should be able to paint there' (p. 343).

What he can do, however, and finally does out of his instinctive understanding, is 'to close the door on his impression'. It is not, after all, their 'seeing' so much which wakes up the Sleeping Beauty, as his 'raving' and Addie's 'yelling' (p. 337). It is in his hands at least to stop the former and to keep his perception at its bare essential – in other words, to refrain from expressing it again. Another of James's observers, Shirley Sutton of *The Two Faces* (1900), has acquired this rare skill, and recommends it to his interlocutress:[7]

'Never notice anything.'
'That's nice advice from you,' she laughed,
'who notice everything!'
'Ah, but I speak of nothing.'

But we know that for Granger to see something is 'to see [it] . . . primarily as a picture', to recreate immediately his impression. The two parts are so intricately linked as to make a single activity – seeing – which it is impossible for him to separate into passive noticing and 'reproduction'. Expression does not even require a conventional medium, and the picture he has created is made without paint and brush.

Hence, in order to close the door on his impression effectively, he must leave Flickerbridge and its Sleeping Beauty, for in Miss Wenham he has an inevitable partner for the communication of his impression, a witness to his active imagination. And this not even because he is talking to her; he could remain silent, and yet his impression would find a resonance in her: she would grow conscious that he is conscious. And he must also leave his bride, with whom he could not but share his constant observing. What he thus saves, however, is not Flickerbridge and its innocence, but his precious private glimpse of it. It may be a work of art, though of a peculiar 'medium-less' kind; and he, like any artist, leaves his model behind. He certainly now behaves like a member of the guild of artists, shunning the intimacy of marriage. Indeed, another glimmer of intimacy also alarmed him and helped him to reach his awareness as an artist–Miss Wenham's response to his tale of the Sleeping Beauty.

She gazed at him with her queerest, kindest look, which he was getting used to, in spite of a faint fear, at the back of his head, of the strange things that sometimes occurred when lonely ladies, however mature, began to look at interesting young men from over the seas as if the young men desired to flirt. (p. 341)

He has declared himself her 'fairy prince' (p. 341), but the suggestion that she might take him literally, suspecting him of a desire to flirt, and maybe even respond, shocks him out of his dream. He is talking, of course, of his impression, of the Sleeping Beauty he has made with his perception, as well as of its creator who may guard her or wake her. She, on the other hand, thinks quite naturally of Miss Wenham and Frank Granger. Nor is it entirely her fault, since it is to her, the original, that the words are spoken. But this may be for Granger the beginning of his understanding that he cannot, must not, have 'incestuous' conversations about his 'work'. There follow, in any case, some further allusions to his extraordinary 'conversational freedom' (p. 347): 'He was really scared at moments at some of the liberties he took in talk – at finding himself so familiar . . .' (p. 346).

The 'freedom' and the 'liberties' come naturally to him, since he is speaking in the capacity of artist, while the social situation would have called for more decorum. Yet he is participating in a social situation, which he thus allows to develop into an intimacy that threatens to impinge on his 'art' and to induce that impermissible fusion of the two.

We have traced the 'marriage laws' of the literary tribe and what I have called the literary 'incest taboo'. I gave the latter its name for its constitutive function and its force as a taboo, rather than for any intrinsic similarity with its social counterpart, which is based on blood relations and the demarcation of the family. The literary incest taboo seemed at first to have little to do with the other marriage laws; and the fact that the artist finds marriage a distraction from work and may fare better as a celibate can stand independently of the taboo.

The first peripheral connection begins to appear with the implication that the intimacy of marriage may on the one hand encourage literary incest, say, between a writer and his wife, and on the other hand act as a preventive, namely if the reader or critic is married. Only, literary incest can occur between a writer and a critic of the same sex, whose relations cannot be regulated by marriage laws.

Through that link the two kinds of intimacy are put on a par functionally, in so far as the writer – or the prospective writer – must make a choice. The only intimacy open to him *qua* writer is the intimacy with the Muse.

We then discussed two tales which illustrate a particular type of artistic intimacy between the artist and his work, which emphasises its affinity with ordinary social intimacy, the conversion of passion into aesthetic excellence.

Finally, in the fifth section, we began to open the rank of works of art to the insubstantial products of the imagination, revaluating at the same time the notions of observation and imagination. Observation need not be passive or receptive, nor does imagination perforce entail concrete productions.

This leads us to a kind of Saussurean triangle,[8] where the original (object, referent) is not directly translated into its representation (word, sound-image), but first of all into a *concept*:

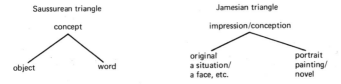

The formation of the concept from the original already involves the creative imagination, although no concrete work of art results. Or we may put it differently, preferring to call such conceptualisation creative observation.

We must be aware, however, that the Jamesian triangle is of a different order and a higher complexity. I have referred above to the danger of a simple analogy between the simple and the complex sign. In the former, the relation between the concept and its representation is one of symbolic attribution, while in the latter a complex process of 'translation' or 'superisation'[9] is involved. Similarly, the relation between the original and the conceptualis- ation is not simple attribution, but already contains, for example, a conceptualisation of a concrete medium; Granger of *Flickerbridge* 'sees' in pictures, while Maud Blessingbourne fantasises in stories. That is to say, the 'subsequent' translation from concept into text is already part of the conceptualisation. The triangles pertain to the conceptual, with the sound-image unsounded and the text un- written; and a separate diagram would have to represent actual articulation and expression. Rather than have recourse to Saussure's problematical distinction between *langue* and *parole*, one might use the one Chomsky made between sentence generation and sentence production or utterance:[10] the conceptualisation involves the 'tacit knowledge' by the artist of his medium and its 'grammar', but none of the productive motor activities of expression. In the case of the literary work this is not, however, a matter of the tacit knowledge of language; the conceptualisation of the medium is 'treatment'.

With the last two themes in mind – that of passion and that of 'conceptual art' – we can go on to the next section and the analysis of *The Sacred Fount*.

III The Sacred Fount

11 The concept of the fount

> Th' expense of Spirit in a waste of shame
> Is lust in action . . .   *Shakespeare*

The conjunction of the literary incest taboo and the literary marriage patterns suggests a peculiar relation between intimacy, sexuality and the literary or artistic, with the neutral or not further qualified term 'intimacy' verging on one of the others on either side: sex – intimacy – 'literariness'.[1]

The former connection hardly needs further comment, while of the latter we have so far discussed only its distributional social aspect, and the particular transformation of unfulfilled or restrained passion into masterpieces. But such a conversion of Life into Art is only a special case, and by no means a necessary condition for the artist's creativity. We have assumed on the contrary that the 'ideal' artist's involvement with his Muse excludes such human passions. Yet passion it is – or so the symmetry of the formula would suggest.

With *The Sacred Fount* we hope to fill in this last missing element, namely the question whether art, besides being a substitute for love and marriage, is itself of the very nature of passionate love. The novel is well known for its analysis of social passion, which moreover is properly understood to be an euphemism for sexual relations;[2] and many critics have read it further as an allegory of the creative imagination gone wild. But allegory is of course an arbitrary style of reading, and we have yet to close that gap between the narrator's actual activity and the activity of the artist which the allegoric equation simply straddles. Moreover, the image of the 'sacred fount' usually falls by the wayside in such allegorical readings.[3] I will instead let the narrator give his own demonstration of his felt affinity with the artist. It will be for him too to lead us from his presentation of love affairs and of his own fate to a conclusion about the nature of creative passion.

The 'plot' of *The Sacred Fount* consists entirely of the narrator's self-set task to observe and analyse the relations of two couples, during a weekend he spends with them at the same house-party. On his way up to the party at Newmarch, he forms the first intuition about the promise of such a study, following a quick succession of impressions of and exchanges with Mrs Brissenden and Gilbert Long, two fellow-travellers on his train. His suspicion is that a passionate relation is not so much a state of affairs between the two, as the positive flow of a mysterious substance from one to the other – a flow necessarily unidirectional. For the Brissendens the waters of the 'sacred fount' seem to be Briss's youth, which is drained from him and absorbed by his rejuvenated wife. A disequilibrium existed from the start, since Briss is more than a dozen years his wife's junior. Now Mrs Briss looks younger than ever, while Briss himself, as the narrator is soon to discover, has aged considerably.

The other couple seem to exchange a different substance: cleverness. Gilbert Long has suddenly grown so 'clever',[4] and his secret mistress is to be found out as the person most 'idiotised' (p. 103). But the necessary basis for either fount must be a 'relation . . . so awfully intimate' (p. 36) or, as the narrator wishes to improve on it, '*intimissima*' (p. 36). It is not a matter of mere infatuation or flirtation, but of a fully developed passion, virtually secret in its intensity, and certainly exclusive. This passion, however, is something to be consumed; it is a fount not bottomless, but with a strictly limited quota of fluid.

If the artist's passion for his Muse were to be of this very kind, it would corroborate our conclusion that his intimacy is of an insufficient quantity to stretch for both marriage and art.

The concept of the fount recalls venerable beliefs about sex and the life juices, flourishing, for example, in Bacon's time and still a presupposition in Herbert Spencer's.[5] Every loss of precious fluid means a reduction of the overall stocks, and the individual is advised to husband it prudently to last him a lifetime. In particular, such 'vital capital'[6] governs mental as well as physical wellbeing. A more general and cosmic theory of life fluids was articulated in Mesmer's 'animal magnetism' and remained, despite controversy, widespread throughout Europe and influential well into the nineteenth century.[7] Today, the myth of the more explicitly sexual theory of life fluids has faded out in its literal form,[8] but has survived in a metaphorised manner. Freud's theory of civilisation as sublimation selfconsciously makes that link from literal quantum of fluid to the general and abstract notion of mental potency which previously had been taken for granted, but in the age of rationalism needs 'scientific' justification. Achievement of the mind is for Freud a sublimated form of repressed sexuality. The energy (energy rather than life juices) is channelled elsewhere and discharged in another form. The implication remains, however, that the original quota is given since it accounts for output at large; and since we compare, in *Civilisation and its Discontents*,[9] the civilised but sexually repressed society with the 'primitive' one where sexuality is fully lived out, but nothing remains to be sublimated. The idea of substitution is maintained, as one form, the sublimated, appears in the place of another.

Yet, rather than apply simply a Freudian terminology and say that the artist's work is sublimated sexuality, we will return to the image of the fount in James's novel. And before a full analogy can be seen to hold between the artist's passion and the passion of the world, it also remains to be examined if the artist's fount is as fatally limited as the 'sacred founts' he observes, or if it is not after all of a different order.

12 That frivolous thing an observer

> Mad in pursuit and in possession so,
> Had, having, and in quest, to have extreame,
> A blisse in proofe and proud and very wo,
> Before, a joy proposd, behind, a dreame . . .   *Shakespeare*

After following for some time innocently the natural inclination of his talent, observing and refining his intuition about the lovers, as well as looking for the unknown fourth partner, the narrator is suddenly overcome by a sensation of personal danger, 'the scared presentiment of something in store for myself' (p. 75). Admittedly, it is brought about mainly by his rash involvement of others in his happy pursuit, the particular threat of which he comes to realise more sharply:

> I suddenly found myself thinking with a kind of horror of any accident by which I might have to expose to the world, to defend against the world, to share with the world, that now so complex tangle of hypotheses . . .   (p. 125)

It is 'the peril of the public ugliness' (p. 127) which threatens the work exposed to the world prematurely. Rarely would an artist let the public participate in the progress of his work, would expose its frail growth to the critical judgement. 'A great work needs silence, privacy, mystery even',[1] says one of James's painters; the artist must work in solitude, and bear the responsibility for its completion alone: 'the mere brush of Lady John's clumsier curiosity made me tremble for the impunity of my creation' (p. 125). The answer to this sudden anxiety he finds in calling his preoccupation 'my private madness' (p. 118), an 'obsession' better got rid of (p. 72). But as in a true artist, the creative impulse overrides the concern for personal welfare; and he resigns himself to finding it 'the best wisdom to accept my mood' as one accepts the 'law of one's talent': 'It was a force that I at this stage simply found I had already succumbed to' (p. 76). That this impulse and its pursuit stand up to the comparison with art is implied by his description of them: 'the full-blown flower of my theory' (p. 122) recalls the garden of *The Aspern Papers*, as does his assurance that there is 'not a single flower of the garden that my woven wreath should lack' (p. 177). It is a thing 'all mine' (p. 101), as its 'beauty perhaps was only for *me*' (p. 96), but it is a 'kingdom of thought I had won' (p. 176). The sense of private ownership, of total disregard for any outside opinion, is the characteristic of the working artist. Although his work will eventually be published, the creative process must be influenced by no thought of it. He is working for his own satisfaction, heeding but his own standards, and exhibiting the egotism and keen desire for privacy appropriate for a lover. The sensation of his creation is private too: 'the beauty and the terror' (p. 121), and 'the joy of the intellectual mastery of things unamenable, that joy of determining, almost of creating, re-sults' (p. 151).

The question remains, of course, as to the medium of this creative achievement, which moreover has also the signs of a scientific construct. But it is a commonplace that artistic creativity and scientific originality bear crucial resemblances.

This 'glittering crystal palace' (p. 145) is made of 'accumulations of lucidity' (p. 177), of 'plunges of insight' (p. 151), 'intensity of consciousness' (p. 127), of vision. The skills of the art are letting 'the wandering vision play and play' (p. 122), and seeing, seeing even 'too much' (p. 180). The potential of this faculty of sight dawns on the narrator early: 'To see all this was at the time, I remember, to be as inhumanly amused as if one had found one could create something' (p. 81). Seeing, moreover, is knowing – if one knows how: 'I was sufficiently aware even then that if one hadn't known it one might have seen nothing; but I was not less aware that one couldn't know anything without seeing all' (p. 122). He is almost intimidated by this *hubris* of a 'superior vision' (p. 127): 'Didn't I perhaps, in proportion as I felt how little she saw, think awfully well of myself . . . for seeing so much more?' (p. 127). 'Transcendent intelligence' (p. 114) in fact combines these twin demons of knowing and seeing perfectly; it is creative imagination which works this particular medium and fits together the bits one by one to make 'the larger sense, every way' (p. 96). For it is all a matter of fitting, of fitting together cogitations, perceptions, 'like a

sudden picture and with a click that fairly resound[s]' (p. 176). Like
a work of art it relies on 'artificial proportion' (p. 130), a 'real
principle of composition' (p. 121), and selection from this 'affluence
of fine things' (p. 121).

The 'rewards' of the artist we have already begun to name – the
joy, the beauty, 'the taste of success' (p. 96), the 'personal privilege,
on the basis of the full consciousness' (p. 131); yet they are
ambiguous enough to become questionable and verge on madness.
A passage from James's prefaces restores a balance to this oscillation
between privilege and price, beauty and terror, of 'the particular
intellectual adventure':[2]

> Here lurks an immense homage to the general privilege of the
> artist, to that constructive, that creative passion . . . the exercise
> of which finds so many an occasion for appearing to him the
> highest of human fortunes, the rarest boon of the gods. He values
> it, all sublimely and perhaps a little fatuously, for itself – as the
> great extension, great beyond all others, of experience and of
> consciousness; with the toil and trouble a mere sun-cast shadow
> that falls, shifts and vanishes, the result of his living in so large a
> light . . . Robert Louis Stevenson has . . . said the right word:
> that the partaker of the 'life of art' who repines at the absense of
> the rewards, as they are called, of the pursuit might surely be
> better occupied. Much rather should he endlessly wonder at his
> not having to pay half his substance for his luxurious immersion.
> He enjoys it, so to speak, without a tax; the effort of labour
> involved, the torment of expression, of which we have heard in
> our time so much, being after all but the last refinement of his
> privilege. It may leave him weary and worn; but how, after his
> fashion, he will have lived!

Our 'artist' of *The Sacred Fount* feels that he even pays, 'vicariously,
the tax on being absurd' (p. 131) and thus earns his 'own
constructive joy' (p. 155). Also, a touch of social masochism quite
becomes the artist: 'It was absurd to have consented to such
immersion, intellectually speaking, in the affairs of other people.
One had always affairs of one's own, and I was positively neglecting
mine' (p. 72). On the other hand, terror and beauty are combined
in the intercourse with the Muse. The temporary 'toil and trouble',
in fact, lies only in the wrestling, soon outshone by the fullness of the
light:

[my relation], so far as [Mrs Server] was concerned, was unexpressed – so that I suppose what most, at the juncture in question, stirred within me was the wonder of how I might successfully express it. I felt that so long as I didn't express it I should be haunted with the idea of something infinitely touching and tragic in her loneliness – possibly in her torment, in her terror.   (p. 76)

In other words, he might himself be suffering the torment and the terror of compassion and empathy. But the remedy lies in its expression, its relegation to the realm of signification. Expression for this artist, as opposed to the novelist, does not however consist of putting it into words; his medium is pure significance, 'the larger sense', and the resulting 'consciousness [being] aware of having performed a full revolution' (p. 137), being aware, in other words, of itself. To express his relation to Mrs Server, then, is to fit 'this deeper vision of her' (p. 76) into his larger scheme and to assign it a place in the complex tangle of hypotheses, in order to bring it finally 'through a magnificent chiaroscuro of colour and shadow, out into the light of day' (p. 156).

Some critics have taken the position, shared by some characters at Newmarch, that the narrator must himself be in love.[3] Opinion however varies as to the beneficiary of his affection, and none of the choices seems to be derived from good grounds. Evidence for the narrator's frame of mind, for what I shall call a 'third sacred fount', consists not only in the hints of other characters that he may be in love with Mrs Server, but first and foremost in allusions in the narrator's own unselfconscious words. While I thus agree as to the clues which may lead us to suspect the narrator's 'sacred fount' and partly take them for granted, I suggest that a different receptacle can be seen to accept its flow.

The passage cited on 'expression' is one of many that cast doubt on the narrator's serious infatuation with May Server, and gives a different idea of his interest in her. If it were personal and emotional, the haunting 'idea of something infinitely touching and tragic in her loneliness' would not be successfully staved off by expressing his own relation to her. It might be explained, understood better why it is touching and tragic to him, if he were to become articulately aware of his love for her; yet with its recognition he would also hope to know how to put an end to her loneliness. But no indication of any such plan of relief is anywhere given; on the contrary, 'the question of her happiness was essentially subordinate' (p. 161). Nor would we quite expect, in a lover, the tone of his subsequent references to her person:

> She had her whole compromised machinery of thought and speech, and if these signs were not, like [Briss's], external, that made her case but harder, for she had to create, with intelligence rapidly ebbing, with wit half gone, the illusion of an unimpaired estate . . . . Was not that embarrassment, if one analysed a little, at the bottom of her having been all day, in the vulgar phrase and as the three of us had too cruelly noted, all over the place? (p. 77)

She is of as much interest to him as is Madame Bovary to Flaubert, and he follows her unfortunate lot with as much clinical detachment and cold observation. But while Flaubert is a creative writer (and Madame Bovary a character rather than an acquaintance), the narrator is an artist of seeing, a creative *voyeur*:

> I might from this moment have, as much as I liked, my own sense of [wonder], but I was definitely conscious of a sort of loyalty to her that would have rendered me blank before others: though not indeed that – oh, at last, frankly, quite the contrary! – it would have forbidden me to watch and watch.   (p. 77)

With a certain amount of self-recognition he calls his attitude 'conscientiously infernal' (p. 77). His 'blankness' is loyalty to his theory, which he protects from 'the public ugliness' by protecting May Server. And as a further sign of his lacking intention of coming to her rescue:

> How I remember saying to myself that if she didn't get better she surely *must* get worse! . . . It became present to me that she possibly might recover if anything should happen that would pull her up, turn her into some other channel. If, however, that consideration didn't detain me longer the fact may stand as a sign of how little I believed in any check.   (p. 78)

He does not believe in upsetting the natural balance of fate and of 'founts', and 'all [he] cared for' now was 'Mrs Server's quandary' (p. 79). A lover, surely, in the confidence of his own passion would have felt certain of his ability to 'pull her up', to turn her, even, into some other channel. Particularly if, as some characters and some critics hold, Mrs Server showed equal signs of affection for the narrator. No, Mrs Server does not serve the narrator as the receptacle for his own overflow of sacred waters; and if she is, as the narrator suspects, the object of Gilbert Long's passion, she is not even free to do so, since such passion must be exclusive. The narrative ambiguity of course allows for these other possibilities, especially if we were to trust Mrs Briss's final verdict that Long is 'a prize fool' (p. 201), is 'perfectly stupid' (p. 202) and hence never the beneficiary of anybody's cleverness. Then, also, we might believe Obert's observation that Mrs Server has 'changed back', that 'her misery . . . has dropped' and she is 'all right' again (p. 160). These two external views in combination could at this point still be true without entirely destroying the narrator's theory; and they serve in fact as the points of intersection at which we might try out a set of different 'if' – interpretations. The narrator in fact spends some thought on the question of what would happen in the event of a passion extinguished, and whether the victim would 'change back' and recover. We shall come back to his considered opinion in a moment. It remains for us to consider if we should allow these outsiders to daub in our artist's work, since they are as much subject to 'structural ambiguity' as is the narrator with his account. But since their statements are themselves recounted by the narrator and thus in their selection and arrangement part of his edifice, we shall continue to follow his own interpretation.

Instead, I suggest that the receptacle of the narrator's secret but overflowing spring is his 'crystal palace', the flower of his theory, into which all his strength, his energy and his intelligence are poured. Can we observe, then, a similar disequilibrium, a sign of the effect of the drain on this particular substance, and apart from the hints by other characters? If his theory is growing in strength, can we detect depletion in its benefactor? We can, and in more ways than one.

To start with, intelligence and intellectual curiosity, 'wonder and wisdom', are the very substance of which the narrator claims to have a surplus: 'My extraordinary interest in my fellow-creatures. I have more than most men. I've never really seen anyone with half so much . . . ' (p. 108). The substance is measurable, so that a want or an excess of it becomes manifest, just like Long's initial dullness and Briss's youth in comparison to his wife's age. Hence, also, it calls for a strict sense of economy: 'I had better waste neither my wonder nor my wisdom' (p. 30). This sets out at least one part of an initial situation for a sacred fountain's flow. Then there are those testimonies by other characters which concern effects rather than interpretations and which suggest, simply, that the narrator now shows himself the signs of 'sacrifice' (p. 35), is himself arrayed and anointed (p. 122). But it is above all an unselfconscious remark by the narrator, delivered casually and as an aside, which announces an already latent awareness that he, supreme subject of his kingdom of thought, might also be an object of observation – as indeed he is, at least, for us:

> I daresay that, for that matter, my cogitations – for I must have bristled with them – would have made me as stiff a puzzle to interpretative minds as I had suffered other phenomena to become to my own. I daresay I wandered with a tell-tale restlessness of which the practical detachment might well have mystified those who hadn't suspicions. (p. 74)

Again a testimony to the peculiarity of his interest in Mrs Server, but it is mystifying only to those who do not recognise its origin in his flowering theory and who might, banally, put it down to 'silly infatuations' (p. 80). For, not to have 'suspicions' is to suspect mere superficial relations – 'vulgar flirtation' (p. 38) – that show by the conventional signs of excessive interest; while the passions traced by the narrator betray themselves by avoidance, by covering up. A stiff puzzle he will certainly be since with him, as with May Server and unlike with Briss, the symptoms are not 'external' (p. 77); they are his cogitations, and the paradoxical combination of a 'tell-tale restlessness' and a 'practical detachment'. His latent selfawareness leads to recognition in others, his response to which, however, shows clearly that it *is* only latent. Mrs Server, coming upon the narrator unexpectedly, puts the question to him: 'What is it that has happened to you?' (p. 101). He finds this ironically funny, and replies with a laugh and the same question, intended already before she put hers: 'Oh . . . what is it that has happened to *you*?' (p. 101). But he locates the irony only partly, thinking it simply ironic that she should ask *him* the question properly to be put to *her*. For the reader wielding 'the torch of [the narrator's] analogy' (p. 152) so as to include him too in the circle of its light, the irony casts a longer shadow; just as the narrator is overwhelmed to see the 'victims', Mrs

Server and poor Briss, relax together in mute communion, in a 'fellowship in resistance to doom' (p. 107), so we detect an equally congenial pair in Mrs Server and the narrator,' [he], as well as [she], on the mope, or on the muse, or on whatever you call it', in '[not] half a bad corner for such a mood' (p. 100). If he follows the traces of two victims and two beneficiaries, we are on the scent of three of each kind. And if we know that each pair requires a number of screens and manoeuvres in order to disguise their burning passion, we have examples of this aspect in the narrator's dread of public exposure, in his 'protection' of Mrs Server, and most pointedly, in the last colloquy with Mrs Briss.

The rhetorical verve of the narrator again betrays connections he may himself not have fully recognised:

> It would be well, for aught I could do *for* [Briss], that I should have seen the last of him. What remained with me from that vision of his pacing there with his wife was the conviction that his fate, whatever it was, held him fast. It wouldn't let him go, and all I could ask of it now was that it should let *me*. I *would* go – I was going . . . (p. 142)

But if Brissenden's fate holds him fast, the narrator's, 'whatever it [is]', equally retains its grip on *him*. We fairly see him dangle:

> The admonitions of that moment . . . were that I should catch in the morning, with energy, an earlier train to town than anyone else was likely to take, and get off alone by it, bidding farewell for a long day to Newmarch. I should be in small haste to come back, for I should leave behind me my tangled theory, no loose thread of which need I ever again pick up, in no stray mesh of which need my foot again trip. It was on my way to the place, in fine, that my obsession had met me, and it was by retracing those steps that I should be able to get rid of it. (p. 142)

We may suspect, and have it confirmed soon after, that alas the 'energy', so emphasised, to 'break off sharp' (p. 142), is no longer at his disposal, is, rather, turned already into some other channel and to a different purpose. But we are surprised most of all by his sweet hope that 'retracing those steps' will do the trick, or undo the harm, for we know that the sacred fount flows in one direction only. A little earlier the narrator raised the problem of 'changing back', again

entertaining the illusion that he himself might still be 'free' (p. 137),
though he gives us at the same time a vivid example of the contrary.
Much as he cherishes the imagined freedom, he 'still want[s] to
know!' (p. 137). The flow, once begun, cannot be dammed and
presumably continues until the fount is dry. And if the narrator may
consider, as he does, whether there is a possibility of correcting the
imbalance of passion, he has in his own the strongest evidence to the
contrary, as there is certainly none of making knowledge, once
gained, unlearnt. But a termination of the fountain's flow, he
concludes, can only be imagined along the lines he defines for Briss:
'he would have quitted the world, in truth, only the more effectually
to leave it to her' (p. 79). Just so the narrator's hasty retreat would
not leave the theory lifeless behind, nor would he save himself from
its snares by cancelling his authorship; rather, he would quit the
scene 'only the more effectually to leave it to [it]'. And as 'Gilbert
Long might die, but not the intensity he had inspired' (p. 78), so this
particular crystal palace might crumble and yet 'the torch of [his]
analogy' continue to burn for ever. Leaving Newmarch, then, is no
guarantee of freedom, nor against tripping again in stray meshes
and living in 'the strained vision' (p. 137).

In one of his smoking-room colloquies with Obert the narrator
himself employs the argument of the irreversibility of knowledge,
yet not without giving another demonstration of his slackening
'energy' in his persistent blind spot regarding himself. Obert has
tried to evade the subject altogether, denying having any part in the
theory, but the narrator will not let him off so easily:

'Yes, precisely. That *was* the torch of my analogy. What I showed
you in the one case seemed to tell you what to look for in the other.
You thought it over. I accuse you of nothing worse than of *having*
thought it over. But you see what thinking it over does for it.'
The way I said this appeared to amuse him. 'I see what it does for
you!'   (p. 152)

Secure in the logic of his argument, the narrator assumes that 'the
one case' and 'the other' exhaust the possible cases. Hence he fails to
catch the signification of Obert's allusion, for which he himself has
paved the way, and which conjoins rhetorically the 'torch', 'the
other case', the 'analogy' and 'thinking it over': 'I see what IT[4] does
for you', what my thinking it over, your thinking it over, does for the

analogy and for you. It is not until later when Obert spells it out that we find his reference to the third 'case' confirmed. The narrator boasts:

'For I, you see, have watched . . . everyone, everything *but* you.'
'Oh, I've watched *you*,' said Ford Obert . . .   (p. 154)

Yet even such explicit reference to himself fails to alert him. Of course we do not know how much Obert really sees, whether he simply suspects the narrator of being in love with another person at Newmarch or recognises his special passion for what we take it to be. But he is certainly aware of the symptoms in the 'victim', while his hints concerning them are lost on the narrator, who takes any reference to himself as one to the conceiver of the theory. He continues the dialogue after Obert's claim to see what 'it' does for *him*:

'No, you don't! Not at all yet. That's just the embarrassment.'
'Just whose? . . . Just yours?'
'Well, say mine . . . '   (p. 152)

Embarrassment is of course a sure sign of the lover found out, and especially, we have seen, in the victim. It is the victims who carry the burden of preserving the secret, of screening and shielding the sacred fount, so that it is also they who incur the embarrassment of discovery. The narrator claims it voluntarily when it was left open to him to refute – 'say mine'.

'Blind spot' we must call it, for he does not lack the astuteness to perceive such blindness in others. Grace Brissenden shows a persistent imperviousness to any allusion to her own case, although she herself is a beneficiary. The narrator is talking to her about Long and his secret mistress, who he asserts must be present at Newmarch:

'It's my belief that he no more goes away without her than you go away without poor Briss.'
She surveyed me in splendid serenity. 'But what have we in common.'   (p. 41)

Her lack of comprehension of what they have 'in common' may at this point still be genuine, though the absence of a question mark may indicate protest rather than surprise. In their last interview, on the other hand, her consciousness has been alerted and she has a deliberate design to persuade the narrator that his theory was wrong from the start. The resulting complex *double entente* of their dialogue plays between their discussion of the theory of vision and the actual objects of that vision. Apparently their talk is about the precise moment at which Mrs Briss ceased to believe in the narrator's 'miracle', 'stopped thinking' (p. 187) as she calls it. He pretends to be in search of her recipe for the 'cure', and to 'catch' her (p. 199) at the earliest stage it began to work on her. Of course he has no such innocent reason, and on the contrary finds in her new position just the last missing element for his theory: if she suddenly wishes to deny the relevance of his fantasy altogether, it must be because she has grown conscious of the fact that she plays her own part in it and that the analogy lights up her own relations with Briss. 'Your . . . change is quite sufficient – it gives us all we need' (p. 179), says the narrator, pleased by the richness of her blind spot and the eloquence of her denials. He seems for ever to 'trap' her words, and to help at least the reader to read them in his way:

> 'I persuaded you apparently that Long's metamorphosis was not the work of Lady John. I persuaded you of nothing else.'
> She looked down a little, as if again at a trap.
> 'You persuaded me that it was the work of somebody.'
> Then she held up her head. 'It came to the same thing.'
> If I had credit then for my trap it at least might serve. 'The same thing as what?'
> 'Why, as claiming that it *was* she.'
> 'Poor May – "claiming"? When I insisted it wasn't!'   (p. 186)

On a surface of rhetoric he firmly leads her into this last contradiction, namely that he 'claimed' it was Mrs Server, while he had precisely always denied it. But what his trap really serves for, beyond trapping her in contradiction, is her unavowed admission of understanding the analogy, of conceding that to grant Long's transformation as the work of somebody 'came to the same thing' as admitting Briss's premature age as the work of Grace Brissenden, or inversely, her youth and beauty as the work of Briss. It is this awareness, the narrator is convinced (and collecting proof of), which lies at the bottom of her present change of mind.

Uneasiness is similarly betrayed by her anxious attempt to confirm explicitly that she and Briss are out of the game. She asks:

'Are we accusing each other?' And the narrator replies with a laugh:

> 'Dear no . . . not each other; only with each other's help, a few of our good friends.'
> 'A few?' She handsomely demurred. 'But one or two at the best.'
> 'Or at the worst!' – I continued to laugh.   (p. 185)

'One or two at the best' would suit her fine, as being Long and Mrs Server. For the narrator this would be 'at the worst', since he is anxious to 'catch' the Brissendens as well – just as the reader would like to catch the narrator in addition.

The narrator muses about the particular excitement this *double entente* affords him, though he entirely missed that of his talk with Obert:

> It could *not* but be exciting to talk, as we talked, on the basis of those suppressed processes and unavowed references which made the meaning of our meeting so different from its form. We knew ourselves – what moved me, that is, was that she knew me – to mean, at every point, immensely more than I said or than she answered; just as she saw me, at the same points, measure the space by which her answers fell short.   (p. 188)

We are following in the first instance the narrator's passion, however, and looking out for the familiar symptoms. In the same final chapters of his ultimate talk with Grace Brissenden we discover a more pronounced policy of screening and deception on the narrator's part. It is partly his tactics for trapping Mrs Brissenden that he pretends to deny still, as from the first, the identity of May Server as Long's secret lover; yet he also has his own pressing reasons. Indeed, to himself he admits 'to know little now of [his] desire to "protect" Mrs Server': 'She was certainly, with Mrs Briss at least, past all protection . . . But I none the less, on a perfectly simple reasoning, stood to my guns . . .' (p. 173). What standing to his guns means is to gather, in a grand finale, the beautiful edifice, the 'kingdom of thought', back into the subjectivity of his singular authorship, to make sure that in the last analysis and despite his earlier indiscretions, he can establish his 'superior vision' and will know and see 'so much more' than anyone else at Newmarch; even though the only personal privilege I could, after all, save from the whole business was that of understanding. I couldn't save Mrs Server, and I couldn't save poor Briss; I *could*, however, guard, to the last grain of gold, my prècious sense of their loss, their disintegration and their doom; and it was for this that I was now bargaining.   (p. 189)

Perhaps he cannot even save himself, and the 'embarrassment' claimed so insistently with Obert is a signal of the precious sense of *his* loss. And, like the victim who guards the secret, he now jealously demands the privilege of his theory back from Mrs Briss, who had a share in it: 'Nothing *is*, I admit, a miracle from the moment one's on the track of the cause, which was the scent we were following. Call the thing simply my fact' (p. 187). She answers, somewhat vaguely: 'If it's yours it's nobody else's!' (p. 187). She might more clearly have pointed out his own contradiction of wanting it to be both a 'fact' and his very own; both, that is, an 'objective' or public truth, and a personal secret. His notion of a fact, however, begins to emerge more distinctly when he emphasises the subjective position of the observer, who may be right, simply, owing to the self-consistency, the beauty, of the vision he constructs:

'Long *isn't* what he seems?'
'Seems to whom?' she asked sturdily.
'Well, call it – for simplicity – to *me*. For you see' – and I spoke as to show *what* it was to see – 'it all stands and falls by that.'
(p. 181)

He is of course an expert at seeing, and selfconscious of his art to the extent of spotting even the most trivial allusion in a manner of speech – 'you see'. No wonder Grace Brissenden is so exasperated by his slippery discourse, which she feels obliged to take up and dispute even at the level of rhetoric, let alone that of its reference:

'. . . it's precisely because you regard it as rubbish that I now appeal to you.' . . .
'Appeal? I thought you were on the ground, rather,' she beautifully smiled, 'of dictation.'
'Well, I'm that too. I dictate my terms. But my terms are in themselves the appeal.' I was ingenious but patient. 'See?'
'How in the world can I see?'
'*Voyons*, then . . .' (p. 191)

In her defensive despair Mrs Briss unwittingly employs terms more fitting than either is aware for the narrator's emerging resemblance to a victim: 'I mean you're carried away – you're abused by a fine fancy . . .' (p. 181). In her terminology, this is simply synonymous with being 'crazy', and her calling him mad is her 'lateral' way of getting out of the argument. While the shorter synonym remains virtually insignificant, we will have reason to consider 'abuse' again, as a typical relation of beneficiary to victim.

In the course of their long final conversation the narrator's initial self-assurance seems gradually to wane, while more and more doubts insinuate themselves – a certain dawning but not quite conscious suspicion of unhappiness despite the bliss of passion, which we have observed in Briss as well as Mrs Server, a growing awareness of being exploited by their lovers and having the additional burden of hiding it. So it becomes the narrator's privilege to bargain for his 'precious sense of their loss' and, as we add, of his own. But it makes for a special complication that in his own case the subject of the 'sense' and the observed subject of the loss are one and the same consciousness. Thus there follows a struggle between his duty to assert the victorious theory, at least to himself, and his own depletion which cannot but show through at the same time and which he tries, moreover, to hide:

> 'Well,' said Mrs Briss, 'I think you're crazy.'
> It naturally struck me. 'Crazy?'
> 'Crazy.'
> I turned it over. 'But do you call that intelligible?'
> She did it justice. 'No: I don't suppose it *can* be so for you if you *are* insane.'
> I risked the long laugh which might have seemed that of madness. '"If I am" is lovely!' And whether or not it was the special sound, in my ear, of my hilarity, I remember just wondering if perhaps I mightn't be. 'Dear woman, it's the point at issue!'   (p. 192)

When Mrs Briss takes another side jump in her argument, now asserting that Long's woman is Lady John, the narrator again seems insecure in the face of her confidence: 'She was all logic now, and I could easily see, between my light and my darkness, how she would remain so' (p. 209). It is not her 'logic' that really worries him, which after all, in its blatant inconsistency, is following perfectly the path of proof he has mapped out for her with his higher logic, and

every step of which he ticks off with a mental *QED*. But his
statement recalls an allusion which, somewhat unconnectedly,
followed the passage cited above: '*Voyons*, then. Light or darkness,
my imagination rides me . . .' (p. 191). The light of seeing, the
sacred substance of his fount, is contending with the darkness of his
depletion, a darkness now growing more and more in the place
where the light had been and is nearly spent. This dialectic of his
fount is naturally reflected in his language, as in his comment earlier
on facing Briss, 'never . . . so much poor Briss as at that moment':

> That ministered to the confusion as well as to the brightness, for if
> his being there at all renewed my sources and replenished my
> current – spoke all, in short, for my gain – so, on the other
> hand . . . his particular aspect was something of a shock.   (pp.
> 157–8)

When, to his question 'I'm to understand that you *know*?', Mrs
Briss retorts, with some hesitation but nonetheless with syntactic
decisiveness, 'I know', he gives free rein to his doubts – at least 'for a
little':

> It was the oddest thing in the world for a little, the way this
> affected me without my at all believing it. It was preposterous,
> hang though it would with her somersault, and she had quite
> succeeded in giving it the note of sincerity. It was the mere sound
> of it that, as I felt even at the time, made it a little of a blow – a
> blow of the smart of which I was conscious just long enough
> inwardly to murmur: 'What if she *should* be right?' She had for
> these seconds the advantage of stirring within me the memory of
> her having indeed, the day previous, at Paddington, 'known' as
> I hadn't. It had been really on what she *then* knew that we
> originally started, and an element of our start had been that I
> admired her freedom.   (p. 210)

The great seer finds it difficult indeed to get used to the mist
which is spreading over his eyes, and as this one faculty begins to fail
him, tries to compensate with the second best, hearing. It is a
strained ear now, instead of the 'strained vision', that just catches
'the note', 'the mere sound of it', as in the passage before it is 'the
special sound, in [his] ear' which provides the sensory information
for his knowledge. With her strong instinct for survival Grace Briss

has switched from the futile attempt to make the narrator 'un-see' what he has seen, to an attack on his vision with her 'tone'. But we now also see the intense conflict of the narrator's split self, the struggle between the author in subject position of knowing and seeing, and the vulnerable and weakened victim, compelled passively to receive impressions on his ear – the supplier at the source of the sacred fount. The former would not at all believe it, while the latter is in the oddest way affected, with few resistances to fend off the attack. The memory of Paddington, stirred up to his disadvantage, may at first seem only connected to the selfishness with which he wishes to hug the authorship of the 'crystal palace'. Yet her knowing then as now is based altogether on different grounds – not on seeing with 'transcendent intelligence', but on the mere gossip from which society breeds rumours. Indeed we learn that she now has it from Briss, and that she 'take[s] his word' for it (p. 211). It is neither understanding, nor even 'fact' with its sources confirmed; it is sheer assertion, and with the tone of defiance with which she also declares him mad.

It can therefore have been little that the narrator took from her at Paddington, and it certainly was not his methodology. It was a mere hint she gave, a sketching out of the area to which he might apply his faculties, and what provided the incentive was in fact 'her freedom'. This cue prompts an unexpected sequel:

> . . . and an element of our start had been that I admired her freedom. The form of it, at least – so beautifully had she recovered herself – was all there now. Well, I at any rate reflected, it wasn't the form that need trouble me, and I quickly enough put her a question that related only to the matter. (p. 210)

It is not as if the 'form' of her freedom did not interest him and the matter did – it would be difficult indeed to conceive what exactly these two entities were. The freedom *is* the form, while the 'matter' is whatever purpose she puts it to. In the first instance at Paddington, it was the boldness (freedom) of her conception, her hypothesis that 'what's the difference in Mr Long' (p. 21) is that 'a very clever woman', Lady John, has taken an interest in him and given him a 'lift' – 'Lady John's company *is*, you see, a lift' (p. 22). We might note that the content of her thesis is the same as the one she penultimately reverts to; it is also a matter on which the narrator disagrees. But the real 'matter' of her second demonstration of freedom, and which now troubles him, concerns her new change of mind, her liberty not only to dispose of his theory, but to dispose as freely of her own. It is freedom so evidently for not being subject to logic and consistency.

What is interesting, however, is the narrator's reflection 'that it wasn't the form that need trouble [him]', while at Paddington it was the 'matter' that did not; and it brings out the frailty of his fallacious distinction between 'form' and 'matter' of freedom, as well as the ambiguity of 'troubling'. If he minds the 'matter', he must by implication resent the freedom with which it was embraced. But to say that he 'minds' is not to do him full justice, for if he minds Mrs Briss's present idea for being wrong, he likes it for leading her into his trap; just as to say that it need not trouble him may mean both that it is not worth bothering about because unimportant (though false), or that it is no cause for worry since he agrees with it. Still, if from this wealth of commutations he chooses to put aside her freedom (or its 'form') and consider the matter only, it may be an indication – a subconscious admission – that he himself is no longer in a position to hanker after freedom, that he is a slave to his wild theory which when conceived was conceived with great freedom, but which now imposes the limitations of its stringent logic on him. He has chosen bondage, and he will act to the last in the interest of his 'master', which means investigating this last piece of the mosaic: Grace Briss's change of mind and its significance.

He leads her gracefully and with ease into another self-contradiction, flattering her at the same time for her apparent astuteness. The topic is Briss's 'proceeding', that is, his coming up with Lady John on a later train than his wife; and the narrator reminds her:

'. . . you described to me the purpose of it as a screening of the pair.'
'I described to you the purpose of it as nothing of the sort. I didn't describe to you the purpose of it,' said Mrs Briss, 'at all. I described to you,' she triumphantly set forth, 'the *effect* of it – which is a very different thing.'
I could only meet her with admiration. 'You're of an astuteness – !'
'Of course I'm of an astuteness! I *see* effects. And I saw that one. How much Briss himself had seen it is, as I've told you, another matter; and what he had, at any rate, quite taken the affair for

was the sort of flirtation in which, if one is a friend to either party, and one's own feelings are not at stake, one may now and then give people a lift . . .'   (p. 213)

She seems to have forgotten that there was indeed talk of purpose, and that purpose one conceived by herself, namely for Lady John 'to give [poor Briss] a lift' (p. 22). Moreover, she did also impute a purpose, an intended effect, to Lady John's travelling with Briss, which was to 'cultivate, to cover their game, the appearance of other little friendships' (p. 22). But while the purposes, in one and the same matter, of Grace Briss, of Lady John, and even of Briss himself if he has any at all, may differ, the effects should be in more general evidence, and it is in terms of effects that she further contradicts herself; it is now a lift to Lady John – a lady hardly in need of lifts if she is herself so very uplifting. That Briss himself is not a man of purposes – a man whose single purpose is his passion – we hardly need to be told; yet Grace Brissenden, as if to clear him of such imputations, gives herself away again, and we understand how the narrator, following *his* single purpose, need only lead her along and pick up the morsels as she drops them: 'He's peculiar, dear old Briss, but in a way by which, if one uses him – by which, I mean, if one depends on him – at all, one gains, I think, more than one loses' (p. 213). Nobody of course knows Briss more intimately than she, and her description of his 'use' is as appropriate as the narrator could wish. Her correction, prompted probably by a subconscious recognition of what it is she is saying, in no way diminishes its incrimination, since 'depending' on him in the way she does, not only to the extent to which he is dependable and trustworthy, but depend on him for her most vital nourishment, is hardly less severe than to 'use' him.

In the narrator's struggle the creator of theories is still scoring triumphs despite the growing blindness of the victim, as indeed the moments of lucidity of the former must increase simultaneously with the shadow of the latter:

'I seem myself to see [my perfect palace of thought] again, perfect in every part,' I pursued, 'even while I thus speak to you and to feel afresh that, weren't the wretched accident of its weak foundation, it wouldn't have the shadow of a flaw. I've spoken of it in my conceivable regret,' I conceded, 'as already a mere heap of disfigured fragments; but that was the extravagance of my vexation, my despair. It's in point of fact so beautifully fitted that it comes apart piece by piece – which, so far as that goes, you've seen it do in the last quarter of an hour at your own touch, quite handing me the pieces, one by one, yourself and watching me stack them along the ground. They're not even in this state – see!' I would up – 'a pile of ruins!'   (p. 214)

But he is yet to tell her why he let her do it at all, how he agreed to take the structure apart piece by piece:

> I should almost like, piece by piece, to hand them back to you . . . I believe that, for the very charm of it, you'd find yourself placing them by your own sense in their order and rearing once more the splendid pile.   (pp. 214–15)

What he does not tell her is that he would in this hypothetical case slip in a piece or two concerning herself, pieces which she had not been conscious of handing him, but which fortify the apparently weak foundations and which would 'start [her] off' (p. 215) quite by herself. Indeed, he does hand her one, but to no avail: 'I held it up before her, but I couldn't make her look at it' (p. 215). One thing the beneficiary will never do is look at his or her situation.

Meanwhile, the narrator's 'double' game has become highly complex and indeed 'multiple', for slowly he leads Mrs Briss to negate all the points which are important to his system, only some of which, however, he has ever admitted to her. By contending May Server's place in the scheme from the start he has made her look at it all the sharper, and by feigning defeat where she expects it, he steers her firmly into denying what he never asserted. Thus she betrays her dim comprehension, finally, of his fully worked-out scheme, with herself and Briss as two of the cornerstones. But his internal triumph must, 'to defy all leakage' (p. 177), be covered up by a convincing outward defeat, a 'superficial sacrifice' (p. 177): 'It brought light, but it brought also, I fear, for me, another queer grimace' (p. 218). Both his perfect pretence and her complementary 'victory' turn out almost too convincing: 'I gasped – she turned it out so' (p. 218). The narrator's ensuing remarks contain little that straightforwardly tells us how in fact he is totally satisfied with his crystal palace, which gleams in a finish of irony. With reference to the repeated 'awfully sharp', intended by Mrs Briss to describe May Server, the narrator conjoins: 'It was she herself whom the words at present described!'

(p. 218). For the first time he has betrayed to her that he might indeed see the signs of the victim in Mrs Server; while his silent and ironic compliment to Mrs Briss, who is after all rather late with her recognitions, is paid for his and our amusement only. Yet he remains almost as oblique to the reader of the last page as he does to Mrs Briss:

> The strange mixture in my face naturally made her ask it [what on earth *do* you believe], but everything, within a minute, had somehow so given way under the touch of her supreme assurance, the presentation of her own now finished system, that I daresay I couldn't at the moment have in the least trusted myself to tell her.   (p. 218)

It is the threat of the 'fortress of granite' (p. 214) against the glass palace, which makes his sense of protection against her full sight contend with his sense of protection against the 'stones' she 'throw[s]' (p. 214), so that he cannot trust himself 'to tell her' – what he really believes or what he needs to make her believe he believes. But it is not, finally, her stonethrows – her vulgar facts – which make everything give way, but the 'touch' of her assurance and her tone of triumph – as well as the accuracy with which she hits precisely where he expects it. He has nothing to equal her assurance; his palace of thought is already taking off and he has 'achieved [his] flight into luminous ether' (p. 177), while her sturdy fortress rests firmly on the ground. Her 'now finished system', the evidence which, in giving her evidence, she has adduced, corroborates absolutely the plans for his own: 'I had no use . . . for your stupid idea, but I had great use for your stupidly, alas! having it' (p. 215).

In what follows we see the other side of the coin, the simultaneous effect on the feeder of the theory once the theory has assumed autonomy – its effect, which means also its visible appearance:

> She left me, however, in fact, small time – she only took enough, with her negations arrayed and her insolence recaptured, to judge me afresh, which she did as she gathered herself up into the strength of twenty-five. I didn't after all – it appeared part of my smash – know the weight of her husband's years, but I knew the weight of my own. They might have been a thousand, and nothing but the sense of them would in a moment, I saw, be left

me. 'My poor dear, you *are* crazy, and I bid you good-night!' (p. 218)

We are no longer on the level of theories and crystal palaces, but in the midst of the sacred fount. Mrs Briss, vampire of youth, becomes greedy with time and leaves the narrator but little, gathering up all her resources and consciously displaying their splendour. The narrator is made to feel a victim at the feet of a victor, and if he does not know the full measure of Briss's loss, he certainly knows that of his own. Were their founts but issuing the same waters, he would reckon his loss at 'a thousand years' gained, which he uses metaphorically for his own. It appears part of his own 'smash' that he cannot calculate the exact number of Briss's years – though the sacred fluid is youth rather than years – calculate it, that is, as a 'fact' and with her assurance; though his latest estimate was 'two centuries – ten!' (p. 159), exactly what he assigns himself now. Still, it *appears* a smash only, just as the 'sacrifice' was 'superficial', and in the common context with Mrs Briss, who considers herself an absolute winner, and who is now 'to judge [him] afresh' from the vantage of her fortress. What is left to him, once his theory has taken flight, is 'nothing but the sense of [his thousand years]', the 'precious sense of [the victims'] loss, their disintegration and their doom', instead of the 'exact weight' – just as he takes in Mrs Briss's 'arrayed negations' rather than the facts of her denials. It is the last thing, before he is 'all gone', for him to see, and of course he does: '. . . nothing but the sense of them would, I saw, be left me.' And on seeing, last instance of active authorship, there follows the feeling,[5] the actual experience of the hollowed victim, now object of the seeing and subject of the loss. 'I see' has become disengaged vision, disengaged from its original subject, and we witness the visionless agent with what is left him:

> Nothing but the sense of them – on my taking it from her without a sound and watching her, through the lighted rooms, retreat and disappear – *was* at first left me; but after a minute something else came, and I grew conscious that her verdict lingered. She had so had the last word that, to get out of its planted presence, I shook myself, as I had done before, from my thought. When once I had started to my room indeed – and to preparation for a livelier start as soon as the house should stir again – I almost breathlessly hurried. Such a last word – the word that put me altogether

nowhere – was too unacceptable not to prescribe afresh that
prompt test of escape to other air for which I had earlier in the
evening seen so much reason. I *should* certainly never again, on
the spot, quite hang together, even though it wasn't really that I
hadn't three times her method. What I too fatally lacked was her
tone.   (pp. 218–19)

Sight – the sense of active seeing – has taken off with the completed
vision, and he only passively watches her disappear, while the
compensatory sense of hearing once more takes over. Her audible
verdict lingers, and its presence, as before, becomes threatening in
his darkness. 'Such a last word', not easily accepted, does above all
put him 'altogether nowhere' – a phrase familiar and special.
'Where one is' is a place in the mental landscape, a conceptual locus
defined, at least, by a coefficient of knowledge and one of
consciousness thereof, which is precisely the space our narrator was
so busy mapping. Such points are never 'quite fixed' (p. 213),
though Mrs Briss treats them, like 'facts', as absolute constants. But
now that the narrator's knowledge has all been invested in his
theory, he also grows anxious about his consciousness of it, as if
drained of all faculty of knowing. To hear that he is 'crazy' thus
leaves him 'nowhere', a place he is now unable to determine – on the
map because it is completed already, and in the landscape because
he no longer can 'see'. But it is, at any rate, not where we would fix
him, for whom he is at the crossroads of his achievement and the
spent fount of his phantasmagoric passion.

What remains to be seen is whether he will be able to escape to
'other air', where he may or may not start building a new palace.
Here at Newmarch he shall certainly never 'quite hang together'
again, for what now does is his 'full-blown flower of a theory', with
the beauty and the terror of its spiralling self-consistency. 'Hang
together' (p. 160) is what arguments do, and we recall the narrator's
wonder when he saw Mrs Briss's 'hang though it would with her
somersault' (p. 210). What goes finally over from the victims to their
beneficiaries is the tone of self-confidence and 'supreme assurance',
which both Long and Mrs Briss have in abundance while remain-
ing, by definition, sublimely blind. The victims, on the other hand,
are in possession of conscious sight but lack the tone of their
partners. Their silence is matched by a growing self-effacement:
Briss turning forever a back bent under the burden of centuries, Mrs
Server flitting about, 'ready for flight, [seeking] fresh perch' (p. 28),

and never alighting with permanence. So also must the narrator look the perfect fool, and pay for 'the condition of light' with the 'sacrifice of feeling' (p. 203): must, like Vereker, remain misunderstood, since he must refrain from elucidating his emancipated theory himself, and like Paraday, suffer to be socially awkward, half dreaded, half feared like epidemics and revolutions. To grant his work perfection, and possible recognition, he forgoes personal recognition and does, metaphorically, 'too fatally lack [Mrs Briss's] tone'.

13 From artist to critic

During the process of creation, that is, up to the moment his theory is 'full-blown', the narrator is indeed an artist, an artist in the conceptual medium of interpretation and imagination. But our reluctance to call his creation a work of art is obviously due to the fact that it so little resembles any of the artistic products we know. Some critics have evaded the problem by reading the novel simply as allegory;[1] while we have refined and redefined the concept of artistic creation. We have already encountered a number of similar figments: the Beldonald Holbein, Granger's Flickerbridge, Maud Blessingbourne's little drama, and the vision of Nona Vincent. Mrs Briss calls the narrator's a 'bubble' which she would like to 'burst' (p. 213), an 'incubus' (p. 213) – almost a tumour implanted in the narrator's mind. What happens at the end of the novel is, however, crucial. The latent contradiction of this state of affairs – of the intangible 'work of art', or of the one-man sacred fount – has come to a head; the theory is fully grown and becomes detached from its author's mind. A real work of creation cannot remain for ever imprisoned in the subjectivity of its maker who alone watches over it, and this conflict resolves itself in the narrator's case in the simultaneous 'disintegration and . . . doom' of the supplier, the victim of the sacred fount. Both the theory's perfection and the narrator's salvation lie in fact in the severing of their connection, to which the narrator 'almost breathlessly hurrie[s]'. This is precisely what one imagines happening to the relation between the artist and his work, a severing of the umbilical cord which leaves the artist, at the release of his work, in that classical unprivileged position: a reader or critic, a receiver like any other. Once the work is autonomous and is said to have a 'life' of its own, a public exist- ence, its maker is no more competent to approach it than any reader. From the subjective role of an author he moves into that of an 'objective' critic; from being an insider he becomes an out- sider.

For the rather peculiar case in *The Sacred Fount* of the narrator's insubstantial work we find a fitting image in James's preface to *The American*, *à propos* of romance:[2]

> The real represents to my perception the things we cannot possibly *not* know, sooner or later, in one way or another. . . . The romantic stands, on the other hand, for the things that, with all the facilities in the world, all the wealth and all the courage and all the wit and all the adventure, we never *can* directly know; the things that can reach us only through the beautiful circuit and subterfuge of our thought and our desire. (pp. 31–2)

Let me simply point out the resonance of this passage with our narrator's curious art – the courage, the wit, and the adventure he employs and enjoys but which do not suffice, as well as the 'beautiful circuit and subterfuge' which recall the circular fount that feeds on itself, and in which flow both thought and desire – the passion which is all-absorbing. But let us return to James's passage on romance; for what, if not romance, is this *intimissima* affair of the narrator's?

> The only *general* attribute of a projected romance that I can see . . . is the fact of the kind of experience with which it deals – experience liberated, so to speak; experience disengaged, disembroiled, disencumbered, exempt from the conditions that we usually know to attach to it and, if we wish so to put the matter, drag upon it, and operating in a medium which relieves it, in a particular interest, of the inconvenience of a *related*, a measurable state, a state subject to all our vulgar communities. (p. 33)

We may indeed say that the narrator's is a projected romance – projected first of all on to the screen of his own consciousness – and liberated from all the conventions of commonsense we usually attach to the experience of a party like that at Newmarch, or indeed to an account of it. It is a peculiar feature of the narrator's working method that the conventional road to information, linguistic discourse, is almost entirely excluded: although he discusses some of his hypotheses with Obert and Mrs Briss, he does not otherwise try to extract any statement of fact from any character he is concerned with. One might say that rather than extract from Mrs Briss and Obert, he gives his projection a trial run on the screens of their minds; while nothing that Mrs Briss 'straightforwardly' communicates is accepted at face value. It merely serves as evidence of 'unavowed references' (p. 188), and to 'measure the space' by which what she says 'falls short' – short of the significance he is interested in. He does in fact regard it as the 'fine manner' in which to play this game, not to 'say' and not to 'ask' (p. 58). He is positively horrified when there is a suggestion that Mrs Briss might inflict such direct and explicit information on him unasked:

> 'But now the truth shall be told . . . !'. . . . I for an instance almost miscalculated her direction and believed she was really throwing up her cards. It was as if she had decided, on some still finer lines, just to rub my nose into what I had been spelling out; which would have been an anticipation of my own journey's crown of the most disconcerting sort. I wanted my personal confidence, but I wanted nobody's confession . . . for a confession might, after all, be itself a lie. . . . My friend's intention, however, remained but briefly equivocal; my danger passed . . . (p. 208)

If he has been 'spelling out' things, it has certainly been only in this 'personal confidence' between him and himself, while for the larger audience the spelling is in this unfamiliar but idiosyncratic medium of his rather than in the letters of the alphabet.

There is therefore no 'related state' by which to measure the narrator's theory, and the last colloquy with Mrs Briss shows that it is not 'subject to vulgar communities': none of her objections can now affect it, whether or not Briss 'knows' some 'facts' – facts moreover acquired exactly in vulgar communities. Facts of that sort are not part of the inventory of the narrator's medium (apart from what he calls 'my fact'); the *interpretandum* is a surface of effects, of 'signs' (p. 77) and 'impressions' (p. 167), of things that 'show' (p. 159) and that are so 'marked' (p. 99); and to interpret any of these means to follow their 'scent' along the 'track of [their] cause' (p. 187).

What James describes in the passage quoted is ultimately of course the *writing* of romance, for the concern which follows is how not to 'betray' the romance too rashly to the reader. Hence what he calls the 'balloon of experience' relates to the experience in fiction (a related and measurable state), rather than to experience in real life, and it is tied by the rope of verisimilitude. If we remember, on the other hand, the discussion of 'conceptual works of art', and the fact that experience – perception and cognition – are already themselves

creative and fictionalising activities, the relevance becomes obvious. In *The Sacred Fount* the narrator's theory is at first firmly
grounded in the 'real' (from his point of view, rather than the
reader's), and then follows this course of 'romance':

> The balloon of experience is in fact of course tied to the earth, and
> under that necessity we swing, thanks to a rope of remarkable
> length, in the more or less commodious car of the imagination;
> but it is by the rope we know where we are, and from the moment
> that cable is cut we are at large and unrelated: we only swing
> apart from the globe – though remaining as exhilarated, nat-
> urally, as we like, especially when all goes well. The art of the
> romancer is, 'for the fun of it,' insidiously to cut the
> cable . . .   (pp. 33–4)

One has, at the end of *The Sacred Fount*, a distinct impression of the
'rope' of the balloon (or the 'bubble') having been cut, while the
cable throughout has been of remarkable, of prodigious, length.
The problem, in the narrator's case, is that he himself is seated in the
'more or less commodious car of the imagination', having, admittedly, for the most part an exhilarating time; yet this particular car
plummets to the ground once the cable has been cut, while the
balloon soars alone to its 'flight into luminous ether'. The fact of the
matter is that for Henry James, or the literary romancer in general,
there is an 'experience' manning the balloon, although the drive
and the guidance come from the pilot imagination. This experience,
we have already implied it, is the consciousness of the reader, which
in the romance James discusses teams up with the imagination of the
writer. The experience, in fact, is only properly viable if such a crew
is intact.

There are signs, however, of a specification of the conceptual
medium, just as Granger conceptually 'paints', while Maud
Blessingbourne 'writes' romance. The beginnings of the earlier
chapters abound in hints that this is a retrospective verbal account,
with all the familiar features, especially tense distinction. There is a
present time in which the narrator, now properly narrating,
'recovers' in tranquillity; and if he does not tell us directly that he is
also writing, the image of a book with 'chapters' is not very far from
his mind:

> I recover . . . a full sequence of impressions, each of which, I

afterwards saw, had been appointed to help all the others. . . . They formed, nevertheless, the happiest little chapter of accidents, though a series of which I can scarce give more than the general effect.   (p. 24)

These references are vague enough to prevent us from 'fixing' him as a writer. To the extent that the narrative of *The Sacred Fount* is a delayed account we may properly call the narrator its author, so long as we do not confuse him with Henry James, who turned it into a novel and gave it a title. But we cannot extract, as has been done, a moral of the story that the narrator, after his experience at Newmarch, became a novelist. Rather, I wish to emphasise that his theory, but for the present account of it, would indeed have gone up in a bubble, with no experience enjoying the ride.

A 'moral', if at all, can be drawn in another way. We must first of all acknowledge that the narrator's consciousness as reporter gradually recedes in the course of his account and in the heat of the recounted drama. Instead, I am following another scent. In the previous section we noted how the narrator's vision is gradually replaced by hearing, since his growing insight leads him to blindness. But what does this actually mean, and what is its greater significance?

The narrator's visual faculty, though also metaphoric to the extent that it becomes knowledge and inner vision, is founded at the beginning on the real and is a literal scanning of visual effects. Discourse is spurned as an object of interpretation, until the final chapters when he reaps the fruits of Mrs Briss's speeches. Thus he moves from the concrete 'stuff' of visual reality to a more literary dimension – discursive at least, but at any rate lingual.

An interesting analogy can be found in the breakthrough of Freud's psychoanalysis, which presents just such a shift from the 'eye' of the nineteenth-century physician and quack-healer to the 'ear' of the analyst of discourse.[3] The matter is of course not quite so simple, and the Freudian analysis involves more than just audible speech. The language of the body, the symptom as 'a symbol written in the sand of the flesh',[4] forms part of the text to be read. In the literary interpretation which goes beyond linguistic decoding, as well as in the narrator's method of discourse-analysis, symptoms also play their part; and it is above all the 'third ear'[5] which listens to the *parole pleine*.

As mentioned already, it is not what Mrs Briss communicates

with intention and as information that the narrator chooses to hear; neither that Long is 'a prize fool' and Lady John his lover, nor that May Server has 'enough of her left' (p. 217) not to qualify as a victim. It is, in the narrator's words, 'what you say you *don't* say' (p. 217) that he finds of interest and, quoted already, 'to talk, as we talked, on the basis of those suppressed processes and unavowed references which made the meaning of our meeting so different from its form' (p. 188). A Freudian apparatus of interpretation seems indeed required for the narrator's enterprise at large, for his analysis of a society in which repression is a main barrier between reality and appearance. There is a censorship in this society, a consideration for acceptability, which prevents any manifestation and admission of sexual relations. If such relations exist, they must be covered up by careful mechanisms of screening which distort the truth into a deceptive 'manifest content'.[6] If Lady John was in love with Gilbert Long, she had 'kicked up, to save her credit, the dust of a fictive relation with another man – the relation one of mere artifice and the man one in her encouragement of whom nobody would believe' (p. 81). Similarly, May Server's lover will be the man she most consistently avoids. And when Mrs Briss in her defence assures the narrator that Briss has 'not . . . spoken to me since we parted, yesterday, to come down here by different trains. We haven't so much as met since our arrival' (p. 41), she only corroborates the narrator's theory to perfection. Appearance, the 'signifier', is not in a one-to-one correspondence with what it signifies, and special instruments are needed to get at the latter. The deceptive, typological sign language proffered by the society is characterised by its symbolistic mechanism: Mrs. Server's flirtatious smile is 'the mere mechanism of her expression, the dangling paper lantern itself' (p. 101). And like a lantern 'her terrible little fixed smile . . . came back as if with an audible click' (p.109). For the narrator's keener interpretation, the appearance of Lady John's 'fictive relation' becomes a negative signification in which 'nobody would believe', yet which neither gives the meaning in which everybody would. But the resulting problem for the narrator, naturally, is similar to that which has entailed objections to Freudian dream interpretation, namely that a patient's denial of the analysis suggested by the analyst is as good a 'proof' of his interpretation as would be his acceptance, since it only manifests another level of repression.[7] The same apparent paradox arises in the narrator's theory even outside personal interview, in the sphere of detectable phenomena: ' . . . the evident truth that that element [of collateral support] *could* be present only in such doses as practically to escape detection' (p. 172). But the above-mentioned objection to Freud is essentially crude and ignores the entire path along overdetermination which leads the analyst to his interpretation in the first place. Yet it is a commonplace with the sceptic, who resents the apparent double-bind; and since scepticism might well be brought to the narrator's procedures (and to mine) it is worth refuting.

We do indeed get splendid examples of the flexibility of the narrator's tangled hypothesis, which can adopt the anticipated as well as its unexpected opposite. The theory, as in Freud if we read chronologically, is refined through the introduction of new empirical evidence, since it is only properly in the process of being constructed. At the point where we shall arrest the narrator's theory it posits that true couples, those with a sacred fount, never converge for 'more than a moment' (p. 116). At dinner, where he wishes to observe Mrs Server, he is shocked to find that while Lord Lutley is her one neighbour, Gilbert Long is her other. He comments:

> My theory had not at all been framed to embrace the phenomenon thus presented; it had been precisely framed, on the contrary, to hang together with the observed inveteracy of escape, on the part of the two persons about whom it busied itself, from public juxtaposition of more than a moment.   (p. 116)

But a further oddity comes to his aid – an element of overdetermination; for in listing the longer chain of neighbours he discovers also that Mrs Froome was

> not, for a wonder, this time paired, as by the immemorial tradition, so fairly comical in its candour, with Lord Lutley. Wasn't it too funny, the kind of grandmotherly view of their relation shown in their always being put together? If I perhaps questioned whether 'grandmotherly' were exactly the name for the view, what yet at least was definite in the light of this evening's arrangement was that there did occur occasions on which they were put apart.   (p. 116)

So the solution to his problem is already at hand:

if the exception did prove the rule in the one case it might equally
prove it in the other. If on a rare occasion one of these couples
might be divided, so, by as uncommon a chance, the other might
be joined; the only difference being in the gravity of the violated
law.   (p. 117)

It becomes evident, though, that the narrator is a very peculiar
kind of depth analyst, and we need to specify the 'texts' he
interprets. The main overall 'canvas' whose 'vast expanse' of surface
he wishes to embroider and of whose 'boundless number
of . . . distinct holes' he is 'fairly . . . in terror'[8] is the reality – or
better, the appearance – of the three days at Newmarch. Thus,
unlike the psychoanalyst, he deals less with the manifestations of
individual neurotics or psychotics than with the general relations
between the parts of a multicellular organism. The secrets he seeks
to uncover are not traumas of individuals, but the dissimulations of
a collective unconscious.[9] It is society at large, it seems, which
wishes to protect the sacred founts amongst it – to protect them from
the view of an observer as well as from its own. This is how the
narrator can make sense of the table arrangement cited above, how
he can modify his theory at all without giving up its basis, though it
started with the study of individuals or pairs. For if it were only the
victims, or at most the couples, who are anxious to 'cover up their
game', the exception and the rule, particularly in another case,
would have no weight in the matter. It is presumably not in the
hands of these 'guilty' ones to arrange the seating at their host's
dinner-table so as to spare themselves embarrassement.

It is, on the contrary, 'the grandmotherly *view of* [Lord Lutley
and Mrs Froome's] relation *shown* in their always *being put* together'.
We are not told that these two insist on being always together, nor
who it is who takes the 'view' and who puts them together; it is
simply the general opinion that they should be, that in their case the
relation is 'comical' and charming, presumably on account of their
age, if not simply of the 'immemorial tradition'; while in the case,
say, of Long and Mrs Server their being 'put' together would be
scandalous. On the basis of commonsense it would be rather curious
to speak of 'chance', since *somebody* must have worked out the
seating deliberately. But the narrator treats it like a matter of Fate,
as a depersonalised occurrence following its own secret laws or, in
other words, as the output of a collective unconscious, restricted of
course to the collective at Newmarch: 'If on a rare occasion one of

these couples might *be divided*, so, *by as uncommon a chance*, the other might *be joined* . . .' (*my emphasis*). The consideration of the agent of this chance takes its only form in the narrator's presupposition of the mysterious force, whose laws he is about to establish like the scientist with the black-box. For him it is 'machinery' which will have to be 'put into motion consistently . . . to minimise the disconcerting incident' (p. 117), though again, by whom is not clear, just as 'disconcerting' seems intrinsic to the incident rather than its value for specified people. The law by which this machinery works is expected to appeal through its consistency, its economy, and its stringent probability. It looks as if the narrator imagined himself a minor Newton, observing phenomena and inferring their laws, while the notion of 'social codes', or of the structures of structuralists, as well as the ambiguity of their psychological status, seem unfamiliar to his way of thinking.

Thus the 'perceptions' of the rest of the company remain part of the puzzle to be solved, treated rather as 'objective' phenomena than as subjective functions of individuals. It is now no weakness for the narrator's argument that no one else seems struck by the observations which so agitate him. They only *seem* not to notice anything, but it may be part of the collective instinct not to betray what is sensed. Once it all looks so obvious to the narrator, he wonders if not everyone can see it as well: 'I wondered hereupon if the discovery [that something *was* the matter with Mrs Server] were inevitable for each gentleman in succession, and if this were their reason for changing so often' (p. 74). Again, the gentlemen are assumed to have a collective reason for taking turns so often, between them, for being in Mrs Server's company, rather than each deciding that he had enough of her. Thus the verb does not apply to each gentleman individually, but only to them all as a group. Although the narrator grows shy about publicly discussing Mrs Server with the other gentlemen, he is convinced that 'nobody, doubtless, would have said anything worse than that she was more of a flirt than ever . . .' (p. 79). What would be said, in words, would be nothing but the trivial and superficial, and the narrator is gradually convinced that this is all the party at Newmarch will ever allow to its consciousness – the symptom, but not its cause. Although

Newmarch had always, in our time, carried itself as the great asylum of the finer wit . . . . There was a sound law in virtue of which one could always – alike in privileged and unprivileged

circles – rest more on people's density than on their penetrability.
. . . Whatever her successive partners of a moment might have
noticed, they wouldn't have discovered in her reason for
dropping them quickly a principle of fear that they might notice
her failure articulately to keep up.   (pp. 77–8)

Notice again the deindividualised collective of Newmarch which is
allowed to take a single active verb in its self-assured unity. It is on
account of the behaviour of 'Newmarch' that the narrator ceases to
care if he is believed to be in love with May Server: 'That was as
good a name as another for an interest springing up in an hour . . .'
(p. 75). The name applies to the surface only (it 'might, after all,
be itself a lie'), and it does not give away the deeper meaning,
namely   the   fact   that   the   narrator   knows   'too   much'
(p. 117).

   But, conscious of his consciousness, he himself falls prey to the
collective instinct, to the injunction not to let on that he knows;
hence his fear of public exposure of his theory, and consequently of
his awareness, and hence his own elaborate screening manoeuvres.
The consciousness is, as already said, in his own view somewhat
questionable, yet not so much for his own sake as for the sake of the
others should they discover that he possesses it: 'I was really quite
scared at the chance of having to face – of having to see *them* face –
another recognition' (p. 131). The contextual view does in fact alter
his whole 'estimate of the value of perception':

> To be without it was the most consistent, the most successful,
> because the most amiable, form of selfishness; and why should
> people admirably equipped for remaining so, people bright and
> insolent in their prior state, people in whom this state was to have
> been respected as a surface without a scratch is respected, be
> made to begin to vibrate, to crack and split, from within?
> (p. 131)

In such a society the narrator assumes the position of the collective
ego, the collective censor who on the one hand knows and on the
other rules that the known must not be known, must not be
admitted to the collective consciousness – in other words, he
becomes himself part of the collective suppression agency. It is the
society's instinct for self-preservation to remain in a happy state of
selfishness and ignorance; and the narrator with his morbid sense of

the deeper vision becomes, in terms of the whole social organism, a nasty pathological symptom, an expression of the suppressed consciousness trying to break through to the surface, a 'crack and split from within'. This conflict is necessarily reflected in himself, who feels part of the larger organism at the same time as being an inquiring individual: 'It was as if, abruptly, with a new emotion, I had wished to unthink every thought with which I had been occupied for twenty-four hours' (p. 131). The 'sound law' quoted above (150) expresses a similarly curious feature; given, in the context, the 'density' of people, one would expect it to be paired with 'penetration', since density we take to be the derogatory term for a person's poor intelligence which would result in a lack of penetration. But the narrator looks at it more as a quality of resistance to *his* penetration: if they are dense, they are also difficult to interpret – they are impenetrable or hard to penetrate. Thus the density becomes a mutual social quality of the collective as well as its parts, of not interpreting others and resisting interpretation by others.

This strange transitivity links penetrability with consciousness: the narrator's consciousness having succeeded in penetrating the beneficiaries' shame, has resulted in awareness on their part: ' I had spoiled their unconsciousness, I had destroyed it, and it was consciousness alone that could make them effectively cruel'(p. 203). While the beneficiaries thus retaliate with cruelty, the victims' penetrability generates active penetration in turn, itself easily cruel in a society which shuns knowledge. Poor Briss, not normally too 'sharp', rises to 'supersubtlety' (p. 130). The narrator, this time innocently, wishes him: 'Good-night, Brissenden. I shall be gone to-morrow before you show.' And Briss takes him up with paranoia: 'Show? *What* do I show?' (p. 159). Moreover, what he penetrates with his newly won subtlety is the consciousness of the narrator; he knows that the latter knows.

If the relations between the parts are repressed by the whole, it is only to be expected that discourse should be so, and the narrator speaks of it amply:

[Lady John] would just this once have admitted it, I was to gather, to be an occasion for pleading guilty – oh, so harmlessly! – to a consciousness of the gentleman mutely named between us. (p. 82).
[Mrs Server's] eyes . . . told me from time to time that she knew

whatever I was thinking of to be for her virtual advantage. It was prodigious what, in the way of suppressed communication, passed in these wonderful minutes between us.   (p. 102)

He 'gathers' rather than is told, and the only 'telling' going on is that of expression, of a show of consciousness and speaking eyes. So little danger is there of language being used for the telling of facts or the 'truth' that the verbs of saying, or those commonly associated with verbal communication, can be used for this other type of 'suppressed communication': 'admit', 'plead guilty', 'name', 'tell' and 'pass in communication'. '[Mrs Server] would give herself away supremely if she showed she suspected me of placing my finger on the spot – if she understood the person I had not named to be nameable as Gilbert Long' (p. 105). 'Give herself away' is also what Grace Brissenden does in her last talk with the narrator, and what May Server would be doing if she proved to be aware of what she most represses – not so much from her own consciousness as from that of the narrator and of everyone else at Newmarch – the name of Gilbert Long. If it is 'nameable' it is preconscious already, 'capable of becoming conscious'. If she, too, through the distorting screen of harmless appearances, is aware of the latent content of their colloquy, then she has as good as pleaded guilty of knowing the deceit. But being aware is incompatible with suppression, and it becomes evident that the 'surface', or the consciousness to which the suppressed notion of Long is in danger of rising, is that of the collective – here represented by the interlocutors.

If we consider, along with the narrator, the party at Newmarch as one vast psychic organism, there must be one part which is the 'unconscious', storing all the suppressed material, and which thus 'knows', in itself, the full truth. The beneficiaries of the sacred founts possess in their profit the fullest account of the founts' secret and represent it, while the consciousness of the whole organism is the 'appearance', and properly the discourse, of that society, that which is allowed to be articulated. The narrator, as indicated already, partakes of the knowledge and assists in its suppression, thus embodying the omniscient censor – expressing what 'stirs within' him in his own medium, yet refraining from articulating it in the open discourse of the society. The preconscious at large is seated in those who, like Briss and Mrs Server, are aware and actually in a position to express their knowledge, although they do not. Their awareness, unarticulated, is greater than the proper unconsciousness of their beneficiaries, and is capable of becoming articulated. The society shares in the unconscious and preconscious knowledge which precisely motivates its suppression and the conspiratorial behaviour we witness at the dinner-table, just as the party includes Briss and May Server, Grace Briss and Long, and indeed even the narrator.

Such a conception of 'Newmarch' as a psychic apparatus also bears out Lacan's emphasis on the 'discourse of the Other':[10] the fact that there are different loci within the psyche communicating with one another. If the factor of language has entered, if, in other words, potential consciousness has been reached, the ensuing discourse or text – however much a monologue or soliloquy in the case of the individual – is nevertheless directed at another. In the social terms of Newmarch, where a 'monologue' constitutes a discourse amongst its members according to the principles of suppression and acceptability, this Other, although potentially the collective or any part of it, is first and foremost the narrator:[11]

> Car dans ce travail qu'il fait de la reconstruire [son œuvre Imaginaire] *pour un autre*, il retrouve l'aliénation fondamentale qui la lui a fait construire *comme une autre*, et qui l'a toujours destinée à lui être dérobée *par un autre*.

> (For in this labor which he undertakes to reconstruct this construct [in the Imaginary] *for another*, he finds again the fundamental alienation which made him construct it *like another one*, and which has always destined it to be stripped from him *by another*.)

We have no difficulty in recognising in this last 'other' the self-appointed function of the narrator; just as we recognise May Server's conduct – or construct of the surface discourse – as an alienated construction: her 'principle of fear that they might notice her failure articulately to keep up' (p. 78). It is for *their* benefit that she creates the part for herself of a woman 'all over the place', which will lead *them* to drop her, or think they do, while it is destined to be stripped from her by the narrator.

As the danger increases that the impermissible might be articulated, which at all costs should be suppressed if the happiness and ignorance are to be preserved – as this danger grows with the growing consciousness of the narrator and the victims, the antics of the suppressors, the symptoms of suppression, become accordingly more pronounced. Obert's rather conspicuous refusal, on the last evening in the smoking-room, to discuss things with the narrator and his flat denial that anything is the matter with anyone, as well as the comparable tactics of Mrs Briss, are signs of more desperate measures. Yet earlier the narrator already experiences the dread and the gravity of the situation when he suspects Gilbert Long of guessing his intenser consciousness:

> The state of my conscience was that I knew too much – that no one had really any business to know what I knew. If he suspected but the fiftieth part of it there was no simple spirit in which he could challenge me. It would have been simple of course to desire to knock me down, but that was barred by its being simple to excess. (p. 117)

It would be 'simple to excess' to knock the narrator down, as nothing, of course, would be achieved by it. If the consciousness is there, at Newmarch, it will spread and eventually infect the whole company, and a physical punch would do nothing but aggravate the situation. The prime remedy is a new attempt to repress it, and one of the most effective means of repression and suppression at Newmarch is 'talking', which is just 'the high sport' for which Long has come to the narrator (p. 119). This is how one can make a point of not saying what is most in the air, how one can 'kick up dust', 'describe purposes' and 'make confessions', and can 'tell' that truth which is no harm to anybody, because its 'form' is so different from its 'meaning'.

When his analysis leads him from the whole organism to the individual parts, the narrator more directly resembles the psychoanalyst – particularly the sort Lacan discredits for posing as 'one who knows'. But it is here, in interview with individuals, that he lends like the analyst his 'third ear' and closes, effectively, his other two. Here he is more confident of being a true observer (though observing as much through his ear as through his eye). Thus he fails at first, like the early Freud, to be fully conscious of the extent to which he is an insider, inside the range of transference between his 'patient' and himself. There is the possibility of transference and countertransference in his relationship with May Server, to which Obert early draws attention. But all his other colloquies suffer some such interference, preventing not only him from being the purely detached observer, but his interlocutor from being an ideal object for scientific investigation. His presence counts crucially in their interaction, and the responses of his partners are influenced and determined by it in the way described by Lacan: they construct for his ear to hear.

By the time of his last interview with Mrs Briss he has mastered the technique of the analyst who knows how to extrapolate – or at least recognise – all that is aimed at himself and to interpret altogether at a different level, although as victim he cannot escape the personal repercussions. But his growing analytical sophistication has its match, as pointed out, in Mrs Briss's intensified manoeuvring. She designs her speech carefully for the narrator's ears, gearing it specifically to the sort of consciousness and the particular suspicions she suspects him of having. Only she has not reckoned with his 'third ear', the one precisely attuned to the deception and the design. Although originally an eye-specialist – with at least 'first sight' and 'second [sight]' (p. 75) – he has now also become expert at analysing discourse, which he decodes not only on its surface according to the good manners at Newmarch, but also and above all in its depth.

In this role, however, he has also come closest to the position of the literary critic – an interpreter of an already embroidered canvas. Lacan, on the task of the analyst, gives us also a description of the narrator's, and indeed of that of the literary critic:[12] 'The art of the analyst must be to suspend the subject's certitudes until their last mirages have been consumed. And it is in the discourse that, like verse, their resolution must be scanned'. The narrator never lets Grace Briss (nor the reader) quite see what stage his interpretation has reached, leaving her (and our) certitudes suspended indeed. But rather than positing an imaginary 'third ear' Lacan holds that the analyst can 'regulate the yield of his ears, in line with the use which is normally made of them, according to both physiology and the Gospel: having ears *in order not to hear*; in other words, to pick up what is to be heard'.[13] Lacan puts it epigrammatically simply: 'what is to be heard' is what the ear, in its Gospel use, 'pick[s] up', while the other two ears try *not to hear*; in other words, there are two different verbs of hearing that Lacan does not take the trouble, stylistically, to distinguish in his polemic against the claim of a 'direct transaudition of the unconscious by the unconscious'.[14] Taking for granted that this latter type is not at issue and that we focus, with Lacan, on discourse, I shall, directly contrary to his ruling, retain the term of the 'third ear' so as to be able to tell hearing from hearing, ears from ears.

This use of the third ear corresponds straightforwardly to Henry James's 'mental ear'[15] and to what he calls 'reading between the lines',[16] shortened by the narrator to 'reading in' (p. 202). Although a familiar colloquial phrase, it deserves, or rather, requires formalisation in the context of literary reading, where its looseness might easily be misconstrued. It does not, of course, mean that the interpreter is free to fill in anything he likes 'between the lines', to add from his personal experience at will and without constraint. Rather than properly reading into that empty space, we read out of it the Fullness of the word. Because Freudian analysis, and the interpretation of dreams in particular, has already formulated a methodology, and because a connection between it and literary reading goes beyond Lacan's eminently poetic way of describing his practice, we may turn it to our own use.

What the third ear hears is what I have termed the 'third articulation' processes of literary texts, for the literary analyst is just as convinced that there is overdetermination as is the psychoanalyst. The conviction is basic to the very assumption of the existence of literature – of literary practice – as opposed to sheer verbalism. The first ear is physiological, in the adult native speaker working by reflex and decoding phonetic information – first articulation – automatically. The second ear serves 'communication' and listens to the 'story', the content of a message, or what Lacan rather contemptuously calls the Empty Word (for it 'might, after all, be . . . a lie'). The third ear, however, the literary or, as Jakobson would perhaps call it, the poetic ear, is sensitive to the articulation on the third level, to meaning beyond content, to form which is semiotic. It recognises the text as a 'secondary' and 'contemporary historisation' moulded specifically in its linguistic medium, through which a primary 'story' can be established. But though 'primary', it is neither the truth, nor the goal of our interpretation, since it is the primary fictionalisation. The third ear, through the 'manifest content' seeks to hear the 'latent content', which again is not just the 'truer' story: the whole story is the constellation of desires and processings of semiotic responses which are realised and played out on these contents – the combinations of historisations.

With these terms of manifest text and latent content we have a pair more appropriate for the literary text than those of signifier and signified, form and content, which imply, as we pointed out in a previous chapter, a relation too simple for the two aspects. In the interpretation of dreams, the translation backwards from manifest dream text to latent dream content is known to be a highly complex and, above all, a never-ending process, and thus it is significantly akin to the literary critic's labours. Speaking of the translation in the original direction, of the textualisation of the dream content, Freud has identified some *Darstellungsmittel*, to be taken into account in interpretation: condensation, displacement, and consideration of representability. All of these we have encountered in the various texts of our narrators, but they are all of them, properly considered, familiar poetic features. They are, however, phenomena beyond Segre's connotative icons, and they lead the reader to *his* crystal palace, to the discovery of the deeper 'laws' and the greater significances which fill him with a sense of having been reading a work of art, rather than a story or sentences. In other words, the third ear switches to an 'artistic disposition' and to a practice drawing on his 'literary competence'.

A methodological distinction must, however, be clearly kept in mind, since the reader does not wish to psychoanalyse an author.[17] In fact the psychoanalytic situation constitutes precisely what in literary terms is incestuous if applied to a creative writer, namely a real dialogue between analyst and analysand, and one in which 'checking back' is of prime importance. Conversely, the analysis of an author on the basis of a single text – even his entire work – is psychoanalytically improper besides impossible, precisely because the dialogue cannot be established. But it should be clear from our discussion that the author's mind is never the aim of our proposed literary interpretation, which is focused on the structuration of the text. Similarly, the narrator of *The Sacred Fount* is not really in search of the psychic depths of primal scenes and childhood traumas of those whose speeches and behaviour he studies; rather, he wants to interpret the texts of their conduct in the context of their society, where the laws of the sacred fount are in operation.

Let us take a look at this literary critic, though he is distracted momentarily by some social obligation:

. . . they *were* as one; as one, at all events, for *my* large reading. My large reading had meanwhile, for the convenience of the rest of my little talk with Lady John, to make itself as small as possible. I had an odd sense, till we fell apart again, as of keeping my finger

rather stiffly fixed on a passage in a favourite author on which I
had not previously lighted. I held the book out of sight and
behind me; I spoke of things that were not at all in it – or not at all
on that particular page; but my volume, none the less, was only
waiting. What might be written there hummed already in my
ears as a result of my mere glimpse.   (p. 130)

Notice also the play of light, sight and the humming in the ears
which all contribute to the larger reading of a favourite author. The
fact that he is a favourite also implies that the passage has been seen,
with the first two eyes, many times before, but has opened only just
now to the third. That vision is immediately associated with the ear
for discourse and for the literary. It is a terminology in which he
becomes steadily more fluent, for when he considers Long's stirred
consciousness and Mrs Briss's alarm, he wonders if these might
'precipitate for them, in some silence deeper than darkness, the
exchange of recognitions . . . ' (p. 202).

If we turn to a passage from James's prefaces, describing what it is
to read critically, there can be no doubt that the narrator of *The
Sacred Fount* is trained in that discipline: 'To criticise is to appreciate,
to appropriate, to take intellectual possession, to establish in fine a
relation with the criticised thing and make it one's own' (p. 155).
For he appreciates, appropriates, and takes 'intellectual possession'
of the most jealous kind, establishing, in fine, 'a relation' so intimate
that it gives rise to the phenomenon of the sacred fount.[18] And he
speaks, just as Leon Edel says of James the critic, 'as if he were a
physician who will diagnose but not prescribe'[19] – a physician, in
other words, like Freud or Lacan who know better than to
'prescribe'.

Yet, as we have seen, what becomes so intimately his 'own' will in
the end take flight and leave him bereft once more. We now have
two points to clear up, which go hand in hand. We asked if the
narrator of *The Sacred Fount* can be called an artist, and if so, whether
his sacred fount leads him, like the 'marriage bed',[20] to death. We
have seen that in the narrator's presentation his art *is* like the
passion of a sacred fount, so that it remains to examine his 'death'.

The 'death' of the creative artist – the completion of his work –
leaves him in the unprivileged position of a reader, which thus is,
strictly speaking, the end of his *être artiste*; but we have also shown
him to be, *qua* artist, some kind of a model critic. On the other hand,
The Sacred Fount has not given us any real example of the fount

expiring, and we had to be satisfied with the narrator's speculation. Thus we need not apply the torch of his analogy any further than we have already done. The curious 'death' of the artist does not predict that it is final, or whether a subsequent passion will once more revive him. It is clear that *this* fount has come to an end, but it is the death of the lover and not of the man. Furthermore, the particular combination of levels at which the narrator is a reader and critic suggests a certain other continuity.

This combination should also make us look once more at the relation between writer and 'true' literary reader – the one who is next to the artist on the scale which grades the literary community. For the latter is, in his fashion and however peripherally or parasitically, drinking from the waters that have flown from the writer into his work; similarly, perhaps, to the way the narrator's intelligence 'feeds' on the founts of the couples he 'reads' and who remain not untouched by his absorbing penetration. Thus we have in him also a paradigm of the reader, although it is usually the artist in him that is emphasised:[21]

> Those 'plunges of insight', those adventures in extrapolation, which are a novelist's peculiar privilege and avocation, had been James's for four decades, and now he seemed to be asking himself whether he had a greater grasp of illusion than of reality, those illusory fantasies and dreams which the writer of fiction projects as 'reality' for his readers.

Here we have the best example that to venture extrapolations of this kind is the privilege and avocation of the critic, and it is indeed curious that the narrator should not be acknowledged for his interpretative faculties by his *confrères*. It is equally curious, however, that an immersion in James's fiction as extensive as Leon Edel's has not provoked a suspicion that there might not be such a clear-cut reality to have a 'grasp of' as the opposition of 'illusion' and 'reality' suggests. The 'moral' of this curiosity is, of course, that the novelist is as much an interpreter of 'the canvas of life'[22] as the reader is an interpreter of the novelist's embroidery; that, in other words, the activities of writer and reader are singularly similar.

This similarity takes us further. From our analysis of *The Aspern Papers* we are familiar with sharing our position as addressee or 'narratee' of the text with the narrator's 'self'. In our reading experience we have also participated in the victimisation of a part of the narrator's self, in his blindness and his 'suspended certitudes' to which we too are subjected by the screenings of his own progress and the obscurity of his particular 'spelling out' in a language which is not simply verbal. But with his retrospective narration we are given discourse to analyse and to 'criticise', to take intellectual possession of and make our own. And since our role as narratees is as much open to the narrator's persona, we can conceive of his final recapture of his kingdom in recollection and retrospection. As an outsider, he now can contemplate his work and take the seat of the spectator-experience on his ride into luminous ether. The creative process itself permitted only the author and his beneficiary, since the fount must be exclusive and '*intimissima*', and hence precluded the spectator who, as persona, fell victim. With its autonomy, the palace is open once more to him – to him as a spectator.

We have of course other evidence of the affinity between the writer and the reader, and I shall only cite briefly two further examples from James's fiction. The first is from *John Delavoy* (1898), which at the same time focuses on the difference between the author and the man, the 'split' personality of the writer.

In their angry dispute with the editor of the journal *Cynosure*, Miss Delavoy, sister of a deceased novelist, and the narrator-critic come up against the classical misunderstanding about the author and his work. The narrator, in agreement with Miss Delavoy, has under-taken to write an appreciative article on 'Delavoy', which for him means the author's work. But the editor now turns it down, since he wants a 'life' of the author, an article on the man. Realising that it is truly literary practice which is being rejected, Miss Delavoy flares up at the editor's renewed refusal:[23]

> 'If my brother's as vile as you say –!'
> 'Oh, I don't say *he's* vile!' he broke in.
> 'You only say *I* am!' I commented.
> 'You've entered so into him,' she replied to me, 'that it comes to the same thing . . .'

Instinctively Miss Delavoy equates a slur on her brother's critic with one on the novelist's own work, and when the editor tries to make a distinction explicitly denies that there is one to be made, since the critic has written about that which is truly literary. A practical equation is to be made here, if anywhere – between art and the critique of art, which both pertain to the literary; and not, as is the wont of both public and editors, between the artist as a man and the artist as author of the work he lends his name to.

A subtle indication that the critic deserves like treatment to the artist is given in a curious incident, when the editor, meaning to be rude, gives the critic the due he so consistently refuses to grant the novelist. Customarily he mistakes any reference to 'Delavoy' for one to the person rather than the work, which is what led him to accept, in principle, the proposed article by the narrator. During their interview at his office he realises that he trusted the critic on account of his acquaintance with Miss Delavoy, a live connection, as it were, with the author: ' "I see. That must have been why I trusted you – sent you, without control, straight off to be set up. But now that I see you – !" he went on' (p. 423). What he means, of course, is not 'now that I see you', but now that I see you 'set up' in galley proof, just as it was not the narrator but his manuscript that he sent straight off to the typesetters.

There is a strong bond between the 'true' critic and the writer of James's literary world, the bond of art which commits them both. And if we have seen the artist's passion to be of the peculiar nature of the sacred fount, we may suspect the real devotee's involvement in art of a similar tendency.

We discussed above how the metaphor of the garden in *The Aspern Papers* comes to represent the literary enterprise. At this point we may be interested in the relation implied by the metaphor between the writer and the critic. It is the poet, Aspern, who has created gardens, who has worked the soil and grown flowers from it. But gardens are themselves of such a nature as to allow for ever more flowers to grow. The product of the poet is not definitive and determined, but has itself inbuilt fertility and regeneration. Thus the narrator-critic, himself a (professed) lover of flowers, wants to grow his own. Yet his particular talent requires a garden already set up, landscaped by someone else, for he is not capable of starting from nothing.

This particular critic of *The Aspern Papers*, we have noted, is perversely interested in the 'expanse of ground . . . confined by a high wall' which is attached to Misses Bordereau's palace, though it is a garden only by a stretch of the imagination. Yet being attached to the house it permits the inference that 'the place was a garden' (p. 11). It is the idea of the surrounding water that attracts him; and associating water with the subjective experience of the writer we saw the metaphor extend further. With the metaphor of a liquid and a measure of its quantity a link to the image of the sacred fount is forming. Yet water is by no means all that goes into the making of a garden; it is work in the best sense of the word, including all its associations of labour and working-over of mental material – of the soil – and not least in the sense of Freud's dream work with respect to 'representability' in the medium.

The critic can grow flowers from the garden too, but they are usually of a more modest kind, and his relation to them not always one of an all-absorbing passion; nor is he ever responsible for their original arrangement and plan. Yet the parallelism of his situation and the sacred interest in the beauty of flowers does leave a margin for a more intense involvement also on the critic's part; and the narrator of *The Sacred Fount* – neither novelist quite, nor critic only – can serve as a paradigm.

To round off we may once more return to the schema of the Jamesian triangle, in order to map the critic's share on to it. From the adduced analogy with the dream text and its interpretation it would appear that the reader's activity is tracing back the artist's labour, to arrive from the text at the 'concept' or, as we expressed it in the terminology of psychoanalysis, to construct from the manifest text the latent content.

But the idea is mistaken – or at least wrongly mapped. I have nonetheless given it here, because it represents the fundamental misconception about 'art as communication' which takes for its model the ideal of ordinary communication, where the meaning of the sender is matched perfectly by the interpretation of the receiver, or where the latter arrives precisely at the point from which the sender's intention originated. In actual fact this is obviously only achieved approximately, and by a series of correction moves guided by feedback. The decoder arrives at c_1, is corrected and directed toward c, which leads him to c_2, then c_3, etc.

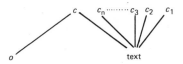

Just so the critic's effort really leads him to a 'conceptual work of art' with the index '1':

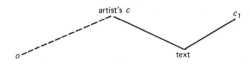

This schema now makes the need for a literary incest taboo obvious, which will prevent a checking and correcting process with the aim of matching c and c_1 that would necessitate further communication from the artist and his 'c'. What the diagram further shows is that the critic's work is real work too, in a creative sense, since he constructs his own c_1.

But what we indeed should say is that 'c' is not a singular conceptual 'point', but rather the entire plane of $c, c_1, c_2, \ldots c_n$. For as pointed out above, the artist's 'c' contains already the conceptualisation of the medium and its text, and hence contains by implication all c_n this text generates or is capable of generating; just as the conception of the garden includes potentially all the flowers that will be growing in the future.

14 On gardening

That the novelist may diagnose but need not prescribe I assume to be generally accepted, and the point here is rather that the critic should not fall into 'normative criticism' but shall, rather, 'for the fun of it' 'appreciate', 'appropriate', 'take intellectual possession' and make the thing criticised his 'own'.

A verb Henry James uses to describe the novelist's task is 'to reproduce',[1] though never overly emphasised and, needless to add, never in the sense of 'imitating nature'. The interest lies not so much in the object reproduced, as in the means and processes of its reproduction (the 'how' – for example pp. 9, 171). Yet my contention is that for James this portentous verb unites rather than distinguishes writer and critic – and indeed any man or woman (including characters) of sensibility. Sensibility, of course, is a key word in James's vocabulary, as it has been for so many poets and aestheticians. James does not pretend not to sort out sharply the good critics from the bad, the intelligent reader from the stupid, though good taste forbids him to be always explicit on the classification of artists and to spell out, as of course he must hold, that he belongs to the right group and serves moreover as its paradigm. It is in his discussion of 'interesting' characters that he can be most open:

> We care, our curiosity and our sympathy care, comparatively little for what happens to the stupid, the coarse and the blind; care for it, and for the effects of it, at the most as helping to precipitate what happens to the more deeply wondering, to the really sentient. (p. 62)

Just so, there is 'criticism based upon perception, criticism which is too little of this world' (pp. 53–4), and which is 'the only sort of criticism of which account need be taken' (p. 169). Thirdly, 'the question comes back . . . , obviously, to the kind and the degree of the artist's prime sensibility, which is the soil out of which his subject springs' (p. 45). Sensibility is evidently a necessary ingredient for any appreciation and reproduction, and for the 'perception' on which good criticism is based.

But to perceive, simply and passively, is not good enough, is to be stupid and insentient because, one would infer, there is hardly any 'effect of it' to care for. What distinguishes the interesting character (or reader, or novelist) is his or her awareness of perceiving, and of feeling 'the urgent appeal, on the part of everything, to be interpreted and, so far as may be, reproduced' (p. 59). He will, with this consciousness, fit his perceptions piece by piece into a larger scheme, a coherent vision, and make something of them, make sense out of them.

The artist's garden, we will see, is made of such perceptions gathered elsewhere, and we may indeed in this context follow the metaphor and find him prowling in the park or the jungle of Nature for ideas for his own planned garden. In his preface to *The Princess Casamassima* we see Henry James walk through the streets of London and pluck 'the ripe round fruit of perambulation' (p. 59):

> 'Subjects' and situations, character and history, the tragedy and comedy of life, are things of which the common air, in such conditions, seems pungently to taste; and to a mind curious, before the human scene, of meanings and revelations the great grey Babylon easily becomes, on its face, a garden bristling with an immense illustrative flora. Possible stories, presentable figures, rise from the thick jungle . . . . [The observer] goes on as with his head in a cloud of humming presences . . . (pp. 59–60)

Thus his literary ear catches the 'humming presence' of 'the history of little Hyacinth Robinson – he sprang up for me out of the London pavement' (p. 60). One is tempted indeed to wonder if this metaphor of flora had already, so many years earlier, worked on the author's mind and induced him to name his hero accordingly. Be this as it may, it is clear that he delights in 'organic form' (p. 84). Elsewhere, defending himself against 'the vain critic's quarrel . . . with one's subject' (p. 43), James gives an exposition of this organic architecture, for which he quotes from his much revered Turgenev. He affirms that the 'germ' of any of his ideas has never consisted in a '"plot", nefarious name': 'but altogether in the sense of a single character . . . to which all the usual elements of a "subject", certainly of a setting, were to need to be super-added'

(p. 42). The particular delight, for him as for Turgenev, is in seeing these characters as '*disponibles*' and in having

> to find for them the right relations, those that would most bring them out; to imagine, to invent and select and piece together the situations most useful and favourable to the sense of the creatures themselves . . .   (p. 43)

Having found the seedling, the horticulturist must select the best spot for it in his garden, where the soil, the conditions of light and shadow, as well as the possibilities for expansion are optimally suited to it. The question comes back again (if I may repeat the quotation)

> to the kind and the degree of the artist's prime sensibility, which is the soil out of which his subject springs. The quality and capacity of that soil, its ability to 'grow' with due freshness and straightness any vision of life, represents, strongly or weakly, the projected morality.   (p. 45)

This last reference to morality is again part of the defence against the vain quarrel with his allegedly amoral subject. I will not enter this particular discussion, and have cited the passage for its botanical significance.

Sometimes these seedlings are found on the botanist's rambles through Nature's park, sometimes the seeds are 'blown in by the wind': 'They are the breath of life – by which I mean that life, in its own way, breathes them upon us. They are so, in a manner prescribed and imposed – floated into our minds by the current of life' (p. 43, from Turgenev). Whether seedling or germ, the fact remains that 'they are so, in a manner prescribed and imposed', that is to say, are 'given' and not, as if the artist were God, created *ex nihilo*. Perception and appreciation precede artistic creation; but far from being a disadvantage, or a lesser privilege:

> These are the fascinations of the fabulist's art, these lurking forces of expansion, these necessities of upspringing in the seed, these beautiful determinations, on the part of the idea entertained, to grow as tall as possible, to push into the light and the air and thickly flower there . . .   (p. 42)

The pleasure of laying out the garden, of selecting and piecing together a multitude of flowers in the best possible combination, is enhanced rather than diminished by the constraint of each plant's 'individuality', its intrinsic principle of growth, its genetic programme. There are hardy plants and weakly seedlings, some made of 'much stouter stuff' (p. 50) and some, like 'the Isabel Archers, and even much smaller female fry' (p. 49), that 'are typical . . . of a class difficult, in the individual case, to make a centre of interest; so difficult in fact that many an expert painter . . . has preferred to leave the task unattempted' (p. 49). But the devoted gardener recognises 'the charm of the problem' (p. 49) and feels 'challenged' in his professional 'honour' to bring, particularly, such fragile and fastidious plants to flower.

As it happens, the garden artist has even his own fertiliser: 'Strangely fertilising, in the long run, does a wasted effort of attention often prove. It all depends on *how* the attention has been cheated, has been squandered' (pp. 41–2). The nourishment of 'wasted effort' seeps, naturally, into the soil of the artist's sensibility, to increase its 'quality and capacity', its 'ability to "grow"' its seeds. What appeals as a most 'nutritive or suggestive truth' is 'the perfect dependence of the "moral" sense of a work of art on the amount of felt life concerned in producing it' (p. 45), which may remind us of our earlier observation that a good deal of 'experience' and 'life' must water the flowers. The imagination of the artist, once a seedling has taken root there, 'detains it, preserves, protects, enjoys it' (p. 47). These are the fascinations of the fabulist's art,

> and, quite as much, these fine possibilities of recovering, from some good standpoint on the ground gained, the intimate history of the business – of retracing and reconstructing its steps and stages. (p. 42)

These latter may be listed in the same breath as the novelist's pleasures, but they are certainly not his exclusive privilege. It gives us beautifully the position of the reader, who chooses 'some good standpoint on the ground' the artist has laid out, from which to survey and appreciate the garden in bloom. The 'intimate history', 'its steps and stages', are perfectly open to his view and are retraceable, to the extent that matters, from the full-blown picture in front of him. In their zeal to educate the perceptive critic, James and Turgeniev may sometimes tell him where he is 'on good ground', where, that is, he is speaking from 'some good standpoint':

'when he points out what I've done or failed to do with [the "subject"], that's another matter: there he's on his ground' (p. 44, from Turgenev). The critic can quarrel, for instance, with the treatment of an unhappy plant which appears to droop and wither, but he cannot reproach the artist for having the little seedling in his garden. But I shall return later to the full training programme for the critic which is offered in James's prefaces. Let us add, instead, an example of the third sentient gardener, a character from *The Golden Bowl*, and one which, though female, has proved a hardy plant in James's park.

The Princess, only waking up fully to her sensibility and imagination in the second book of that novel, grows suddenly aware of her own garden:[2]

It wasn't till many days had passed that the Princess began to accept the idea of having done, a little, something she was not always doing, or indeed that of having listened to any inward voice that spoke in a new tone. Yet these instinctive postponements of reflexion were the fruit, positively, of recognitions and perceptions already active; of the sense above all that she had made at a particular hour, made by the mere touch of her hand, a difference in the situation so long present to her as practically unattackable. This situation had been occupying for months and months the very centre of the garden of her life, but it had reared itself there like some strange tall tower of ivory . . .

The 'tower of ivory' grows into the metaphor of 'the house of fiction'[3], or properly a 'house of perception', with 'apertures' and outlooks it had never occurred to the Princess to imagine as yielding special views on her garden. 'She had walked round and round it – that was what she felt; she had carried on her existence in the space left her for circulation, a space that sometimes seemed ample and sometimes seemed narrow' (II, p. 3). She had not, so far, realised that her own garden is for her to landscape, and had allowed this tower to be erected in it by other hands. She had not, indeed, permitted herself to assume a 'good standpoint' and survey her garden, content to experience it from within. But owing to 'recognitions and perceptions already active' she is able, at her awakening, to reap the fruit of her belated reflection – a sign that she has always possessed a latent talent for gardening. It, and her consciousness of it, are now steadily growing, and recurring references become more specific:

> [Her husband] had 'met' her – she so put it to herself; met her with an effect of generosity and of gaiety in especial . . . which she wore in her breast as the token of an escape for them both from something not quite definite but clearly much less good. Even at that moment in fact her plan had begun to work; she had been, when he brightly reappeared, in the act of plucking it out of the heart of her earnestness – plucking it, in the garden of thought, as if it had been some full-blown flower that she could present to him on the spot. Well, it was the flower of participation, and as that, then and there, she held it out to him . . .   (II, pp. 25–6)

The seed for this little flower had been sown some time ago, naked and modest outside a particular setting, but already with the full potential for its powerful specificity in relation to the environment into which it would grow. Now a 'full-blown flower', it presents 'the idea, so needlessly, so absurdly obscured, of her *sharing* with him, whatever the enjoyment, the interest, the experience might be – and sharing also, for that matter with Charlotte' (II, p. 26). This is a good example of the 'determination' of a little flower to grow as tall as possible with the help of its setting, since 'participation', in this situation, means sharing with a husband and a stepmother, an outcome not entirely predictable from the isolated seedling. But to return to the Princess:

> It may be said of her that during these passages she plucked her sensations by the way, detached nervously the small wild blossoms of her dim forest, so that she could smile over them at least with the spacious appearance, for her companions, for her husband above all, of bravely, of altogether frivolously, going a-maying.   (II, p. 144)

The Princess, after a passive existence of consuming her perceptions, even though with a certain appreciation, has embarked on an active plan of construction, of building her own crystal palace. She goes about it very much in the manner and style of the narrator of *The Sacred Fount*; and the question, here, is again pressingly 'intimacy': ' "They were intimate, you see. Intimate," said the Princess'. And Fanny Assingham replies:

'There's always the question of what one considers – !' 'What one considers intimate? Well, I know what I consider intimate now. Too intimate,' said Maggie, 'to let me know anything about it.' (II, p. 161)

The fact that there had been no sign of intimacy between the Prince and Charlotte, and the absence of any suspicion on Maggie's part, are symptom enough of something very treacherous, something requiring 'screening' and 'covering up'. Charlotte and the Prince work on the inverse assumption that if they 'go about' with and visit each other unreservedly, the very openness of their actions will speak of their innocence. But Maggie, in the words of the Prince, insists on 'drawing immense conclusions from very small matters' (II, p. 193); and she answers Fanny's anticipation of an 'unexplained complication' between her and her husband:

'"Unexplained", my dear? Quite the contrary – explained: fully, intensely, admirably explained, with nothing really to add. My own love' – she kept it up – 'I don't want anything *more*. I've plenty to go upon and to do with as it is.' (II, p. 166)

And she rejects the idea of speaking to the Prince – 'his keeping away from me . . . – what will that *be* but to speak' (p. 167). She does not, in other words, want explanations and 'confessions', but much prefers the speaking evidence of 'the gilt cup' in her own 'personal confidence'. 'The gilt cup' (II, p. 159) may itself be an ironic reflection of the fact that the Princess, despite her efforts, is still an apprentice in the art of 'sentient' appreciation. The dealer in the shop, surely an expert at discriminating beautiful objects, names it 'my Golden Bowl' to Charlotte and the Prince, and the chronicler adds on their behalf: 'and it sounded on his lips as if it said everything. He left the important object – for as "important" it did somehow present itself – to produce its certain effect' (I, p. 112). There is assembled here a trio of connoisseurs of effects as well as of sounds that 'say everything'. It would not occur to them to call the vessel by a lexical equivalent, which, on the contrary, may help to accentuate a comparison: the Bowl is 'larger than a common cup' (I, p. 112). It retains, even for the chronicler, its capital letters, while Charlotte begins to play with the magic of its name.

But it is precisely against Charlotte and the Prince that the Princess is now measuring her sensibility. Intimidated by

Charlotte's radiant presence, she is nevertheless building up her awareness that she and the Prince are 'together':

> The heart of the Princess swelled accordingly even in her abasement; she had kept in tune with the right, and something certainly, something that might resemble a rare flower snatched from an impossible ledge, would, and possibly soon, come of it for her. (II, p. 250)

From the Prince on the other hand she learns the use of a sentient ear: 'when she passed near him and he turned to give her a smile she caught – or so she fancied – the greater depth of his small perpetual hum of contemplation' (II, p. 286). She has learnt, like the narrator of *The Sacred Fount*, to rely on a logic other than causality, and to interpret effect more subtly than with respect to intention: 'Maggie . . . had so shuffled away every link between consequence and cause that the intention remained, like some famous poetic line in a dead language, subject to varieties of interpretation' (II, p. 345). Thus she feels, with the 'participation' in her husband's experience guaranteed, that she has reached the end she has worked for: 'Here it was then, the moment, the golden fruit that had shone from afar . . .' (II, p. 367). And, like any product of perception and imagination, it is accompanied by a sense of terror as well as beauty:

> Closer than she had ever been to the measure of her course and the full face of her act, she had an instant of the terror that, when there has been suspense, always precedes, on the part of the creature to be paid, the certification of the amount. (II, p. 367)

Weakness is paired with the desire at the moment of its fulfilment: 'her weakness, her desire, so long as she was yet not saving herself, flowered in her face like a light or a darkness' (II, p. 352).

Now that we have seen artists, critics and characters in the act of 'reproducing' and 'recovering', we shall take a closer look at how this is done. As we have said, receiving perceptions is not sufficient and something has to be made of them; they must be actively recreated. The direction, as it were, must change and the gathered flower be offered again to some new soil, some other garden. Perceptions of the garden of life are received by many characters of *The Golden Bowl*, though through different apertures in the house of perception; while the private vistas produced differ substantially from each other. Fanny Assingham presents her prodigious scheme at the end of book one, in which we also had the benefit of the Prince's and Charlotte's; the second book opens the view on the garden of the Princess, as she is taking charge of it. We may call them different media, different 'soils', and none is intrinsically better – or truer – than another.

Freud, who wants to account for what is going on inside the house of perception, has devised a psychic apparatus for assembling perceptions into larger wholes. The process of 'regression' is a projection backwards, for a private viewing, on to the screen of dreams, as well as daydreams and fantasy. Linguistic expression, as any action upon the world, proceeds in the opposite direction. If a dream, from the private screen of the mind, is articulated, it is reproduced through a complex process of transformation and translation into the new verbal medium. The finished dream, assembled in hard dream work from material in the unconscious, has to pass through this locus again and come, in the process, to pieces in order to be reassembled according to the laws of the new medium. We could thus associate the dream with the 'conceptual works of art', with the crystal palaces of observation and imagination; and it gives an idea of the complexity of their reproduction.

But the apparent simplicity of the binary directionality of Freud's model must not deceive us, since that apparatus can generate infinitely. The new linguistic expression may itself become a perception, and travel, in the same or some other apparatus, back in the opposite direction, and so *ad infinitum*.

James, student of consciousness, recognises and allows for many channels and media of expression; and he has outlined the first few steps of the infinite regress the flow of consciousness generates. Nature or Life may serve as an arbitrary starting point, yet there is no doubt that all its plants and flowers are already producing patterns and embroideries that cry out for interpretation, for the retracing of their history of perception and reproduction. It may be significant that a favourite term of James's is that of 'the canvas of Life', indicating that this is already a complicated artefact and not a 'natural' beginning.

It serves him as the beginning of the 'literary circuit', namely as the store from which the artist gathers his 'germs'. At his hands they undergo the mysterious process of artistic reproduction; they grow not only in the soil of his private sensibility but turn back into literary expression. For the reader his work becomes a new canvas, appealing for interpretation, for possession to be taken, so as to be rebuilt into new crystal palaces in the reader's mind. If that reader happens to be a practising critic, himself a dabbler in the craft of words, he may even forge these into verbal expression again; though whether this is a fact to be welcomed or simply a contingency to be faced, James does not properly spell out. It is a rare benefit, in the case of the discriminating critic, but certainly not one he may, as novelist, expect:

> He must not think of benefits . . . for that way dishonour lies: he has, that is, but one to think of – the benefit, whatever it may be, involved in his having cast a spell upon the simpler, the very simplest, forms of attention. This is all he is entitled to; he is entitled to nothing, he is bound to admit, that can come to him, from the reader, as a result on the latter's part of any act of reflexion or discrimination. He may *enjoy* this finer tribute – that is another affair, but on condition only of taking it as a gratuity 'thrown in', a mere miraculous windfall, the fruit of a tree he may not pretend to have shaken.   (p. 54)

'Reflexion or discrimination' may stir in the mind of any reader, and it is only a chance – a chance against long odds, James would say – if that reader is a literary journalist and thus succeeds in communicating a tribute to the author. But above all, this fruit grows in another's garden, and he who supplied the seedling of the tree has no right to its harvest.

We will arrest this generative process at this point and refrain from a glance at the further chain of seedlings grown from a critic's tree and all the academic graftings one might envisage. The same infinite production can be seen to go on in the novels themselves, where perceptions are perceived, interpreted, reproduced in discourse, reinterpreted, and where palace is built upon palace, with none at the bottom built on rock.

15 Reader and critic writ large

We shall now look at the critic's role as it emerges from James's *The Art of the Novel*, although references to the reader and critic are few and woeful. 'The vain critic's quarrel' we have already cited, as well as the perceptive criticism which is 'too little of this world'. But particularly sad is this fantasy of Paradise:

> The artist may of course, in wanton moods, dream of some Paradise (for art) where the direct appeal to the intelligence might be legalised; for to such extravagances as these his yearning mind can scarce hope ever completely to close itself. The most he can do is to remember they *are* extravagances.   (p. 54)

Scarcely more flattering is the following estimate of us, the readers:

> The picture of an intelligence appears for the most part, it is true, a dead weight for the reader of the English novel to carry, this reader having so often the wondrous property of caring for the displayed tangle of human relations without caring for its intelligibility.   (p. 63)

But properly paranoid is this grim picture:

> Against reflexion, against discrimination, in [the novelist's] interest, all earth and air conspire; wherefore it is that, as I say, he must in many a case have schooled himself, from the first, to work but for a 'living wage'. The living wage is the reader's grant of the least possible quantity of attention required for consciousness of a 'spell'.   (p. 54)

James is sinking into the cynical realism of *The Next Time*, talking of the critic that is rather than could be. The 'living wage' is the cheap price at which the writer is willing to sell himself: the promise from the reader to fall spellbound at the sight of a 'tangle of human relations', regardless of its intelligibility, to be captured already by a 'story'. A response beyond that, from the 'intelligence', is 'a golden apple, for the writer's lap, straight from the wind-stirred tree' (p. 54).

Nevertheless, Henry James is forever concerned with 'my relation with the reader' (p. 55), the 'provision for interest' (p. 70) or the surprise of romance. This multifaceted term of 'interest' may serve as well as another to light up the ambiguous dividing line between writer and reader, between James the author and James the critic. For, the many times we hear of this 'interest' in the prefaces, it is as often his own as the interest he wishes to provide that is being traced, and we must ask ourselves if the two can at all be different. James's modesty and his pessimistic opinion of the reader make him assume that many a thing giving pleasure to him will remain unshared by the reader. But inversely, it can hardly be doubted that anything received as interesting by the latter is *a priori* so for the writer.

Yet, what must above all be remembered is the fact that *The Art of the Novel* is written not by a novelist, strictly speaking, but by a critic. For the occasion of a collected edition he has reread the works of a familiar and favourite author; and the pleasures, the little excitements he records are most of all a subtle example, a pointer for the critic, of 'work cut out'. It might be thought that through a greater intimacy with the person of the author this critic has an incomparable advantage; but then we must ask how much of a real, a critical, advantage it is. Remember that Miss Delavoy, devoted reader of her brother's work, does not feel she has any advantage over her friend, the narrator, and indeed leaves it to him to express their common appreciation.

Let us see to what use James turns this exclusive 'advantage', when he recalls the incidents of the 'genesis' of a novel or story. We shall find that, when it really comes down to such memories, the real origin of a 'germ', beyond the city whose streets James happened to roam at the time, there is a blank:

> I seem to myself to have waked up one morning in possession of them – of Ralph Touchett and his parents, of Madame Merle, of Gilbert Osmond and his daughter and his sister, of Lord Warburton, Caspar Goodwood and Miss Stackpole, the definite

array of contributions to Isabel Archer's history. . . . It was as if they had simply, by an impulse of their own, floated into my ken . . . (p. 53)

I profess a certain vagueness of remembrance in respect to the origin and growth of 'The Tragic Muse' . . . (p. 79)

I had, no doubt, a groping instinct for the right complications, since I am quite unable to track the footsteps of those that constitute, as the case stands, the general situation exhibited. They are there, for what they are worth, and as numerous as might be; but my memory, I confess, is a blank as to how and whence they came. (p. 53)

The only apparent road to the 'origin' and the memory of it seems to be the text he is rereading, and of how far back it goes we now have a testimony. We may want to consider what the gain is when the memory is somewhat more substantial and anecdotal, as for instance in the case of *The Sacred Fount*. From the *Notebooks* we learn that James, during a story told at a dinner conversation, suddenly perceives the possible theme of 'vampirish relations'.[1] But what we must ask, in the face of such evidence, is why *this* story, at *this* dinner, and why not some other piece of gossip told in different circumstances? What makes the 'spark' in the one case, and not in the other? It is a question James asks himself, without, needless to say, giving an answer (p. 159). We have truly got no further than if we did not possess these 'confessions' of an author, as concerns the intimacy of the conception of ideas.

James almost apologises for his failing memory (though can the memory be said to have failed when the 'knowledge' was presumably never there?); and he answers his own question:

If the apparition was still all to be placed how came it to be vivid? . . . . One could answer such a question beautifully, doubtless, if one could do so subtle, if not so monstrous, a thing as to write the history of the growth of one's imagination. (p. 47)

The thing would be so uncanny as to be all but monstrous, and if we remember that the narrator of *The Sacred Fount* attempts just that and succeeds, one feels, rather better than James in the prefaces, it may be for just that reason that *The Sacred Fount* and its narrator are supersubtle to the point, almost, of monstrosity.

If we look at the opening page of the first preface, we find an intention mapped out which is soon retracted again, or at least weakened in its original claim. A bold factual statement sets our expectations for intimate revelations: '*Roderick Hudson* was begun in Florence in the spring of 1874, designed from the first for serial publication in *The Atlantic Monthly*, where it opened in January 1875 and persisted through the year' (p. 3). Then an explanation, of a far more intimate and 'confessional' tone:

> I yield to the pleasure of placing these circumstances on record, as I shall place others, and as I have yielded to the need of renewing acquaintance with the book after a quarter of a century. This revival of an all but extinct relation with an early work may often produce for an artist, I think, more kinds of interest and emotion than he shall find it easy to express, and yet will light not a little, to his eyes, that veiled face of his Muse which he is condemned forever and all anxiously to study. (p. 3)

For one thing, he is 'renewing acquaintance' after twenty-five years, and therefore speaks from this new, this latter 'standpoint' rather than from that intimate one of an author with regard to a work he is in the process of writing. He studies the Muse, not just the inspiration of yesterday, who moreover may unveil her face 'to his eyes' which does not in itself guarantee us a glimpse. And he is studying, one might add, the 'art of representation' in general:

> The art of representation bristles with questions the very terms of which are difficult to apply and to appreciate; but whatever makes it arduous makes it, for our refreshment, infinite, causes the practice of it, with experience, to spread round us in a widening, not in a narrowing circle. Therefore it is that experience has to organise, for convenience and cheer, some system of observation – for fear, in the admirable immensity, of losing its way. (p. 3)

How can he then not discuss – indeed, 'appreciate' – the early work with this enlarged 'experience' of twenty-five years? And what needs to be organised is a 'system of observation', observation implying precisely an 'external', a critical, point of view, as we discussed it with regard to *The Sacred Fount*, where the 'objective' view of the observer is that of the severed and retrospective critic. As to the claim we said was strongly put and announcing the prefaces seemingly as authorial 'inside' documents:

> We see [the experience] as pausing from time to time to consult its notes, to measure, for guidance, as many aspects and distances as possible, as many steps taken and obstacles mastered and fruits gathered and beauties enjoyed. Everything counts, nothing is superfluous in such a survey; the explorer's note-book strikes me here as endlessly receptive. This accordingly is what I mean by the contributive value – or put it simply as, to one's own sense, the beguiling charm – of the *accessory* facts in a given artistic case. This is why, as one looks back, the private history of any sincere work, however modest its pretensions, looms with its own completeness in the rich, ambiguous aesthetic air, and seems at once to borrow a dignity and to mark, so to say, a station. This is why, reading over, for revision, correction and republication, the volumes here in hand, I find myself, all atttentively, in presence of some such recording scroll or engraved commemorative table – from which the 'private' character, moreover, quite insists on dropping out. (pp. 3–4)

The most significant and almost Freudian stylistic oddity is the phrase 'the explorer's note-book strikes me here as endlessly receptive'. Our expectations are all set for the notebook to be bountifully providing – instead, it is receptive. And from the passage following, which I will not quote in full, one gains a sense that the 'continuity of an artist's endeavour', his development over the years, is read as a 'thrilling tale, almost for a wondrous adventure', not out of the notebook, but from the 'volumes here in hand' back into it. We do then get in the prefaces at large extensive analyses of the works, yet hardly of the notes; and of the latter mainly those details count from which the 'private' character 'quite insists on dropping out' – that is, those which are aesthetically relevant and have correspondences in the novels, and no private or personal ones. The associative clues come largely from the works and may – who knows – make James glance at his notes. But in this we can follow him in every step; and, it is my contention, there is nothing in the prefaces apart from some trivial biographical data of little interest, that we as readers should not be able to trace on our own.

Thus it is that we can learn from the prefaces our job as critics, but not the master's craft. His 'terror' of the temptation to be 'led on by "developments"' ' beyond the point of 'interest' tells the critic to look out for the structure of that 'development' – not only for what it is, but for what it could have been, and to recognise the vast 'sea' of alternatives that presented the temptation. It will increase our appreciation to realise the 'selection' before us, the selection from the 'boundless number of [the canvas's] distinct perforations for the needle' of the 'embroiderer' (p. 5). The constant gauge in front of the novelist's eyes is the balance, 'the very condition of interest, which languishes and drops' without these 'developments' (pp. 4–5).

> To exhibit these relations, once they have all been recognised, is to 'treat' his idea, which involves neglecting none of those that directly minister to interest; the degree of that directness remaining meanwhile a matter of highly difficult appreciation, and one on which felicity of form and composition, as a part of the total effect, mercilessly rests. (p. 5)

The appreciation, therefore, of the directness with which these relations minister to interest is needed by us for the appreciation of the total effect, of 'felicity of form and composition'. Inversely, if the novelist has to appreciate it, he has to be a critic himself throughout the time of authorship. This is, of course, no news, and it is spelt out in another preface: 'The teller of a story is primarily, none the less, the listener to it, the reader of it, too . . . ' (p. 63). This sums up the complicated tangle into which the narrator of *The Sacred Fount* got himself, of the subjectivity and the objectivity in opposition. They need be in no graver antithesis than that of dialogue and dialectic, and it is the narrator's peculiar fate to suffer from it 'passionately'.

Once it is recognised that the writer contains the critic it is also more understandable that the narrator of *The Sacred Fount* is so often associated with James himself. The activity which the narrator illustrates is precisely the one that writer and reader share – and, for that matter, the characters of 'interest'. The point I am making is that on the differentiating qualities of the writer James has little to say even in the prefaces. He cannot remember the real origins of his ideas, nor can he describe their translation into the literary text. His commentary in the prefaces concentrates on the critical perception of his growing ideas and thus instructs us, as it were, on how criticism ought to be practised. This is also reflected stylistically, since the James of the prefaces frequently slips into the third person

form when talking about James the author, while including himself
in the 'we' of the readers and critics. Passages already quoted, like
that on *Roderick Hudson*, illustrate this feature. It might be seen
simply as a form of expressing general ideas about the art of the
novel, as opposed to the personal experience concerning a particular work. But such a generalisation speaks precisely of a shift from
the perspective of the author to that of the critic and theoretician,
which is evidenced in the following passage by the 'critical question'
in subject position. From relating the personal failure of having
'named' rather than 'done' Northampton – always in the first
person – he goes on:

> Since I do insist, at all events, I find this ghostly interest perhaps
> even more reasserted for me by the questions begotten within the
> very covers of the book, those that wander and idle there as in
> some sweet old overtangled walled garden, a safe paradise of self-
> criticism. Here it is that if there be air for it to breathe at all,
> the critical question swarms, and here it is, in particular, that
> one of the happy hours of the painter's long day may strike.
> (p. 10)

James almost delights in this fault in *Roderick Hudson* for providing
him with an opportunity for excelling all the more as a critic. This
particular pleasure, surely, also indicates how little he feels it still
has to do with him, the James of the 1900s: 'A "fancy" indication [of
New England] would have served my turn – except that I should so
have failed perhaps of a pretext for my present insistence' (p. 10).
He has discovered this other pleasure of gardens, besides creating
them, namely the one we are familiar with, of taking 'some good
standpoint on the ground' and surveying the finished product. A
paradise it may be for him to perform this in his very own garden,
although he has also visited many others.[2] It may be the more
paradisiacal for not demanding that delicate diplomacy called for in
dealing with his colleagues' work, or it may be simply because it is so
fruitful a garden. But certainly the shortness of the memory is
responsible again, since the critic of the present cannot remember
fully the achievements of the novelist of the past, and there results a
certain suspense:

> the very uncertainties themselves yield a thrill, and if subject and
> treatment, working together, have had their felicity, the artist,

the prime creator, may find a strange charm in this stage of the connexion. (p. 10)

The revived anxieties and the forgotten motives 'fall together once more' with 'the actual appearances . . . and a lesson and a moral and a consecrating final light are somehow disengaged' (p. 11). The thrill is as great for the critic, who after all is exactly looking for that felicity of subject and treatment 'working together', and all he has to abdicate of the share is the knowledge of having created it himself. But the case is even closer to this anxiety of the 'prime creator' in the critic who also rereads a favourite author, whose achievements he cannot fully and in detail remember. Uncertainties accompany this 'reading over' and 'revision', as to whether subject and treatment merit the earlier enthusiasm, and whether the widened experience will find them 'working together' as perfectly. At any rate, he too will 'disengage' a lesson and a moral – or rather, will see 'a consecrating final light' being disengaged and emerge from the finished product thus surveyed. James further qualifies: 'All this, I mean of course, if the case will wonderfully take any such pressure, if the work doesn't break down under even such mild overhauling. The author knows well enough how easily that may happen . . .' (p. 11). So does the practising reader. 'The author' is now in the third person, as it is the critic rather than he who does the overhauling. This last term, however, is interesting, for in the present context of 'revision, correction and republication' we might easily take it as a metaphor for the reworking of an earlier work. Instead, the overhaul is precisely the 'critical apprehension' of its present effect, which 'insists on becoming as active as it can' (p. 11), with no parts exchanged, retouched or readjusted.

There follows a final refutation of the apparent claim that any private 'accessory' facts would be revived: 'The old reasons then are too old to revive; they were not, it is plain, good enough reasons to live' (p. 11). This is to say that the only valid 'reasons' are those which have their traces and their marks in the work, 'buried as they are in the texture of the work' (p. 11), while those recorded in some private diary – or unrecorded and forgotten – are irrelevant. It amounts to the contention above that the critic and reader can achieve as much in this paradise of criticism as can its rereading author, can trace as well as he the growth and the history of a novel. James confirms this again for us in his preface to *What Maisie Knew, In the Cage* and *The Pupil*:

The second in order of these fictions speaks for itself, I think, so
frankly as scarce to suffer further expatiation. Its origin is written
upon it large . . .   (p. 154)
The composition before us tells in fact clearly enough, it seems to
me, the story of its growth . . .   (p. 155)

And the first person plural once more gathers together the critics
and the James of the prefaces in a common enterprise. And they
watch the 'scenic' law: 'To read [the three tales] over has been to
find them on this ground never at fault . . . . Going over the pages
here placed together has been for me, at all events, quite to watch
the scenic system at play . . .' (p. 157). 'For me, at all events' does
not mean for him as their creator, since he is reading these pages
now and 'watching'. Rather, the phrase is a result of his caution not
to generalise to 'the reader', and it qualifies 'this critic, at all events',
whatever other critics may say. For preceding this passage there is
another realisation that despite the prominence of the 'scenic law'
the critics seem not to have noticed it, or at any rate have not
commented.

> These finer idiosyncracies of a literary form seem to be regarded
> as outside the scope of criticism – small reference to them do I
> remember ever to have met; such surprises of re-perusal, such
> recoveries of old fundamental intention, such moments of almost
> ruefully independent discrimination, would doubtless in that case
> not have waylaid my steps.   (p. 157)

Were the critics to have said it all before, he would not feel the need
to enlarge upon it now. Although it is re-perusal and recovery of 'old
fundamental intention', it is the critic and not the author who now
discovers it, all alone in the field of discrimination, with his fellow
critics left far behind. Nor is his term 'intention' a slip into fallacy,
for it is the intention he speaks of elsewhere and which is the
'growth' and the 'history' of a tale written large upon its text,
intention which can be *seen* fulfilling itself. James knows well how to
dissociate such intention from a consciously held design of the
author – one that may or may not become realised in the work: 'If I
speak . . . of the *action* embodied, each time, in these so "quiet"
recitals, it is under renewed recognition of the inveterate instinct
with which they keep conforming to the "scenic" law' (p. 157).
These tales have full autonomy and follow their 'instinct' – so much

so that James prefers to make them syntactical agents: 'they keep conforming . . . they demean themselves for all the world – they quite insist on it, that is, whenever they have a chance – as little constituted dramas . . . ' (p. 157). All the author does in the face of such autonomy and independence is prepare the ground:

> The point, however, is that the scenic passages are *wholly* and logically scenic, having for their rule of beauty the principle of the 'conduct', the organic development, of a scene – the entire succession of values that flower and bear fruit on ground solidly laid for them. (p. 158)

And once again he modestly retreats into the company of critics, marvelling as much as they at the literary drama unfolding before their eyes:

> The great advantage for the total effect is that we feel, with the definite alternation, how the theme *is* being treated. That is we feel it when, in such tangled connexions, we happen to care. I shouldn't really go on as if this were the case with many readers. (p. 158)

He feels by no means that it is he who treats the theme; the theme is being treated in the ground so prepared for it and according to a law that exists outside the author's will. James's distinction again is not that he is an author while others are critics and readers, but that he is almost the only reader of perception and discrimination, one who cares for the 'intelligibility' of a tangle.

If we saw the metaphor of the garden unite writer, reader and character, we also find them bound by the 'critical spirit' (p. 156). There is Henry James, the novelist and author of *In the Cage*, referred to by the James of the prefaces as 'this most beset of critics', for at the time of that story he is a 'student of great cities' (p. 155), a student in the park of urban Nature, who with his obsession of interpreting all its plants is in danger 'inevitably of imputing to too many others, right and left, the critical impulse and the acuter vision' (p. 155). From this, needless to say, the characters of his novels also suffer, if they are of the sentient type:

> The range of wonderment attributed in our tale to the young woman employed at Cocker's differs little in essence from the

speculative thread on which the pearls of Maisie's experience, in this same volume – pearls of so strange an iridescence – are mostly strung. She wonders, putting it simply, very much as Morgan Moreen wonders; and they all wonder, for that matter, very much after the fashion of our portentous little Hyacinth of *The Princess Casamassima*, tainted to the core, as we have seen him, with the trick of mental reaction on the things about him and fairly staggering under the appropriations, as I have called them, that he owes to the critical spirit. (p. 156)

And through Maisie, for instance, our position is again defined:

To that then I settled – to the question of giving it *all*, the whole situation surrounding her, but of giving it only through the occasions and connexions of her proximity and her attention; only as it might pass before her and appeal to her . . . for better or worse, for perceptive gain or perceptive loss: so that we fellow witnesses, we not ·more invited but only more expert critics, should feel in strong possession of it. (p. 145)

And if it seems as though the author were for once 'going behind' his subject as if to assert his authorial presence, which in other instances he stresses he does not do (pp. 91, 111, 117), it is only because behind the mirror of Maisie's consciousness he inserts yet another one, initiating an infinite regression of possible reflections of reflections of the 'facts', yet without providing that authorial looking-glass which would finally give the real facts or the 'truth'.

Maisie's terms accordingly play their part – since her simpler conclusions quite depend on them; but our own commentary constantly attends and amplifies. This it is that on occasion, doubtless, seems to represent us as going so 'behind' the facts of her spectacle as to exaggerate the activity of her relation to them. The difference here is but of a shade: it is her relation, her activity of spirit, that determines all our own concern – we simply take advantage of these things better than she herself. (p. 146)

All he does, he affirms, is provide her 'activity of spirit' with another medium of expression beyond her limited and childlike one, and translate the picture from the screen of her mind into the communal medium of the text. 'The manner of the thing may thus illustrate the author's incorrigible taste for gradations and superpositions of effect' (p. 153). The quotation, in fact, regards *The Pupil*, but the author's illustrated taste is a general one.

Since we are talking about truth again, James shall be allowed a final word to dispel those arguments about Reality and Truth *versus* imagination, illusion and fancy, once and for all: 'Extravagant as the mere statement sounds, one seemed accordingly to handle the secret of life in drawing the positive right truth out of the so easy muddle of wrong truths . . .' (p. 123). Extravagant indeed it must sound to the ear attuned to the singular Truth. The 'right truth' is the one which is right for the work and its plan, where another truth would be wrong – not so much intrinsically wrong as to make it a falsehood, but wrong for the particular case. And to those who think not only that James's characters are sometimes led astray by fancy but who impute, through equation of James with such characters and narrators, a similar weakness to him, one has to cite James's low opinion of that Reality he calls Life. He comments at all because he just related how he had found a 'germ' in the storeroom of Life, 'the merest grain, the speck of truth' (p. 119) which suffices him as a situation, while declining to hear any further details about the real case and its development.

> It at the same time amuses him again and again to note how, beyond the first step of the actual case, the case that constitutes for him his germ, his vital particle, his grain of gold, life persistently blunders and deviates, loses herself in the sand. The reason is of course that life has no direct sense whatever for the subject and is capable, luckily for us, of nothing but splendid waste. Hence the opportunity for the sublime economy of art . . .   (p. 120)

It is from this premise, 'the fatal futility of Fact' (p. 122), that James is led to the necessity of the 'logic of the particular case' (p. 121) and 'the positive right truth'; for:

> If life, presenting us the germ, and left merely to herself in such a business, gives the case away, almost always, before we can stop her, what are the signs for our guidance, what the primary laws for a saving selection, how do we know when and where to intervene, where do we place the beginnings of the wrong or the right deviation?   (p. 120)

Where, in other words, does he get guidance if an imitation of life is not good enough? Verisimilitude, in a strict sense, would lead to poor art. And when, although he declined, James's informant 'had already begun all complacently and benightedly further to report', he triumphs:

> I saw clumsy Life again at her stupid work. For the action taken . . . I had absolutely, and could have, no scrap of use; one had been so perfectly qualified to say in advance: 'It's the perfect little workable thing, but she'll strangle it in the cradle, even while she pretends, all so cheeringly, to rock it; wherefore I'll stay her hand while yet there's time.'   (p. 121)

He 'didn't, of course, stay her hand' (p. 121) since there was no time, nor did he have the authorial power to interfere with her work. But the situation, 'if arrested in the right place', is excellent, even if the 'Real' development shows a turn to the 'classic ineptitude' (p. 122).

> It was not, however, that this in the least mattered, once the seed had been transplanted to richer soil; and I dwell on that almost inveterate redundancy of the wrong, as opposed to the ideal right, in any free flowering of the actual, by reason only of its approach to calculable regularity.   (p. 122)

So again, when he comes across the 'germ' for *What Maisie Knew*, he selects immediately the right and workable thing, and substitutes, where necessary, 'the ideal right':

> I recollect, however, promptly thinking that for a proper symmetry the second parent should marry too – which in the case named to me indeed would probably soon occur, and was in any case what the ideal of the situation required.   (pp. 140–1)

Life has no 'sense for the subject', because 'she' has no appreciation, no perception, of her facts; that is, none of that critical spirit which is essential for the interpreter. Her 'stories' embody no principle of selection – 'life being all inclusion and confusion' (p. 120), a mere accumulation of facts.

While the 'ideal' which improves on Nature is the 'symmetry' of the situation in *What Maisie Knew*, it is not, of course, a constant ingredient, and is appropriate only in this particular case. Elsewhere James mentions 'the "scenic" law', the 'economy of art',

or the 'law of entire expression' (p. 144), but these are names rather
than descriptions or explanations.[3] Thus the suspicion grows that if
the novelist cannot give away his secret, neither can the critic, and
we begin to grasp more fully the significance of 'the secret of life' (p.
123) which serves James as an image. He describes how once he 'has
borrowed his motive' (p. 122) from Life, the artist

> only lends and gives, only builds and piles high, lays together the
> blocks quarried in the deeps of his imagination and on his
> personal premises. He thus remains all the while in intimate
> commerce with his motive, and can say to himself – what really
> more than anything else inflames and sustains him – that he alone
> has the *secret* of the particular case, he alone can measure the truth
> of the direction to be taken by his developed data.   (pp. 122–3)

We are getting close to the mode of expression in *The Sacred Fount*,
with the building of crystal palaces out of the 'blocks quarried in the
deeps of [the] imagination', through the 'intimate commerce' that
binds the artist to his work, to the knowledge of having sole
possession of the secret. 'There can be for him, evidently, only one
logic for these things; there can be for him only one truth and one
direction – the quarter in which his subject most completely
expresses itself' (p. 123). The secret is tautologically locked in these
circumlocutions: the 'case' has to follow its own direction, according
to its own truth, the truth is the logic and the logic is the truth of the
situation, while the direction to be taken is the one which leads to
the ideal and complete treatment of the subject.

> The careful ascertainment of how it shall do so, and the art of
> guiding it with consequent authority – since this sense of 'au-
> thority' is for the master-builder the treasure of treasures, or at
> least the joy of joys – renews in the modern alchemist something
> like the old dream of the secret of life.   (p. 123)

Again we are reminded of the narrator of *The Sacred Fount*, whose joy
is concentrated in his authorship of the beautiful theory – an
authorship which is as ambiguous as the 'authority' of James's
passage. For while he jealously claims it on the one hand, part of the
responsibility – at least for its origin – is devolved on to something

else, on to Life. It is after all from the facts – the visible effects – that the narrator starts out, just as James takes his 'speck of truth' from Life's storeroom. The 'authority' lies in the possession taken of the little treasure – in its recognition, and in the responsibility assumed after its transplantation to 'richer soil'. It is not the authoritarian power exercised over a seedling, manipulating and forcing its growth. We have already cited many passages in which James asserts how he is guided by his subject, how it 'quite insisted' on following its own organic principle. The attitude recalls the cliché that Michaelangelo only carved out of the block of marble what was already latently contained within it. Finally, we come to the ambiguity of the 'secret', which, in its invoked presence, holds the promise of the secret discovered, the secret known, and yet remains 'the old dream of the secret of life'. Just such a secret is the narrator's full-blown theory at the moment it takes flight, letting him glimpse the fulfilment of his dream for an instance but carrying its secret away with it. It retains its status as secret embodied in the fabric of the finished work, as a puzzle for the observer. And James, impatient that the reader should take up his task, is pointing at it to goad him:

> I might give a considerable list of those of my fictions . . . in which this curious conversion is noted.   (p. 188)
> As to which in my list they are, however, that is another business, not on any terms to be made known.   (p. 86)

'I might' tell my secret, but I won't.

> If it be asked how then we were to have assisted at the copious passage I thus incriminate without our privilege of presence, I can only say that my discovery of the right way should – and would –have been the very flower of the performance. (p. 137)

If it had not long been evident, James now spells it out for us that the literary enterprise is an elaborate game. On the same page he refutes the more pedestrian course of '[reporting] the matter quite straight', which

> had indeed every merit but that of its playing the particular game to which I had addressed myself. My prime loyalty was to the

interest of the game, and the honour to be won the more desirable
by that fact. (p. 137)

We have encountered the notion of the game already in the context
of *The Turn of the Screw*, that 'piece of . . . cold artistic calculation,
an *amusette* to catch those not easily caught' (p. 172). The notion of
game relates, of course, particularly to 'form', if such a distinction be
still allowed, since that 'cold artistic calculation' is in contrast with
the 'matter' to be 'reported'; just as it is a device of technique which
constitutes 'the real fun':

> The real 'fun' of the thing would have been exactly to sacrifice my
> comparative platitude of statement . . . without sacrificing a
> grain of what was to be conveyed. The real fun, in other words,
> would have been in not, by an exceptional collapse of other
> ingenuity, making my attack on the spectator's consciousness a
> call as immediate as a postman's knock. (p. 137)

And he adds, in anticipation of a sceptical question:

> To what degree the game was worth playing, I needn't attempt to
> say: the exercise I have noted strikes me now, I confess, as the
> interesting thing, the imaginative faculty acting with the *whole* of
> the case on its hands. (p. 171)

Other pleasures we quoted already, concerning the 'art of the
romancer', which is ' "for the fun of it", insidiously to cut the cable,
to cut it without our detecting him' (p. 34). Note again James's
position with 'us' as those who fail to detect the romancer's trick.
Concerning *The American*, which he finds somewhat lacking in
'soundness', he admits: 'Had I patched it up to a greater apparent
soundness my own trick, artistically speaking, would have been
played; I should have cut the cable without my reader's suspecting
it' (p. 35). This does indeed throw some light on what it is to play the
game; it involves 'tricks', 'covering one's tracks' (pp. 108, 166),
'catching the reader', 'hocus-pocus under cover' (p. 168) and even
drugging the reader surreptitiously: 'There are drugs enough,
clearly – it is all a question of applying them with tact, in which case
the way things don't happen may be artfully made to pass for the
way things do' (p. 34). Above all it is 'fun', and not, for instance,
simply a matter of conveying (or extracting, respectively) a moral

judgement on the society portrayed, for which so many critics of James's work are out. And as the fun lies mostly in the 'how' of the game – how it is played, how the story is made – the fun, for both players, would indeed be taken out of it if all were told and the 'case' given away.

This brings us back nearly to the beginning of our argument, which we will illustrate once more with the example of *The Figure in the Carpet*. There the 'secret' of Vereker's work is, as in the image of James's, objectified into the 'figure' the critics are looking for. The author cannot reveal 'it' himself; but, interestingly, neither can Corvick when he has apparently found it. He refuses to cable the results of his studies and announces instead an article of his own – a repartee, as it were, to the work of Vereker. The secret of the 'figure', it appears, is not quantifiable: it cannot be told, it must be shown, for it is 'the very flower of the performance'.

For just this reason the other literati of the tales cannot prevail upon the public with their articles. Although the narrator of *The Next Time* is, to his mind, absolutely 'plain' in his praise of Limbert's work, both the work and the review fall flat with the public. Only the fellow literati understand, appreciate, and indeed decipher the 'message' of the review; and so the 'literary circuit' continues its course without ever ending in the definitive, the final word. For as there are right and wrong truths, so there are many 'last words': 'The retort to that . . . was . . . the restrictive truth exactly contended for, which may embody my critic's last word rather of course than my own. My own, so far as I shall pretend . . . to report it, was . . .' (p. 168). He oscillates between James, the author who has been criticised, and the James of *The Art of the Novel*, who becomes a critic answering a fellow critic, both 'pretending' to report another final word in the infinite cycle of literary words.

16 A word on critics

A word might be in order concerning the status of my own critical argument and its position within the larger critical context. My reading of *The Sacred Fount*, rather than claiming to be 'final', is 'primary', that is, textual. It takes up the narrator's hypothesis about sacred founts and follows it through to the end, and with the consistency that makes it necessary to include the narrator in our analysis, as well as our own act upon the text. I call it 'primary' for not being exhaustive, but also for the fact that it enters the text on its own level.

Many readings by other critics take place on a level above the text, on a plane of parable or allegory which adduces an entirely new stratum of meaning, to be superimposed on the text.[1] Any reading identifying the narrator as an artist, or indeed as Henry James, is based on such an allegorical assumption.[2] Conversely, we find discussions of the novel which reject its terms from the beginning, claiming that sacred founts cannot exist, on grounds of commonsense and personal experience.[3] These arguments rather resemble Mrs Briss's response of declaring the narrator mad while refusing to contemplate the theory in its own terms.[4] But while Mrs Briss is at least justified to the extent of living in the same universe as the narrator and sharing a plane of reference, the critic is not, and his personal experience and his commonsense are misapplied to the 'reality' of a work of fiction. Then, there are interpretations which want to 'have it both ways' (reflecting Obert's conduct?), pandering both to commonsense and to the narrator's speculation in an untenable synthesis. These are represented by the new creation of a circular fount involving almost all characters in the novel, if not also Henry James. Refusing to accept the fount's constitutive definition as an exclusive and intimate relation between two partners only, critics compete with the narrator and evolve fountains of 'life', 'vitality' or 'conscience', which distribute their substances, more or less fairly, all round.[5] One need hardly point out that the image of the sacred fount has thus been transformed out of all recognition and has nothing more to do with its original conception. Other critics again lose themselves in the ambiguity of the 'reality' represented in the narrator's account, trying to find some fixed point of truth on which to peg their argument. This may be the statement of one or another character in the novel, though, needless again to say, on no sufficient grounds; or it may, besides common-sense, be the beliefs of 'Henry James'.[6] But these choices are all motivated by the recognition that the narrator's position is unverifiable, with no recognition, apparently, that all other positions are equally unverifiable.

It is a curious feature of frustration in the face of ambiguity, and especially ambiguity generated by an 'unreliable' first person narrative, that the critic who recognises the narrator's pretence, deceit or even lie, expects to be able automatically to get hold of the truth this lie covers up. But rather than revealing the hidden truth, the recognised pretence opens up the plural of possibility, just as the fake relationship of Lady John is one in which no one believes, yet permits no one to know the truth. In my analysis of *The Aspern Papers* I have indicated that an ambiguous text offers a number of interpretations, which one might call 'if-interpretations'. Each one holds fast, so to speak, one of the variables, supposing it to be constant, and then reads the text through under this perspective. Thus my own reading of *The Sacred Fount* supposes the sincerity of the narrator in his account. One may then start again with a different premise, say, 'If Mrs Briss were having an affair with Long . . .', and see how the clues would fit such a reading. What is unsatisfactory is the changing of premises in the middle of a reading, choosing them *ad hoc* each time. However, the most important premise is the recognition that whatever variable we hold, it is not the 'true' one, or the one intended by James, and its unverifiability remains. This means that faced with a structurally ambiguous text we must subscribe to a 'literary relativism' regarding the 'real events' of the story, whether or not we would wish to be committed to a phenomenological relativism as a personal life philosophy. Whether or not we believe in some stable and 'objective' reality in real life, we cannot infer such a reality and its 'facts' for a text which refuses to give them.[7] Hence no interpretation of an ambiguous text is ever going to be complete, or 'correct'; but every consistent interpretation which is faithful to the text is spelling out a part of the work's ambiguity.

However, one also has to recognise that ambiguity and the

possibility of 'lies' are concerned with the relation of the narrative to a fictional plane of reference – that reference being the fictional reality of 'what really happened'. I have argued that this plane is not necessarily the most important one in a work of fiction, and certainly not the only one worth considering. Apart from this 'story' which has no solution in Truth, we are looking for artistic resolution:[8] a coherence between 'form' and 'content', a dialectic of subject and treatment, which override the consideration for the truth of the matter. This is the 'scent' I have been following, leading to a 'larger mystery (and thereby a larger "law")' (p.30), from the 'law' of the sacred fount to the formal law of *The Sacred Fount*. Close adherence to the narrator's tale has led to its own reward, for in following it we have outlined, so to speak, the plot of the novel's form. Concerned not solely with 'what really happened', the very stuff of which plots are made, and concerned as much with the formal aspects of the narrator's telling and presenting, we have discovered another 'affair', a passion betrayed by its form. We have, in other words, followed a secondary hermeneutic, and read the novel on the level of its third articulation.

J. A. Ward has emphasised the importance of 'motion rather than static arrangement'.[9] We found that this is true also of James's notion of 'character', which he thinks of less as an ingredient or element of 'subject', than as a principle of growth, a plant or a 'germ'. Just as meaning of deep structure affects syntactical structure in the sentence, and syntax itself is expressive of meaning, so the 'subject' for James has formal implications and the treatment reflects its meaning. Hence a discussion of form should also take account of formal *principles* rather than simply patterns and structures, if it is to lead to the artistic synthesis of form and subject that is typical of James.

Many critics have discarded *The Sacred Fount* as an inferior work, and for various reasons.[10] Despite the disparity of judgement there are uniting features in their criticisms, in that these are based more often than not on matters of 'content' and a simplistic conception of its relation to form: the narrowness of vision and of novelistic scope, the lack of an emerging morality that would place the novel, its characters and its society unequivocally. Even J. A. Ward's article on form and 'structure' leaves *The Sacred Fount* out of its account. Despite Norma Phillips's prediction and prescription that 'no one will or should pretend that the qualities of *The Sacred Fount* are those of James's great novels',[11] I am defending *The Sacred Fount* on the grounds of its astounding fusion of form and content, of subject and treatment, quite apart, of course, from the 'fun'.[12] Norma Phillips's claim is, however, somewhat weakened, deliberately or unwittingly, by her reference to plural 'qualities'. One intuits that she means 'quality' and imputes a lack of it to *The Sacred Fount*, while of course no one would pretend that the qualities of one novel are the same as those of another. In length and breadth, for instance, *The Sacred Fount* certainly does not equal the 'great novels', though it is doubtful that it competes; nor of course in its exceptional form – for novels – as a first person narrative. But while these are 'qualities' or attributes, they do not have intrinsic values attached to them, and by saying that the qualities are different nothing is said about why these other novels are 'great'.

While the subject of the novel is the idea of the sacred fount, its formal principle is the attempted discovery of sacred founts by a single investigator who is also the narrator. This makes for the apparent resemblance to the structure of the detective novel which is often noted by critics, though they base the similarity in the reader's response.[13] But while Sherlock Holmes, Philip Marlowe or Maigret try to recover a lost plot whose outcome is known, and the plot of the detective story is the detective's investigation of this *fait accompli*, the narrator of *The Sacred Fount* explores a 'case' which is going on in front of his eyes, and the novel's 'plot' is his subsequent account in front of a reader-jury. The task of the private eye resembles that of the historian, whereas the narrator's, as said before, is more akin to that of the anthropologist and the psychoanalyst, and his quest, as opposed to the historian's retrospection, is projected along the axis of evolving time. As such, however, the form of his quest reflects directly its object, the sacred fount, the continuous acquisition by one lover of the precious substance his or her partner possesses.

We have brought this form into relief in our exposition of the narrator's exploration as a passionate 'sacred fount' on a higher level. We too, therefore, find ourselves in quest of sacred founts just like the narrator, shining his torch on him and his search. Like him, we are in pursuit of a 'large reading' (p. 130), so as to make 'the larger sense, every way' (p. 96), when we know the narrator 'to mean, at every point, immensely more than [he] said' (p. 188). And while our 'underhand process' may not be 'crowned . . . with . . . the beauty of having been right' (p. 96), we can at least attain the gratification of not being wrong. Our ultimate search, projected along the progressing narrative, has for its goal not the 'final meaning' of the novel, but the 'larger law' and the vindication of the critical disposition assumed towards the text. For my analysis began when

> I was just conscious, vaguely, of being on the track of a law, a law that would fit, that would strike me as governing the delicate phenomena – delicate though so marked – that my imagination found itself playing with.   (p. 30)

'A part of the amusement they yielded came, I daresay, from my exaggerating them – grouping them into a larger mystery (and thereby a larger "law") than [other critics might feel] the facts, as observed, . . . warranted.' But this may be the 'common fault of minds for which the vision of [art] is an obsession'.

'The obsession pays, if one will; but to pay it has to borrow.' And the price, for one player as for the other is the same in this literary game, and I close by echoing James's words when he had finished writing *The Sacred Fount*: this 'fine flight . . . *into* the high fantastic . . . has rather depleted me . . .'[14]

Epilogue

The theory, as well as the practice of the literary approach in this book have, I hope, implied sufficiently strongly that they do not lead to 'conclusions'. Just as Henry James's tale *is* the message, the 'final meaning' and the 'moral', so this essay *is* the thesis and its conclusion. It is the demonstration of the literary analyses of James's works that must bear out the implications and consequences of the theory outlined; just as the theory may be considered the conclusion of practised analysis.

At the outset I pointed to the proposition – made famous by Barthes, though not his invention – which I regard as essential for literary interpretation, namely that the reader is the producer of his text. We can now subjoin a complement and say that the writer is the reader of his text. We saw that not all textual features can be called 'intended' by the writer in a strong sense, determined as they are also by the constraints of the medium. But we can say that they are all *approved* by the writer, who acts simultaneously in his 'subjective' (productive) and 'objective' (critical) roles. Some of his control over the medium consists in the 'appreciation' of its effects – a critical act in James's sense: 'to appreciate, to appropriate, to take intellectual possession'. If passed by this critical editor, a textual effect is rightly called 'intended', meaningful and significant. Such criticism, however, is part of the total creative process, for it is as a creator that he 'saw everything that he had made, and, behold, it was very good' (*Genesis* 1: 31; Authorised Version). He saw, and you behold – the creator and the beholder united in the same appreciation.

Appendix

Critics and *The Sacred Fount*

Shlomith Rimmon has given an excellent account of the secondary literature on *The Sacred Fount*, exposing in particular the critics' inability to sustain the ambiguity of the text in their readings, and their arbitrary choices of false certainties.[1] Christine Brooke-Rose has given another brilliant example of how to clear up the jungle of Jamesian criticism in the case of *The Turn of the Screw*.[2] One could indeed construct a parallel study for *The Sacred Fount*, since its secondary literature shows an equally astonishing record of mutual contradiction and disagreement. However, Christine Brooke-Rose's 'Essay in Non-Methodology' has value beyond its application to *The Turn of the Screw* and needs no repetition, particularly since the basis of her approach also underlies my own argument. Also, the task of exposing the worst in criticism is somewhat unsavoury, quite apart from being prohibitive in size in the case of *The Sacred Fount*. Nor can I see much profit in recapitulating the critical argument from point zero, since early pronouncements are, for obvious historical reasons, founded on notions about the proper nature of the novel which appear unsophisticated today, besides being coloured by much outraged national chauvinism.[3] Such critical résumé is a well-established tradition of critical practice, but it has two worse effects, generic and related. First, it tends to channel the argument into the same groove in which all the previous critics' has ground itself, and to keep it there; and secondly, it tends to assign priority to the 'intercritical' discourse instead of textual analysis. Thus in the bulk of criticism on *The Sacred Fount*, the number of references to other critics easily outweighs quotation from *The Sacred Fount*, while points are scored for or against an established critical controversy rather than 'off [the critic's] own bat'. In other words, such intercritical practice is detrimental to the conception of new ideas and to revaluations of a well-canonised work. I have therefore chosen to discuss one representative and recent essay on *The Sacred Fount* in detail, and with a further consideration in mind. Since my main criticism of the general secondary literature is that it lacks method and discipline, documentation must needs be extensive. To expose the *ad hoc* nature of single judgements these must be quoted in comparison and context, for it serves only the perpetuation of *ad hoc* criticism to cite one appropriate statement from an essay which would otherwise fail to support the point.[4]

Before I turn to the main discussion I will briefly introduce some examples of non-methodological criticism.

SUPPOSITION–PRESUPPOSITION

There are many ways by which personal opinions, guesses, surmises, are turned into critical 'facts' which then serve as a basis for argument instead of being subject to inquiry. Oscar Cargill uses the device of suggestive rhetorical questioning:[5]

> In *The Spoils of Poynton*, in *What Maisie Knew*, and in *The Awkward Age* (to say nothing about shorter things) James tried out various points of view; why not suppose that he continued his trials with *The Sacred Fount* and regard it as his experiment with telling a story through a narrator who has an obsession? In the second place, why not suppose that obsession itself the product of the very corrupt society James has been so actively portraying?

Why not? Because supposing is not good enough as a critical method. But we then witness how Cargill slips from suggestion into the assumption of a 'fact'; the suggestion just cited becomes, a few pages later, a presupposition: 'If, then, the primary purpose of *The Sacred Fount* is the revelation of an obsession 'natural' in a corrupt society because stimulated by it . . .' (p. 288). The conditional if-clause has only rhetorical value, since the condition is accepted and a presupposition for the following argument. What should be questioned – whether the society *is* corrupt or merely imagined so by the narrator,[6] and whether he 'has an obsession'[7] or is only held to have one by the society – are now removed from inquiry on no other grounds than Cargill's 'why not suppose'.

Another favourite device for introducing opinion is the critic's

taking shelter behind 'Henry James'. Wilson Follett[8] asserts that
The Sacred Fount is

> expressly a parable of the relation between reality and art, as Mr
> James saw that relation. In this story he was trying to illustrate
> the ineptitude and pointlessness of life, as contrasted with the
> rounded symmetry of art . . .

Did Mr James illustrate it, or was he only trying to, perhaps even
failing? And how do we know how he saw this relation?

MISREADING AND MISREPRESENTATION

Blackmur's 'circular fount' is perhaps the most striking example of
textual misreading, since Blackmur does not follow the narrator's
account and instead competes by creating his own version. In the
text the phenomenon of the sacred found occurs in an exclusive and
intimate relation between two partners only, while the circular
fount flows between the narrator – often 'James' – and all other
characters, its substance being conscience or, for other critics, the
fountain of life and the source of vitality, of which all partake except
the narrator.[9]

MISREADING AND DISAMBIGUATION

The examples of arbitrary disambiguation are too numerous to cite,
and one instance must suffice. Thus James Reaney:[10]

> Long's strange new brilliance is established in such a way that it
> cannot possibly be a delusion on the narrator's part. . . . I
> purposely stress that we have a fact here since this is the sort of
> thing brainwashers attempt to flush out of the mind, and Mrs
> Brissenden at the end turns out to be such an expert brainwasher
> that even the sanest reader must nail down certified facts long and
> well beforehand.

Certified is precisely what these facts are not, and if we nailed this
one down there would be many more, possibly contradictory ones,
to be equally nailed. But a great number of critics feel the need to

determine at least one such fact to provide them with a sense of orientation for their interpretation.[11]

This is a more selfconscious mode of determining fact by an allegorical assumption. Parker Tyler speaks of 'the Narrator (who sometimes shall be called, here, HJ)';[12] and Cynthia Ozick, similarly: 'The protagonist, whom we shall call J. (for at first he half seems to be James in much the same way we feel K. to be Kafka)'.[13]

THE AUTOBIOGRAPHIC FALLACY

Whether explicit or implicit, selfconscious or unselfconscious, it is by fiat that the analogy between James and the narrator is invoked or that the latter is made into a novelist. Thanks to the intercritical practice, this autobiographic fallacy has become almost 'unavoidable',[14] and hence deserves its own category.

The individual writers might feel that a distinction ought to be made between the narrator's identification with James and his equation with the artist in general, between the analogy with the 'good' novelist and that with its mad parody. But they are all equally unfounded and allegorical. It appears that despite its intrinsic naiveté, the temptation to take the narrative 'I' as James's personal pronoun is irresistible to most critics, which is only not surprising in the light of the general habit of finding James's mouthpiece in any of his works, even those with no (marked) first person narrator.

It would be pointless to include all critics involved in this particular issue, since many acknowledge their source in Follett's hypothesis, Leon Edel, Edmund Wilson, or a similar precedent. It is more important to note that while in its original form the analogy is made openly, many of the recent critics lapse unobtrusively – perhaps inadvertently – though no less gravely into the autobiographic fallacy. Thus Walter Isle, after following the text closely and without identifying the narrator with James, suddenly claims that 'through the [narrator's] vision James gives us a profound comment on the effect of the fashionable love-game all these couples are engaged in'.[15] The fact that these couples are so engaged is of course precisely one we cannot verify, much less expect James to comment on. Sidney Finkelstein hesitates before the temptation: 'the narrator's morality . . . is James's morality . . . . If the narrator is not James, the two have much in common'.[16]

REFUSAL TO CONSIDER THE NOVEL AS ART
AND TAKING IT AS REALITY INSTEAD

Blackall treats the narrator as if he were her next-door neighbour, and hence uses 'common sense and a sense of the ridiculous'[17] in her assessment of his tale. Nor can she thus accept an elaborate theory like the narrator's 'crystal palace' as an explanation of phenomena that 'may all proceed from the most obvious and pedestrian causes' (p. 62). It seems one of the gravest failings of 'Realist' criticism that it has no place for a 'literary disposition', a suspension of disbelief as well as of belief for the encounter with works of art. It is a hangover from the golden days of nineteenth-century popular fiction, when 'the act of reading [was] . . . – quite literally – the act of life itself'.[18]

A similar lack of expectation of an artistic resolution characterises Tony Tanner's treatment of *The Sacred Fount*, which he sees as subjecting the 'morbid imagination' to its 'most damaging criticisms'.[19] But though he cites a 'key-statement' about the narrator who is on 'the track of a law', and having seen an analogy between him and the artist, he maintains that art 'can only console by recording . . . and lamenting' (p. 51), and that our text stalls before a draw between 'pros' and 'cons', between gains and losses, of the artistic imagination. But given that we as readers face a similar confusion of clues 'for and against', it would be for us to seek the 'larger law' of the text's resolution.[20] I do not mean, of course, such analytic solutions and 'final meanings' as have been extracted from, or read into, the novel, be it James's moral disapproval of promiscuous society or 'salvation through art'.[21] It would not tell us the truth about love affairs and whether or not vampires exist: what an artistic solution of a conflict can meaningfully be is a formal one. And the way to find it would be to be 'conscious, vaguely, of being on the track of a law, a law that would fit, that would strike [one] as governing the delicate phenomena – delicate though so marked', that the critic's imagination finds itself playing with. But the consciousness of artistic order seems for the most part but vague, and 'law' hardly the method of the imagination's play.[22]

What these examples suggest, and what makes me present them as various misreadings, is that the most general critical weakness is a lack of respect for language. But this bad habit is carried even beyond the Jamesian text to the texts of fellow critics, and ultimately to the critic's own writing. Hence the need to posit a category of writing, although it too results from a failure to read correctly what one has just written:

MISHANDLING OF THE SIGNIFIER, OR INATTENTION TOWARDS SIGNIFICATION

Weinstein writes with respect to the 'awkwardness of the metaphor' of the sacred fount:[23] 'Considered literally or physiologically, the relations posited . . . strain credibility when they are not actually embarrassing'. No metaphor will stand up taken physiologically, though it is no reason for embarrassment.

It is also a consequence of *ad hoc* practice and misreading that astute perceptions may be recorded and yet not be followed up. Thus I would have had no difficulty in citing supporting statements from other critics regarding the interpretative as opposed to the artistic nature of the narrator's enterprise;[24] yet I have found no other exploration of the theme I have pursued. This may further be due to the fact that critics are ready to read the novel as a parable or allegory of almost anything except themselves, and to perceive analogies between the narrator and James, the writer in general, or 'any man', except, again, the critic.[25] For Weinstein does seem to conceive of such an analogy and states it clearly: 'The narrator's speculations are likened to the responses one makes to a work of fiction' (p. 104). Needless to say, these 'responses' are not further specified, and in the context of my present critique one would like to exclude some of those Weinstein himself makes to *The Sacred Fount*, which include the apparently 'unavoidable' autobiographic fallacy and the misreading which leads to Blackmur's circular fount, as well as the faults of the present category. However, Weinstein then goes on to emphasise the narrator's likeness to the novelist, sliding back into the groove of the Follett-hypothesis he had already severally invoked. Yet he tries to clinch the new idea once more: 'Furthermore, the "text" he is studying, like *The Sacred Fount* itself, is endlessly suggestive' (p. 104). But the sense that the novel is Henry James's is so strong as to obliterate the fact that it is the critic's when he is 'studying' its text. And together with the overpowering presence of the 'haunting biographical relevance' (p. 97) and the 'unavoidable analogy' (p. 98), it sets up a barrier too strong for any new idea to establish itself, even if this is already immanent in the writer's own thinking.

But I shall now return to the detailed discussion of Bernard Richards's monograph, in which perceptiveness is unhappily paired with the absence of critical rigour we have been deploring. I must emphasise that Richards's essay has been singled out because it is an illustration of a well established critical tradition, rather than for any particular dismerit.

'*The Ambassadors* and *The Sacred Fount*: The Artist *Manqué*', announces both a conventional theme and a by now traditional comparison. I have alluded (in note 24 of this chapter) to Richards's potential awareness of the 'epistemological theme' that might include the reader, but which is marred by the strong hold of the traditional views. Stylistically Richards makes no firm distinction between the narrator and the author, between data in the story to be interpreted by characters, and data of the text to be puzzled out by the reader; which leads him to slip from one to the other without, it seems, noticing. In the second paragraph he states that *The Sacred Fount*, as opposed to *The Ambassadors*, is 'autobiographical'.[26]

It might be only unfortunate, though permissible in the context of fictional method, to call the first person narrative 'autobiographical'. Yet it becomes clear that Richards continues the illustrious tradition of Follett and followers:

> [James] may have had slight, or even acute guilt feelings about his fictional method . . . . It could be that the maturing James felt that his works were less and less related to the way people actually live, and decided to put his misgivings on record in this whimsical and self-abusing fable. (p. 221)

It 'may' well be, but then, it might not; and 'it could be' as Richards says, and again, it could be quite otherwise. Of course, from this rhetorical hesitation he then goes on to assume that it *is* as he says: supposition goes into presupposition. Here we have the writer's personal opinion and nothing more; as a few sentences later when he 'suspects' that if James had written a preface to *The Sacred Fount*, it would have drawn attention away from the psychic vampirism and towards the narrator's consciousness (p. 219). I suppose I am free to suspect, in my turn, that if James had not already written a preface to, say, *Roderick Hudson*, he would have excluded that novel from the New York edition, or, that if he had written one to *The Sacred Fount* it would not have been in English. But Richards has 'proof' for his suspicion: 'The entries in the *Notebooks* do not concentrate on the theme of subjectivity, and this is a case where the preliminary notes should not be used as the main pointer to the achieved work' (p. 219). Because the entries in the *Notebooks* do not concentrate on subjectivity, and because the *Notebooks* are not indicative, in 'this . . . case', of the work's meaning, subjectivity is what the novel is all about. Nor do the notes concentrate on Red Indians, which may be an inverse pointer to the novel's hidden depth. But now Richards moves to 'the traditional theme of "appearance and reality"' (p. 220), traditional indeed with the critics.[27] He points out that

> Strether and the unnamed narrator of *The Sacred Fount* . . . both have a characteristic in common: that of making wilful assumptions about life, and trusting too much in the truth of these assumptions before they have really had time to test them. Strether is perhaps less blameworthy than the Narrator, because he develops his own theories, whereas the Narrator accepts his basic hypothesis from someone else . . . (p. 220)

It might be argued that a little intersubjective comparing of notes is more promising of approximation to 'reality' than are one's own solitary theories; but it seems that the wilful assumption of someone else's ideas involves more, and more perverse, will than sheer solipsism. Be this as it may, we now have the characteristic slide into the 'James analogy': 'This same quality of fanciful inventiveness is invariably shared by James himself' (p. 220). We started out with 'the way people actually live', 'one's self, one's society and one's relation to it' (p. 220), then moved to characters, and are now talking of James the author, and in particular with reference to his prefaces. This ought, of course, to be quite another matter, since James is discussing his attitude to life – 'clumsy Life . . . at her stupid work' – in relation to the making of fiction. But Richards is talking about Life:

> No one who has lived has ever had the chance to check up on the

validity of the multifarious assumptions, both major and minor,
on which he bases his life; but many people at least make the
attempt, and do not hold up a finger at the dinner-table of life to
say 'I have enough facts now, thank you'. (p. 221)

Do they not, indeed? What, then, is the common basis of prejudice
and 'irrational belief', or belief altogether? And have we not seen
some people even who 'have enough facts' to be sure of James's
intention, or to convince themselves of his guilt about his fictional
method? But more serious, to use the metaphor of 'the dinner-table
of life' as a figurative extension from real incidents of 'germs' picked
up at literal dinner-tables is disingenuous: the 'germs' with their
limited factuality are not what James bases his life upon, but what
he bases his fiction upon. Besides, Richards blamed both Strether
and the Narrator for not testing their assumptions before they
believe in them, while he now offers them a feeble excuse. Both the
reproach and the reclaimer testify to a naive scientism, to a
cognitive model of hypothesis forming and verification. The latter,
for Richards, is lacking in most people's experience, not so much
because it is actually impossible, as because there is not enough time
or chance. In James's work there are plenty of characters engaged in
extensive 'verification' of their ideas, not least the narrator of *The
Sacred Fount*, who is an avid collector of 'proof'. But it is verification
with different standards, based much upon the same method as the
original conception of the hypothesis; it is interpretation in the light
of a conceived suspicion, but the reading of signs and the drawing of
inferences are still the main characteristics. Indeed, if verification
were so simply possible, hypothesis need not precede it and the truth
could be read straight away.

Richards warns that if one holds up one's finger at the dinner-
table of life one runs the risk of withdrawing into a 'private world',
but that James maintained that 'the relations between life and
art . . . should mutually sustain each other' (p. 221). He then
suggests that James, 'if he took this seriously', would have had guilt
feelings about his fictional method. As pointed out already, if a
contradiction exists it is in Richards's own assumptions, while
'mutually sustain' does not mean 'be identical'. James did indeed
take this seriously, to the extent of realising that fiction-making is a
large component of life. But as so many other critics, Richards wants
James to treat art as if it were 'life'. What he is consequently also

implying is that the art of James is all 'lies', since James did not hear out Nature till the end of her plots, and which should thus explain his guilt and his 'self-abuse.'

Once again Richards hints at an analogy between the narrator and the reader, but with reservations:

> The 'parable' of *The Sacred Fount* is admonitory in that it refers not only to the author, but also to the readers. James was well informed of the habits of his readers . . . he always bore in mind the potential for dimness and insensitivity . . . (p. 221)

These are above all, Richards holds, those 'overconfident' and 'imperceptive' readers who divine the 'secret' of *The Sacred Fount*, while

> The perceptive readers will see that there is no 'secret' to learn, because the deluded witness is the sole purveyor of information, and his evidence is not enough to go on in framing an absolute picture of the state of affairs at Newmarch . . . (pp. 221–2). [Those who speculate about the relations at Newmarch] will be trapped into the same situation as the hero – of building castles in air. (p. 222)

Note again that the analogy between the 'deluded' narrator is on the one hand to James, and on the other to the dim and imperceptive reader, while only the sensitive reader escapes such admonitory caricature. Moreover, the perceptive reader is he who abstains from interpretation altogether. But from the basis of recognising that there cannot be formed an 'absolute picture', it is the aim of finding such a picture that should be given up rather than interpretation. It may be 'building castles in air', but at least enters the terms of the novel; while the construction of fictions, of 'elaborate theories' (p. 222), readerly or writerly, leads to 'castles in air' by definition.[28] Thus I would suggest that it is the reader's duty to construct all possible interpretations that fit the evidence of the text, and so describe a part of its plurality. Moreover, the causal 'because' of the quotation is misleading: it implies that if only we had, say, two unreliable points of view, the two would cancel each other out – two subjectivities making one objectivity. *The Golden Bowl* offers precisely more than one unreliable view point and a number of different sources of 'information' and 'evidence', yet we have by no means an 'absolute picture of the state of affairs'. It looks as if Richards would like to close again any novel beginning with 'I'; yet he not only reads on, but later in the essay indulges in the very same insensitive constructing of hypotheses about the love affairs at Newmarch (p. 229). What we might say, then, in answer to the charge of this particular imperceptiveness is, in allusion to Richards's own words, that 'many people at least make the attempt' to read the relational puzzle as far as it will be read; but also that we might read the narrator's *discourse* which allows us to understand something about his consciousness, to which Richards earlier wanted attention drawn.[29] Since neither the 'events' at Newmarch nor the narrator's consciousness are as 'absolutely' pictured as most readers would wish, it would be natural to turn from these to the 'picturing', that is, the text. A picture of the 'events', unfinished and prefixed by many 'ifs', serves as a means in the interpretation, but it is not its end.

Despite Richards's hypothetical preface and his promise to investigate 'method', the 'absolute picture' of 'what is going on' (p. 223) has the strongest hold on his attention. In discussing point of view he is most interested in what this reveals, or conceals, of the absolute picture, rather than in the constitution of the said point of view. With respect to the elusive voice in *The Ambassadors* he states that this chronicler sometimes offers, but sometimes withholds, his commentaries and judgements:

> The reader is at a particular disadvantage, as he is denied means of checking up on almost everything that happens in the novel. In real life, and in the theatre, we have some basis for judgement of others by observing facial expression and listening to their tone of voice. (p. 223)

We are back to verification: the reader cannot check up on things, on what happens in, or rather outside, the novel.[30] If this is what the reader really wants to know, I should suggest that he go to the theatre, or study the intrigues of real people instead of fictional characters; yet I should also warn him that even facial expression – in our sophisticated theatres – might occasionally deceive or withhold information, which could make checking up on the real meaning difficult. I must add in fairness, yet also in surprise, that Richards seems to be aware of this too, for he goes on: 'But by virtue of the nature of this novel, and novels in general, we are deprived of this useful adjunct, and are in a sense blindfold spectators of the three-legged race' (p. 223). He essentially knows that it is in the nature of novels (fiction, writing) that checking up on dramatic events is not possible. Yet in this last and generalised admission he is also unmaking his original point about 'this novel': if it is in the nature of novels that we are blindfold, why discuss at such length and with regret the inadequacies of this particular narrator and his point of view? At the basis of this tangle is the nostalgia for an omniscient and 'unselfconscious' Author, who has the power to present dramatically besides telling the truth and commenting; if it is not indeed a desire to be present at the live spectacle of the events the story 'portrays'. Richards began by saying that *The Sacred Fount* is 'an autobiography' while *The Ambassadors* 'has an omniscient narrator who presents events from the point of view of the hero' (p. 222). But he is obviously not omniscient enough, or if he is, he is not 'omnidicent', which is wilful and unpopular. What is gained, on the other hand, for Richards by this whimsical recorder of Strether's consciousness is that 'the reader can distance himself from Strether more than he could if he were seeing events entirely through Strether's eyes, and gain a more composite and scenic picture of what is going on' (p. 223). We have just been told that the narrator's (and hence our) point of view is over Strether's shoulder (p. 222), so that the most we could gain of such a distancing would be a view of Strether's back. On the other hand, and speaking for myself, I find I can distance myself perfectly well from the narrator of *The Sacred Fount*, distance myself in fact enough to gain a more composite (though not absolute) picture of this blindfolder. To come to the main point: one must not confuse eyes with mouth – or the eyes of the detective with the ears of the judge. We are neither seeing through a first person narrator's eyes, blindfold as we are constitutionally as novel readers and far from Newmarch or Venice; but we are reading, if we like, through the narrator's discourse.[31] What we most certainly do not do in James's fiction, nor even in the theatre or in real life, is take up residence inside a skull and look out of the eye sockets. 'What is going on' is going on always only on the level of narration, and not somewhere behind it. Though there is of course a sense in which we do talk of the events in the story, for us, the readers, they must remain a castle in air, a verbal construction of signifieds and fictions; and we do not see them, but analyse their construction. The 'facts' that concern us never exceed the facts of the text.

Yet 'facts' are what are highest in demand – facts of reference and even beyond it, see, for instance, Chad's 'transatlantic state' (p. 223), which is of the order of Lady Macbeth's children. Richards is looking for facts, and imputes them as Strether's goal, who is said to be on a 'fact-finding mission' (p. 228). Or: 'In both novels the game of pretending to be in possession of knowledge, while at the same time fishing for facts, is played' (p. 227). Knowledge, it appears, is identical with the possession of facts. We have shown that 'facts' enjoy a very dubious status in James's work, while knowledge goes far beyond them. Strether avoids some 'facts' while striving for understanding,[32] while the narrator of *The Sacred Fount*, possessed already with knowledge, seeks only to 'verify' it. Richards's 'facts' betray a binary conception of such things as reality and knowledge, which leads to the misconception already discussed, namely that 'pretence' is the reverse of the Truth. It is implied that both the narrator and Strether have a picture not absolute, but with distinct holes which ought to be stopped with facts. But rather, they have *a* picture, which is in permanent formation and absorbing always new 'facts'. The interest in Strether's making of pictures is precisely this flexibility: he does not simply reject the facts of Woollett and substitute the facts of Paris; instead, he is refining and expanding his art of conceiving them. It is not as though a 'point of view' cut out a particular and partial view of the 'absolute picture' (except in the technical sense of dramatic point of view); but the personal vision gives a 'total' picture which may differ from any other. We are invited to contemplate it, while it depends on our awareness of its relativity whether the 'blanks', either of blindness or deceit, can be located. But picture it remains, that is, perception or report, and it is never even partially the reality, or life, or 'what is going on'.[33]

Richards then points out that the Narrator's view of relationships can also be discovered in Strether's way of thinking: 'They both have a view of human relationships that would make anyone quiver in his boots . . . . As they see it, the partners in an intimate and amorous relationship sustain losses or reap gains of a physical and psychomatic kind' (p. 228). Another metaphor taken physically – does it cause Richards 'psychomatically' to quiver in his boots? He takes refuge, in any case, in the less unnerving domain of castles in air, indulging the hypothesis of Mrs Briss's affair with Long; and he concludes: 'If *The Sacred Fount* is to be read as a comedy of manners, and I believe it is, then an interpretation of this kind, though not necessarily *this* interpretation exactly, is what is needed' (p. 229).

Needed for what exactly? For the satisfaction of Richards's belief, on which the if-clause is founded. If it were an interpretation of 'this kind, though not necessarily *this* interpretation exactly', then the narrator's own would certainly do beautifully, since it is of the very kind. Besides, it has the merit of far more detailed and consistent hypothesising, of fitting more 'evidence' into its scheme, and of having a more complex theory of translation between manifest appearance and latent meaning.[34] It may not be the conclusion Richards would like drawn; but reading the narrator's interpretation certainly makes for a comedy of manners.

Of Strether, Richards says: '[He] has a similar faith in external signs, and if it were well-founded it *would* enable him to learn secrets in life without revealing his ignorance, or being involved in vulgar snooping' (p. 229). What we have seen in both novels is that neither Strether nor the narrator in *The Sacred Fount* have any direct faith in external signs at all, but on the contrary suspect them of carefully hidden or suppressed meaning. What signs, if not external ones, are to be considered instead I am not sure. Nor does Richards hint at how a 'faith in external signs' could be well-founded, and how it would lead to 'secrets in life'. The 'vulgar snooping' has enjoyed considerable attention from critics already,[35] although the narrator himself points out that it is going on in his own mind, not without wondering if this in fact absolves him from the epithet. But he is certainly never at the 'key-hole', and specialises in that scanning of facial expression, tone of voice, and behaviour generally which Richards enjoys doing in the theatre and in life and regrets not being able to do for the narrator in the novel. Strether is 'reading surface data' (p. 235), external signs like the narrator, which are thus public and at any rate the sole text to be read; yet they are cited deprecatingly by Richards. This brings us to the final point: Richards, (in company of some other critics) thinks such 'reading', as well as fantasy, altogether reprehensible.[36] He reproves Strether for perceiving the French countryside like a picture by Laminet instead of confronting its hard reality. Although he holds that the 'real' breaks into 'this crystalline world of artistic perfection' (p. 234), he finds that it 'does not cure Strether of imagining himself and the rest of society in a "scene" or a "picture"' (p. 234). Imagination, particularly if cultured, is apparently a disease in need of curing, while a mature and realistic man of the world should not, it is implied, allow himself to indulge it. Again this suggests a binary conception: there is reality on the one hand and morbid fancy on the other, while the straight and narrow is quite clearly on the one side of the boundary. In his fiction James demonstrates a living dialectic: the perception of the real being achieved by the aid of the imagination, and the imagination nourished by the perception of reality. But Richards asserts that we learn from James's letters that he does not 'endorse this habit of mind' (p. 235). Only he does not quote the letters he has in mind, which leaves room, in one's own mind, for remembering James's travel sketches which are rather an eloquent monument to such a habit of mind, though this may be beside the point. Instead, Richards gives us once more his own legislation, quoting first this passage from *The Ambassadors*:

> [Strether] had positively motions and flutters of this conscious hour-to-hour kind, temporary surrenders to irony, to fancy, frequent instinctive snatches at the growing rose of observation, constantly stronger for him, as he felt, in scent and colour, and in which he could bury his nose even to wantonness. (Book 10, chapter 1)

Then Richards 'proves' James's disapproval of 'this habit of mind':

> In the Jamesian family of images, burying one's nose in the rose is an emblem of indulgence in decadent experience. An example from *English Hours* . . . will suffice:
> 'Pending these righteous changes, one would like while one is about it . . . to attach one's self to the abuse, to bury one's nostrils in the rose before it is plucked.' (p. 238)

It does not, of course, suffice. To say that a particular image means, or is the emblem of, *X* is to mistake literary imagery for mathematical symbolism, where each sign is given its one and only fixed meaning.[37] We can no more have a dictionary of Jamesian images than we can have an encyclopedia of dream symbols, to name a similar and familiar dispute. But Richards goes on to accuse the narrator of *The Sacred Fount* of the same flowery imagery, concluding magisterially: 'The flowers of fancy cultivated by Strether and the Narrator are not to be cherished, but discarded as rank weeds' (p. 238). Who does the weeding, and by what criteria? We remember the extensive flower imagery James uses also in his prefaces, not to mention his view on the 'subject', the seedling, which no critic can denounce, however humble – or genteel – it may strike him, and that the sole permissible criticism is of the use which has been made of it. But it is not with the use, or the lack of it, that Richards finds fault: it is the very flower of fancy. James nowhere (to my knowledge) talks of weeds; for him the entire flora is one great potential for the gardener of genius, the unassuming 'smaller fry' presenting moreover the greater challenge. It is only for the binary mind that the flora falls into neat categories of good flowers and bad weeds, and it makes one wonder why the world, and the garden of literary fancy, have not long been weeded clean.

It is presumably for similar reasons that some critics find the novel itself immoral, or at least unsatisfactory for refusing to give the true and the false clearly. The moral verdict of the moralistic critic must perforce come down heavily against ambiguity. And indeed, whether with greater or lesser moralistic overtones, ambiguity is still a quality largely regretted by critics.[38] Charles T. Samuels regrets, with respect to the paragon of ambiguity, *The Turn of the Screw*: 'Unfortunately, the tale offers evidence for both readings'.[39] Jean Frantz Blackall is defending James against a charge of 'sheer perversity':[40]

> In this instance, however, if James is willfully ambiguous, I suggest that he is so not out of perversity, but because the kind of story he wished to tell required the kind of central figure he has adopted.

The ambiguity is not perverse, it simply is the hazard of a form which James has chosen, but wilful it remains. Moreover, it haunts not only his fiction, but even his letters (might it be because these are first person too?). From James's 'explanatory letter to Mrs Humphry Ward' it is regretfully clear to Blackall 'that he was perfectly able to explain the relationships and motives of characters, though he did so, unfortunately, in an allusive and elliptical way' (p. 10). And some doubt, some unease, is expressed in James K. Folsom's hesitation: 'fortunately or unfortunately, we are given the account of the happenings at Newmarch only through the eyes of the too fallible narrator'.[41] Though the combination with 'only' and 'too fallible' seems pretty much to have made up his mind for him. Arnold P. Hinchcliffe speaks of 'the indecision on James's part',[42] thus translating the neutral ambiguity of the text into a morally more loaded description of James's mind. Robert Andreach, who analyses the narrator's 'way of thinking', finds that this consists for one in 'thinking in . . . opposites'.[43] With the evidence that most critics are seduced to a way of thinking in opposites, Christine Brooke-Rose's point is once more illustrated: she argues, and shows, that in the case of *The Turn of the Screw* and its critics 'the state of the governess is contagious'.[44] The state – the language, the way of thinking – of the narrator of *The Sacred Fount* seems no less infectious.

Just so there must, for Richards, be 'necessary boundaries between life and aesthetics' (p. 240). When talking about art earlier, Richards wanted it as much as possible like life; yet life must clearly be separated from the infection of 'aesthetics'. It has already emerged that the 'aesthetic' comprises the realm of the mind altogether, not just pictures and books, since both the narrator and Strether (not to mention Henry James at the dinner-table of life, and the critics) are accused of retreating into 'private worlds' (p. 221), 'countries of the mind' (p. 225), of 'escaping from the present' (p. 232) and 'building castles in air'. Thus Richards's *ad hoc* attempt at a separation is neither wholly sincere nor effective when he implies that such fancy may be permissible if a concrete work of art results from it. I have commented already on the possibility – or rather impossibility – of perceiving 'life' and 'reality' without the use of one's private country, the mind; and that reading, of surface data or 'other', is eminently characterised by the parallel construction of mental images. But as the comments on 'vulgar snooping' show, it is rather speculation itself – a mental practice based on data of observation – that strikes the critics as dirty or immoral. For Hinchliffe it is a 'neurotic' tendency: 'From the very first page it is patently obvious that our narrator is . . . given to premonitions and the enjoyment of speculation'.[45] More ominous it appears to Ralph Ranald:[46]

the narrator's meddling, whatever either he or Obert say of it, is as culpable as the attempt of Roger Chillingworth in *The Scarlet Letter* to ensnare the soul and body of Arthur Dimmesdale . . . in the religion of art, as conceived by James, it is the celebration of the Black Mass.

Robert Andreach straightforwardly warns: 'excessive mental activity is harmful if it distorts reality'.[47]

Compare the Reverend John Todd (1835), an earnest edu-

cationalist with advice for young boys, who thinks it is harmful
because leading to even worse solitary, or private, activity:[48]

> I have spoken of the practice of building castles in the air, – a
> practice which will be very apt to steal in upon you till it becomes
> a regular habit, unless you are very careful. You can hardly be too
> solicitous to keep clear of this habit. I have spoken of worse results
> of permitting the thoughts to wander when alone, – evils which
> want a name, to convey any conception of their enormity.

In his penultimate paragraph Richards touches on the question
of morality, and is full of good intensions: one should be wary of
'elaborate moral interpretations of the work, for in such readings
most of the morality is imported by the critic, and is not inherent in
the work' (p. 243). I would agree, and am 'suspicious' of such
statements as 'Strether is probably not as ignoble as the [narrator of
The Sacred Fount]' (p. 241). Or Richards's earlier moral comparison
concerning the assumption of ideas, quoted above. Moralistic they
certainly are, though perhaps not elaborate. But more interestingly,
Richards continues:

> All that is inherent at a moral level is the perilous nature of trying
> to live true to one's impressions. I should hesitate to describe
> Strether's actions as good or bad: the most that can be said is that
> they are necessary and inevitable, considering what he is.   (p.
> 243)

To talk of weeds is of course also to make a moral statement, though
the word is given by the language (yet not by James's) and one may
think that the weeds are given by God. Some further moralism is
imported, though Richards declares it as the goods of Henry James:
'Organized marriage is one of the "crimes" of Europe, in James's
eyes . . .' (pp. 240–1).

But most importantly, where is the moral level of the work? And
what sort of morality is 'the perilous nature of trying to live true to
one's impressions'? If Richards's message is that such a life contains
its dangers, it is a realistic if not a cynical statement, but not a moral
judgement. And if the same critic goes on to say that Strether's
actions are 'necessary and inevitable, considering what he is', he has
removed the last potential element of moral decision involved in
'trying to live true to one's impressions' and has replaced it by a

determinism and a necessity that absolute. Just like 'one has to be content with what is on the page' (p. 242), these last critical recommendations are lip-service to some other creed than the one practised in the pages that precede them.

To round off this discussion on the moral note struck by Richards, it may be interesting to observe that the critics' adduced morality – or the moral sense outraged by *The Sacred Fount* – tends to be of a somewhat naive or idealistic-adolescent, if not a religious stamp.[49] For example, Gorley Putt, after calling the narrator Peeping Tom, Nosey Parker and Paul Pry in the space of three pages, adds a parenthesis: 'It is significant that in the briefest commentary on this novel, antagonistic nursery types like Peeping Tom, Nosey Parker, Paul Pry, come so readily, unbidden, to mind'.[50] It is significant, yes, but perhaps with respect to the mind to which they come so readily, unbidden. William Dean Howells, too, has located the moral scruples of his imaginary 'interlocutress' with unfailing accuracy when he makes her reply to his question, if she finds herself so much the worse for these novels: 'Why, of course not. But it isn't so much what he says – he never *says* anything – but what he insinuates. I don't believe that is good for young girls.'[51]

Notes

1 THE RELEVANCE OF FOLKLORISTICS TO THE ANALYSIS OF
MODERN NARRATIVE

1. Vladimir Propp, *Morphology of the Folktale*, ed. S. Pirkova-Jakobson, trs. L. Scott; *International Journal of American Linguistics*, Pt. 3, 24 iv, Indiana University Research Center in Anthropology, Folklore and Linguistics Publications, 10 (Indiana, 1958). ˙
2. I am thinking for example of Greimas, Genette, Bremond.
3. P. Bogatyrev and Roman Jakobson, 'Die Folklore als eine besondere Form des Schaffens', *Donum natalicum Schrijnen* (Nijmegen and Utrecht, 1929). For a French text, see Roman Jakobson, *Questions de poétique* (Paris, 1973).
4. Bogatyrev and Jakobson, 'Die Folklore', p. 906; French translation, *Questions*, p. 65. The English translation is my own.
5. Claude Bremond, 'La logique des possibles narratifs', *Communications*, 8 (1966).
6. This is of course paradoxical only on account of this epigrammatic formulation, which leaves out precisely those sociological factors which have been discussed, and which affect changes which are not intrinsic to the medium *per se*.
7. Clemens Lugowski, *Die Form der Individualität im Roman*, with an introduction by Heinz Schlaffer (Frankfurt am Main, 1976, first published 1932). Page references hereafter will be given in the text, in round brackets. The translations are my own.
8. Alex Olrik, 'Epische Gesetze der Volksdichtung', *Zeitschrift für Deutsches Altertum*, 51 (1909).

2 EPIC LAWS AND *THE ASPERN PAPERS:* A FIRST ANALYSIS

1. A. Olrik, in *Deutsches Altertum*, 51. The names of the laws are my own translations, and I shall quote the original ones in the notes, retaining the spelling used by the *Zeitschrift* without capitalisation: 'die dreizahl ist auch ein Gesetz für sich', p. 4.
2. Olrik discusses this law in broader terms, as the highest number of individualised things, people or events. Any other, higher numbers that may occasionally occur only express an abstract quantity or mass. Indian folklore is the only exception, where a 'law of four' takes the place of the law of three, owing to the Indian mythology.
3. Henry James, *The Aspern Papers*, New York edition, XII (London, 1909), p. 38.
4. Olrik, in *Deutsches Altertum*, 51, p. 6: 'das *gesetz der zwillinge*'.
5. Ibid.: 'das grosse *gesetz des gegensatzes*'.

6. Ibid., p. 10. Cf. Propp in *Morphology of the Folktale*, 'The Functions of Actants', IX, 1.
7. Olrik, in *Deutsches Altertum*, 51, p. 5, 'das gesetz der *scenischen zweiheit*'.
8. Olrik cites scenes where a third party is present, but has to remain a silent onlooker until one of the others has left (p. 5).
9. Ibid. p. 9: 'Immer gipfelt die sage in einer oder mehreren *hauptsituationen plastischer art*'.
10. Ora Segal mentions an impression of 'the dramatic intensity of the encounter', yet without any account of how such an effect is produced textually – *The Lucid Reflector: The Observer in Henry James' Fiction* (New Haven and London, 1969), p. 92.
11. John Lyons, *Introduction to Theoretical Linguistics* (Cambridge, 1969), pp. 315, 325.
12. Sigmund Freud, *Die Traumdeutung* (Frankfurt am Main, 1972), first publ. 1900. 'Erinnerungsbilder', for example pp. 55, 230, 570; cf. 'visuelle Erinnerung/Vision', pp. 520–22, 580.
13. Olrik, in *Deutsches Altertum*, 51, p. 2: '*eingangsgesetz* und . . . *gesetz des abschlusses*'.
14. Ibid. p.7: 'das *toppgewicht* und das *achtergewicht*'.
15. Ibid, p. 11: 'die *einsträngigkeit*'; definition, p. 8: 'die volkspoesie . . . ist immer *einsträngig*'.
16. Ibid, p. 10: 'Das höchste gesetz der volksüberlieferung ist *concentration* um eine hauptperson'.
17. Ibid., p. 8: 'das allgemeine gesetz: jede eigenschaft der personen und der dinge muss sich *in handlung* aussprechen, sonst ist sie nichts'. Cf. Roland Barthes, 'An Introduction to the Structural Analysis of Narrative', translated by Lionel Duisit, *New Literary History*, 6 (1975): 'popular tales . . . are predominantly functional', as opposed to 'indical', that is as opposed to using 'indicators' or 'informants', pp. 247, 249; 'characters' or 'agents' *vs.* 'persons', p. 257.

3 THE NARRATIVE

1. 'Basic plot' is of course a simplification. Propp, for instance, very clearly limits himself to one specific literary culture, and within it to one particular genre, the *Zaubermärchen*. (See Propp, 1975 in the bibliography).
2. Propp, *Morphology of the Folktale*, p. 40, 'The Functions of Actants', XII, l. Vladimir Propp, *Morphologie des Märchens*, edited by Karl Eimermacher, translated by Christel Wendt (Frankfurt am Main, 1975; first published in German, Munich, 1972), p. 44.
3. Barthes, in *New Literary History*, 6, p. 269.
4. Ibid, p. 270.
5. I borrow this suggestive analogy from a study by Frank Kermode, *Novel and Narrative* (Glasgow, 1972), and shall refer to it again below.
6. I use this term in the sense Barthes gives it in *S/Z* (Paris, 1970): '[la] Voix de la Vérité', p. 28 (Cf. pp. 81f).
7. Henry James, *The Art of the Novel* (New York and London, 1962), p. 336.
8. Christine Brooke-Rose, 'The Squirm of the True: An Essay in Non-

Methodology', *PTL: A Journal for Descriptive Poetics and Theory of Literature*, I (1976), p. 283.

9. She might indeed be Juliana's daughter by Aspern, in accordance with the tradition of the time of calling illegitimate children nephews and nieces – *Daniel Deronda*, for example. Of course Tina's patronage is beyond verification; but much in the narrator's allusions speaks for this possibility, and nothing speaks directly against it.

10. The term is inspired by Jacques Lacan, but it is also self-explanatory – Lacan, *Ecrits I*, (Paris, 1966), pp. 138–9.

11. Roman Jakobson, 'Deux aspects du langage et deux types d'aphasie', in *Essais de linguistique générale* (Paris, 1963), p. 56.

4 FOLKLORISTS AND DETECTIVES

1. Frank Kermode, *Novel and Narrative*, p. 11.
2. Lugowski, *Die Form der Individualität im Roman*.
3. Propp, *Morphology of the Folktale*, p. 106.
4. Propp, *Morphologie des Märchens*, p. 65. The English translation from the German is mine, as are the italics.
5. E. Rohde, *Der griechische Roman* (Leipzig, 1900, 2nd ed.). Cited in Lugowski, *Die Form der Individualität im Roman*.
6. This particular discussion of Butor and the *nouveau roman* is also indebted to Frank Kermode's study.
7. See *Plädoyer für eine neue Literatur*, edited by Kurt Neff (Munich, 1966), especially Nathalie Sarraute, 'Das Zeitalter des Argwohns', translated by Kyra Stromberg, pp. 83–93.
8. Henry James, *The Art of the Novel*, p. 172.
9. Ibid, p. 54.
10. For the distinction between *le lisible* and *le scriptible*, see Roland Barthes, *S/Z*, pp. 10–12, 161, 187.
11. Ibid, p. 28: 'Voix de l'Empirie'.
12. The term is Lacan's, and we shall return to it in Chapter 5 – 'Fonction et champs de la parole et du langage: 1. Parole vide et parole pleine dans la réalisation psychanalytique du sujet', *Ecrits I*, pp. 123–43.
13. It is of course somewhat misleading to use this value-laden term, for while we expect conscious motivation in the murderer for hiding his tracks, we are making no such assumption about a narrator's self-deception.
14. Kermode, *Novel and Narrative*, p. 15. See also Kermode, *The Genesis of Secrecy* (Cambridge, Mass. and London, 1979).
15. Ibid, p. 15.
16. Cf. Barthes, *S/Z*, p. 18: 'L'irresponsabilité du texte'.

5 ANALYSIS OF NARRATION, OR *LA PAROLE PLEINE*

1. This goes beyond the illocutionary act as defined by the language philosopher in his classification of 'telling', 'asking', 'promising', etc., or indeed his assigning of a 'logical status' to 'fictional discourse'. See J. L. Austin, *How to Do Things with Words* (Oxford, 1962); John R. Searle, *Speech Acts: An Essay in the*

Philosophy of Language (Cambridge, 1969); John R. Searle, 'The Logical Status of Fictional Discourse', *New Literary History*, 6 (1975).

2. The association of sex with money is a commonplace for the nineteenth-century mind: 'If the system was economic, then the ejaculation of sperm was equivalent in some sense to the expenditure of money' – G. J. Barker-Benfield, *The Horrors of the Half-Known Life: Male Attitudes Towards Women and Sexuality in Nineteenth-Century America* (New York, 1976), p. 179.

6 A LINGUISTIC FALLACY

1. Barthes, in *New Literary History*, 6, p. 269.
2. Ferdinand de Saussure, *Cours de linguistique générale* (Paris, 1955), first published 1916; *Course in General Linguistics* (Glasgow, 1974), translated by Wade Baskin, Part I, chapter I, Part II, chapters III and IV. Jacques Lacan, 'L'instance de la lettre dans l'inconscient ou la raison depuis Freud', in *Ecrits I*, p. 260. 'The insistence of the letter in the unconscious', translated by Jan Miel, in *Structuralism*, edited by Jacques Ehrmann (Garden City, NY, 1970), p. 111.
3. In 'An Introduction' (*New Literary History*, 6), Barthes sees this freedom diminishing from the sentence to the narrative, owing to the additional constraints of narrative codes and action, the translinguistic codes. By the time of *S/Z* and the conception of the 'ideally plural text', his position has changed to the opposite (p. 18).
4. Cesare Segre, *Semiotics and Literary Criticism*, Approaches to Semiotics, 35, edited by T. A. Sebeok (The Hague, 1973), p. 55.
5. *Collected Papers of Charles Sanders Peirce*, edited by Charles Hartshorne and Paul Weiss (Cambridge, Mass., 1932), vol. II, p. 135. See also Max Bense, *Einführung in die informationstheoretische Ästhetik* (Reinbek bei Hamburg, 1969), p. 92.
6. Max Bense, *Einführung*, p. 91. The translation and the emphasis are mine, the italics are Bense's.
7. Roman Jakobson and Claude Lévi-Strauss, '*Les Chats* de Charles Baudelaire', *L'Homme*, 2 (1962). Cf. Michael Riffaterre, 'Describing Poetic Structures: Two Approaches to Baudelaire's *Les Chats*', in *Structuralism*, ed. by Jacques Ehrmann.
8. Richard A. Lanham, *A Handlist of Rhetorical Terms* (Berkeley and Los Angeles, 1968), p. 8.
9. Ibid, p. 46.
10. C. S. Peirce, *Collected Papers*, vol. II, chapter 3; or Bense, *Einführung*., p. 22. For attempts to sort out terminological confusion, see Oswald Ducrot and Tzvetan Todorov, *Dictionnaire encyclopédique des sciences du langage* (Paris, 1972); Anthony Wilden, *The Language of the Self* (Baltimore and London, 1968), pp. 209–29.
11. M. A. K. Halliday, 'Notes on Transitivity and Theme in English', *Journal of Linguistics*, 3 (1967), and 4 (1968). For an introduction, see Halliday, 'Language Structure and Language Function', *New Horizons in Linguistics*, edited by John Lyons (Harmondsworth, 1970), esp. pp. 160–4.
12. Jonathan Culler, for one, develops this concept in his *Structuralist Poetics: Structuralism, Linguistics and the Study of Literature* (London, 1975).
The term 'literary competence' is intended in direct allusion to Chomsky's

distinction between 'competence' and 'performance'. While the latter notion is obviously more complex than originally conceived by Chomsky and has been elaborated since by 'applied' linguists, his concept of 'competence' serves us well as that of an acquired and internalised skill of a 'generative' order. But while linguistic competence is an internalised 'theory of language' or 'grammar', the literary competence must be of a more indeterminate kind and consist of a set of principles rather than rules, which is borne out by the fact that literary interpretation, unlike linguistic decoding, is not of a fully spontaneous, unconscious and automatic kind, but involves, on the contrary, conscious and rational work. But the factor of acquisition of such competence links the linguistic with the literary kind, since in both cases it depends on 'observation' or experience of 'primary data' rather than on learnt rules. The process of acquisition may differ to the extent that the literary one is a neverending process, since it deals with literature on a diachronic level. For Chomsky's definition of 'competence', see *Aspects of the Theory of Syntax* (Cambridge, Mass., 1969), p. 4; for a brief exposition of 'acquisition', ibid., p. 25.
13. Barthes, *S/Z*, p. 10.

7 A LITERARY TABOO

1. The term is originally derived from E. H. Gombrich's expression 'the beholder's share', for example, in *Art and Illusion* (London, 1968), Part III. But it has in its adapted form already established itself in the literary critical discourse. Cf. Frank Kermode, 'Novels: Recognition and Deception', *Critical Inquiry*, 1 (1974), p. 106.
2. Cf. Tzvetan Todorov, 'Le secret du récit', in *Poétique de la prose* (Paris, 1971).
3. Thomas S. Kuhn's analysis of the 'scientific community' probably served me as a subconscious source of inspiration, and certainly makes for an interesting comparison; in *The Structure of Scientific Revolutions* (Chicago and London, 1962).
4. W. K. Wimsatt, *The Verbal Icon* (London, 1970): 'The Intentional Fallacy', written in collaboration with Monroe C. Beardsley, first published in the *Sewanee Review*, 54 (1946).
5. Henry James, *The Real Right Thing*, in *The Complete Tales of Henry James*, edited by Leon Edel (London, 1961–64), vol. 10, p. 471. All references to the tales are to this edition, and are followed by the volume number.
6. Henry James, *The Birthplace*, vol. 11, p. 417.
7. Henry James, *The Figure in the Carpet*, vol. 9, p. 306.
8. Henry James, *The Lesson of the Master*, vol. 7, p. 284.
9. Henry James, *The Next Time*, vol. 9, pp. 221–2.
10. Henry James, *The Author of 'Beltraffio'*, vol. 5, p. 306.

8 THE LITERARY COMMUNITY IN THE CONTEXT OF SOCIETY

1. Henry James, *The Death of the Lion*, vol. 9, pp. 107–8.
2. This analysis is based on a paper given by G. A. Cohen to the Moral Sciences Club in Cambridge, 'Labour, Leisure and a Distinctive Contradiction of Advanced Capitalism', on 28 January 1976. The definitions are his, and are

taken from a supplementary to a forthcoming paper, which he kindly sent me.

3. Henry James, *The Sweetheart of M. Briseux*, vol. 3, p. 71.

9 TWIN DEMONS

1. Henry James, *The Velvet Glove*, vol. 12, p. 240.
2. Ibid., p. 234.
3. Ibid., p. 237.
4. Henry James, *The Private Life*, vol. 8, p. 202.
5. Henry James, *The Special Type*, vol. 11, p. 179.
6. Henry James, *The Tone of Time*, vol. 11, p. 195.
7. Oscar Wilde, *The Picture of Dorian Gray; Complete Works of Oscar Wilde* (London and Glasgow, 1973; first collected edition, 1948), p. 25.
8. Leon Edel, *Henry James: The Untried Years 1843–1870* (London, 1953), p. 235.
9. Henry James, *The Real Thing*, vol. 8, p. 257. Cf. 'the ideal right', *The Art of the Novel*, p. 122.
10. Cf. W. B. Yeats, 'The Choice' (1933), *The Collected Poems of W.B. Yeats* (London, 1971; first edition, 1933), p. 278; Henrik Ibsen, *When We Dead Awaken* (1899).
11. Tony Tanner, *The Reign of Wonder* (Cambridge, 1965), p. 306.

10 PRODUCTS OF OBSERVATION AND IMAGINATION

1. Henry James, *Nona Vincent*, vol. 8, p. 155.
2. Leon Edel, *Henry James: The Conquest of London 1870–1883* (London, 1962), p. xiii.
3. Henry James, *The Beldonald Holbein*, vol. 11, p. 302.
4. Henry James, *The Story in It*, vol. 11, p. 309.
5. It has been a source of amused surprise to find in my reading of the secondary literature on *The Sacred Fount* that at least three critics cite, of all James's 'artistic' characters, the Colonel as an authority on aesthetic questions – Naomi Lebowitz, *The Imagination of Loving* (Detroit, 1965), pp. 18–9; Sergio Perosa, 'Introduzione', *La fonte sacra*, translated by Sergio Perosa (Venice, 1963), p. xxiii; Tony Tanner, 'Henry James's Subjective Adventurer: *The Sacred Fount*', *Essays and Studies*, 16 (London, 1963), p. 48.
6. Henry James, *Flickerbridge*, vol. 11, pp. 327–8.
7. Henry James, *The Two Faces*, vol. 11, p. 240.
8. Saussure does not in the *Cours de linguistique générale* draw an actual triangle, but it is implied by the combination of the diagrams of signs, and has been interpreted as a triangle since (pp. 65–7).
9. Max Bense, *Einführung*, p. 12.
10. Noam Chomsky, *Aspects*, p. 46.

11 THE CONCEPT OF THE FOUNT

1. 'Literarity' is a term more commonly adopted into the critical vocabulary, but

it is not quite the same as what is here indicated. Literarity signifies directly a quality of text; 'literariness', on the other hand, is a more general concept referring to a disposition, an attitude, assumed towards a text by a writer or a critic. Thus it designates a certain 'literary sensibility', or an internalised competence.

2. Ralph Ranald objects to this direct association of the fount image with sex: ' . . . the sacred fount is undeniably the fountain of life . . .', and 'The relationships among Gilbert Long and Guy Brissenden and Lady John and May Server and Mrs Brissenden cannot be said to be primarily sexual. The sacred fount is the symbol of the life force of which the sexual relationship is only one aspect'. – '*The Sacred Fount*: James's Portrait of the Artist *Manqué*', *Nineteenth-Century Fiction*, 15 (1960), pp. 240, 242. One's immediate response is: what about the fount's requirement that a relation must be '*intimissima*' and how can this 'symbol' be validated?

3. Whether the novel is read as an allegory of life, as in Ranald cited in note 2 above, or else as an allegory of art in general or of James's art in particular, the image of the fount is mostly explained away. Robert J. Andreach's existentialist interpretation sees in the fount not the symbol of life *tout court*, but of 'the real experiencing of the world', which is one part of the 'existential predicament', to which the other part is 'the logical apprehension of the world' ('Henry James's *The Sacred Fount*: The Existential Predicament', *Nineteenth-Century Fiction*, 17 (1962), p. 198). The answer to this must be the same as that to Ranald, since the intimate relation postulated by the narrator has been extended to its most general application, a relation to the world. Another group is masterminded by R. P. Blackmur, who suggested in 1942 that the sacred fount stands for 'conscience', of which the most comprehensive instance is the narrator, and through equation with him James himself: 'Thus we see that as novelist James is the hidden conscience of his characters, and as a conscience he is himself their sacred fount' '*The Sacred Fount*', *Kenyon Review*, 4 (1942), p. 352). This theme is followed up by many others, amongst them J. A. Ward, 'The Ineffectual Heroes of James's Middle Period', *Texas Studies in Literature and Language*, 2 (1960); Landon Burns, 'Henry James's Mysterious Fount', *Texas Studies in Literature and Language*, 2 (1961); Sidney Finkelstein, 'The "Mystery" of Henry James's *The Sacred Fount*', *Massachusetts Review*, 3 (1962); and James Folsom, 'Archimago's Well: An Interpretation of *The Sacred Fount*', *Modern Fiction Studies*, 7 (1961).

4. Henry James, *The Sacred Fount* (London, 1959), p. 22. All page references, henceforth in the text, are to this edition.

5. Francis Bacon, 'The History of Life and Death', *The Works of Francis Bacon* (London, 1861), vol. 5, pp. 213–335. For example:

'Particular care should be taken that the spirits are not too often dissolved. For attenuation precedes dissolution, and the spirit once attenuated is not easily recovered again and condensed. Dissolution is caused by too great labours, too violent affections of the mind, too profuse perspirations, too large evacuations, warm baths, and intemperate or unseasonable gratification of lust . . . All of which should (as indeed the common physicians advise) be as far as possible avoided.' (p. 280)

[Herbert Spencer, *The Principles of Ethics* (New York, 1897)]

6. 'Beyond that constant surplus vitality which, in the female economy, remains after meeting the expenditure of individual life, there is also what we may call a reserve of vital capital, accumulated during intervals in which the surplus is not being demanded.' Herbert Spencer, *The Principles of Ethics*, p. 553, quoted by Elliot Schrero, 'The Narrator's Palace of Thought in *The Sacred Fount*', *Modern Philology*, 68 (1971), p. 277.

7. Franz Anton Mesmer, *Mémoire Sur La Découverte Du Magnétisme Animal* (Geneva and Paris, 1779); translated by V. R. Meyers (London, 1948). Mesmer posits 'a mutual influence between the Heavenly bodies, the Earth, and Animate Bodies which exist as a universally distributed and continuous fluid . . . of an incomparably rarified nature'; quoted by Fred Kaplan, *Dickens and Mesmerism: The Hidden Springs of Fiction* (Princeton, NJ, 1975), p. 7.

8. At least in the West; Mahatma Gandhi is said to have boasted 'how potent – physically, mentally, and spiritually – he had become through seminal continence' (*Observer Magazine*, 12 June 1977, p. 41).

9. Sigmund Freud, *Das Unbehagen in der Kultur* (1930), (Frankfurt am Main, 1972).

12 THAT FRIVOLOUS THING AN OBSERVER

1. Henry James, *The Madonna of the Future*, *The Complete Tales*, vol. 3, p. 23.

2. Henry James, *The Art of the Novel*, pp. 29–30.

3. The most extensive hypothesis of the narrator's amorousness is Jean Frantz Blackall, *Jamesian Ambiguity and The Sacred Fount* (Ithaca, NY, 1965). Contending all other relationships, Blackall suggests that May Server has fallen in love with the narrator, who remains unaware of it until it is too late and she has given him up. Others suggest that the narrator is really in love with Mrs Briss: Norma Phillips, '*The Sacred Fount*: The Narrator and the Vampires', *PMLA*, 76 (September 1961), pp. 408–9, though a more general concession is also made to Blackmur's 'conscience fount'. Parker Tyler, who finds his own original suspicion about a love affair between the narrator and Mrs Briss 'too *simply* ingenious', proceeds to an allegorical reading in which Mrs Briss is 'James's symbol of his own readers'; thus their relation becomes a 'literary flirtation' – '*The Sacred Fount*: "The Actuality Pretentious and Vain" *vs.* "The Case Rich and Edifying"', *Modern Fiction Studies*, 9 (1963), pp. 127, 133.

4. Cf. Seymour Chatman, *The Later Style of Henry James* (Oxford, 1972), for a discussion of the indeterminacy of 'it'–nominalisations.

5. Quite contrary to the interpretation of Tony Tanner, and most other critics, the narrator's 'sacrifice of feeling' (p. 203) does not mean his exclusion from emotional participation, but precisely an intensification of emotional suffering. Feeling is the currency in which he pays his sacrifice, sacrificing the natural priority its protection and gratification usually enjoys. See Tanner, in *Essays and Studies*, 16, p. 48; Andreach, in *Nineteenth-Century Fiction*, 17, p. 207.

13 FROM ARTIST TO CRITIC

1. All interpretations proclaiming the narrator a novelist or identifying him with James are such allegories, notwithstanding the fact that they are mostly unconsciously allegoric. Identification goes from the most explicit equation to the most unselfconscious confusion of the narrator's view with James's beliefs or intentions. But a list of all allegorists would be too long, since the identification with James is one of the standard assumptions, rarely questioned, in Jamesian criticism. Two allegorical readings may, however, be distinguished, since they allegorise self-consciously: Parker Tyler's (in *Modern Fiction Studies*, 9), and Naomi Lebowitz's chapter, '*The Sacred Fount*: An Author in Search of His Characters' in *The Imagination of Loving*.

2. This is a long way from Hawthorne's preface to *The House of the Seven Gables* (1851). While Hawthorne is defending a 'romantic' mode of fiction against the prevalent presupposition of Realism, James takes 'romance' as a mode of experiencing reality, quite apart from its portrayal.

3. John Forrester, 'The Function of Language in Freud's Psychoanalysis', unpublished Fellowship dissertation, King's College (Cambridge, 1975), chapter II. See also: Forrester, *Language and the Origins of Psychoanalysis* (London, 1980).

4. J. Lacan, *Ecrits I*, p. 160, trs. Anthony Wilden, in *The Language of the Self: The Function of Language in Psychoanalysis, by Jacques Lacan*, p. 44.

5. The term 'third ear' is Lacan's, but my use of it differs from his, as I shall presently explain.

6. Sigmund Freud, *Traumdeutung*, p. 152.

7. Maxwell Geismar, in *Henry James and his Cult* (London, 1964), makes precisely such an objection:

> The mental manipulation of all these secondary characters by the omnipotent observer – complacent, smug, perhaps mad – is the final twist in *The Sacred Fount*. He becomes the perfect proto-Freudian analyst, as it were, who is always right, who always understands the peculiar behavior of the 'patients' who may oppose or flatly deny his speculations; the analyst who can rationalize away any action which contradicts his own 'conclusions'. That is also the final enigma of the novel. (p. 208)

8. Henry James, *The Art of the Novel*, p. 5.

9. The term 'collective unconscious' is familiar from C. G. Jung, for example 'Über psychische Energetik und das Wesen der Träume', *Gesammelte Werke*, vol. 7 (Zurich, 1967). But for Jung it is the manifestation of a non-personal, 'objective' and collective 'knowledge' through and in the individual; whereas I am using the term, quite differently from Jung, for a common or shared unconscious operating on a 'collective', that is, public level, as will become clear from the context.

10. Lacan, *Ecrits I*, p. 143, translated by Wilden, *The Language of the Self*, p. 27. For an exposition of the concept of the 'discourse of the other' (after 1955 to become the 'discourse of the Other'), see the whole *Discours de Rome* (1953), 'Fonction et champs de la parole et du langage en psychanalyse', *Ecrits I*, p. 111, *passim*.

For a clarification of the development of the differentiation between 'autre' and 'Autre', see notes 49 and 59 to Wilden's translation, pp. 106, 110. For a clarification of the direction of this discourse 'of' the Other, see 'Subversion et dialectique du désir dans l'inconscient freudien', *Ecrits II*, esp. pp. 174–5.

11. Lacan, *Ecrits I*, p. 125. I have also given the French here, because in English there appears a confusion between *un autre* and *une autre*. The English passage is from Wilden, *The Language of the Self*, p. 11.

12. Lacan, *Ecrits I*, pp. 127–8, trs. Wilden, *The Language of the Self*, p. 13.

13. Lacan, *Ecrits I*, p. 130, trs. Wilden, *The Language of the Self*, p. 15.

14. Ibid.

15. Henry James, *The Scenic Art*, ed., with an introduction, by Allan Wade (New York, 1957), first published 1948, p. 100.

16. Henry James, quoted by Leon Edel in his 'Introduction' to Henry James, *The House of Fiction* (London, 1957), p. 16. Also, Henry James, *Hawthorne*, ed. Tony Tanner (London, 1967): 'the reader must look for his local and national quality between the lines of his writing', p. 119.

17. Of course there are critics, like Elliot Schrero (*Modern Philology*, 68, p. 269) who want precisely to get at James's 'mind'.

18. Tony Tanner, drawing a parallel to Shaftsbury's philosophy, arrives at a diametrically opposed view: 'The beauty of an object is only really felt . . . when all thoughts of possessing, enjoying, or controlling it are absent' – in *Essays and Studies*, 16, p. 52. The passage on Shaftsbury is omitted from the later version of the essay in Tony Tanner, *The Reign of Wonder*.

19. Leon Edel, 'Introduction' to Henry James, *The House of Fiction*, p. 14.

20. Leon Edel, *Henry James: The Untried Years*, p. 57. A fuller quotation is given above, p. 95.

21. Leon Edel, 'Introduction' to Henry James, *The Sacred Fount* (London, 1959), p. 13.

22. Henry James, *The Art of the Novel*, p. 5.

23. Henry James, *John Delavoy, The Complete Tales*, vol. 9, p. 436.

14 ON GARDENING

1. Henry James, *The Art of the Novel*, for example, pp. 59, 64.

2. Henry James, *The Golden Bowl*, New York edition, XXIII and XXIV (London, 1909), XXIV, p. 3. I shall henceforth refer to the respective volumes as I and II.

3. Henry James, *The Art of the Novel*, p. 46.

15 READER AND CRITIC WRIT LARGE

1. *The Notebooks of Henry James*, edited by F. O. Matthiessen and K. B. Murdock (New York, 1947), pp. 150–1, 275.

2. For example, Henry James, *The House of Fiction*; Henry James, *Hawthorne*.

3. Henry L. Terrie, Jr. tries to track down James's laws of 'economy', yet without being able to rise above those relative and subjective terms which precisely

lock in the secret of 'economy' instead of giving it away: 'to . . . stay *within bounds* without omitting any *essential* part of the story'; 'to treat his story . . . dramatically and at the same time to do so within a *reasonable* number of pages', etc. – 'Henry James and the "Explosive Principle"', *Nineteenth-Century Fiction*, 15 (1961), pp. 283, 299 (*my emphasis*).

16 A WORD ON CRITICS

1. See note 1, chapter 13.
2. Wilson Follett has first suggested that the novel is a self-parody, and thus initiated an interminable train of followers, too numerous to be cited individually – 'Henry James's Portrait of Henry James', *New York Times Book Review* (23 August 1936).
3. See, for example, Jean Frantz Blackall, *Jamesian Ambiguity*, pp. 33, 62.
4. Parker Tyler's allegory in fact assigns to Mrs Briss the role of representing James's 'own readers', while Obert is another, 'a male reader' – in *Modern Fiction Studies*, 9, pp. 127–8. While this obviously seems borne out, one would hope that the novel will enjoy also some more sensitive and disinterested response.
5. See notes 2 and 3, chapter 11, for circular founts and the fount of 'vitality'. Giorgio Melchiori specifically attributes 'vital energy' to the fount – 'Cups of Gold for *The Sacred Fount*: Aspects of James's Symbolism', *Critical Quarterly*, 7 (1965), p. 308.
6. See, for example, Landon Burns, in *Texas Studies in Literature and Language*, 2, p. 524. Julian B. Kaye quotes from Quentin Anderson's dictionary of Jamesian characters, according to which American girls are 'givers' and English girls are 'takers', so as to determine that Mrs Briss (British) *is* a vampire – '*The Awkward Age*, *The Sacred Fount*, and *The Ambassadors*: Another Figure in the Carpet', *Nineteenth-Century Fiction*, 17 (1963), p. 348.
7. Joseph Wiesenfarth is almost unique in explicitly referring to this essential literary relativism: 'the ultimate relativity of "objective reality" stands in evidence, and the novel has come to its logically ambiguous conclusion'. And 'for [the reader] the "objective situation" seems to remain one of complete relativity' – *Henry James and the Dramatic Analogy: A Study of the Major Novels of the Middle Period* (New York, 1963), pp. 98, 105.
8. We should not agree with Tony Tanner (in *Essays and Studies*, 16, p. 51) and many other critics who believe fiction to be no more than a tool for the 'historian', that art 'can only console by recording the loss and lamenting the waste' of its incapacity.
9. J. A. Ward, 'James's Idea of Structure', *PMLA*, 80 (September 1965), p. 423.
10. Philip Weinstein: '*The Sacred Fount* has received critical attention beyond the intrinsic merits of the book' – *Henry James and the Requirements of the Imagination* (Cambridge, Mass., 1971), p. 97. Leon Edel: 'The book is slight enough when set beside the major novels' – 'Introduction' (1959), p. 14. Oscar Cargill: 'it is not a good novel' – *The Novels of Henry James* (New York, 1971), p. 295. Arnold P. Hinchliffe: 'it is by no means a success' – 'Henry James's *The Sacred Fount*', *Texas Studies in Literature and Language*, 2 (1960), p. 88. Cynthia Ozick: 'certainly less than a "good" novel' – 'The Jamesian Parable: *The Sacred Fount*', *Bucknell Review*, 11 (1963), p. 57.

11. Norma Phillips, *PMLA*, 76, p. 412.
12. Morris Roberts is virtually alone in thinking, and saying, that 'amusement' might be an excellent reason for reading; as he is among the few who locate the reasons for the bad reception of *The Sacred Fount* in the receivers rather than in the novel – 'Henry James's Final Period', *Yale Review*, 37 (1947), p. 63.
13. Leon Edel, 'Introduction' (1959), p. 15. Walter Isle, 'The Romantic and the Real: Henry James's *The Sacred Fount*', in *Henry James: Modern Judgements*, ed. Tony Tanner (London, 1968), p. 254; Jean Frantz Blackall, *Jamesian Ambiguity*, p. 9.
14. From a letter by Henry James to William Dean Howells (9 August 1900), *The Letters of Henry James*, 2 vols, selected and edited by Percy Lubbock (London, 1920), vol. I, pp. 364–5. Cf. *The Letters of Henry James*, ed. Leon Edel, 4 vols (London, 1975, 1979 and forthcoming).

APPENDIX

1. Shlomith Rimmon, 'Mutual Incompatibility: The Concept of Ambiguity, Illustrated from some Novels and Stories of Henry James', PhD thesis, (London, 1973, to be published shortly), pp. 314–27.
2. Christine Brooke-Rose, 'The Squirm of the True', vol. 1, no. 2.
3. For a sample of the most extreme of this feeling, see Van Wyck Brooks, 'Two Phases of Henry James' (1925); Herbert Croly, 'Henry James and His Countrymen' (1904); Vernon Louis Parrington, 'Henry James and the Nostalgia of Culture' (1930), all in *The Question of Henry James*, edited by F. W. Dupee (New York, 1945). Edna Kenton in turn defends James against the charges of 'snobbery, toadyism, sycophancy, shame of his country and countrymen' in 'Henry James in the World' (1934), ibid., p. 131. One should also point out that among the earlier pronouncements one can come across perceptions, conceived intuitively rather than methodically, which might put to shame some of the pedestrian haggles that dominate subsequent criticism. Thus Bliss Perry feels 'insufferably stupid, like talking with some confoundedly clever woman who is two or three "moves" ahead of you in the conversational game. . . . Only a woman would let you catch up, and James doesn't', (quoted in Oscar Cargill, *The Novels of Henry James*, p. 282). It shows an awareness that James's fiction has the quality of a 'game', as does Frank Moore Colby's more cantankerous observation that James enjoys an unfair advantage over the reader – 'In Darkest James' (1904), in *The Question of Henry James*, p. 25. Henry Adams regrets the 'subject', yet perceives its treatment: 'if [James] had chosen another background, his treatment of it would have been wonderfully keen'. The treatment obviously *is* wonderfully keen, or Adams could not have made this comment, while the conditional mood expresses his deprecation of the 'background'; quoted in Oscar Cargill, *The Novels of Henry James*, p. 282. William Dean Howells is perhaps the most sensitive early critic, reflecting his sensitivity in his own expression, and entering the novel's terms to the extent of writing his own mock-Jamesian dialogue – 'Mr Henry James's Later Work' (1903), in *The Question of Henry James*.
4. It is symptomatic that Leon Edel has been cited by exponents of two opposing camps as one of theirs. Dorothea Krook agrees explicitly with Edel that the narrator is an 'author' – *The Ordeal of Consciousness in Henry James* (Cambridge,

1962), p. 167. Philip Weinstein cites Edel as one who opposes the artist-analogy. Weinstein claims that Edmund Wilson accepted the hypothesis of Follett, *Henry James and the Requirements of the Imagination*, p. 101; while Oscar Cargill quotes Wilson as an opponent, *The Novels of Henry James*, p. 284. Wilson's objection to the hypothesis is spurious, since he holds that the narrator is not a novelist because, if he were, he would be a bad one – which is itself very close to the Follett-hypothesis of self-parody. 'The Ambiguity of Henry James' (1934–38), in *The Question of Henry James*, p. 171.

5. Oscar Cargill, *The Novels of Henry James*, p. 283.

6. For this fact is disputed by other critics, such as Tony Tanner: '[This society] has all the appearance of being James's version of paradise, a sort of Platonic idea of "society" '– in *Essays and Studies*, 16, p. 40. James Folsom: 'Newmarch is more than it appears to be. It is not exactly heaven, nor is it a palace of art, but it is certainly more than an estate in the country' – in *Modern Fiction Studies*, 7, p. 138.

7. Like many others, Cargill talks about 'having an obsession' as one does about having a cold. Some more subtle psychology might be used in such diagnoses – a recommendation also made by Christine Brooke-Rose, op. cit., p. 287, and *passim*.

8. Wilson Follett, quoted in Oscar Cargill, *The Novels of Henry James*, p. 284.

9. See above, chapter 11, notes 2 and 3.

10. James Reaney, 'The Condition of Light: Henry James's *The Sacred Fount*', *University of Toronto Quarterly*, 31 (1962), p. 142.

11. See Walter Isle, quoted below, note 21.

12. Parker Tyler, in *Modern Fiction Studies*, 9, p. 127.

13. Cynthia Ozick, in *Bucknell Review*, 11, p. 61.

14. Philip Weinstein, *Henry James and the Requirements of the Imagination*, p. 98.

15. Walter Isle, 'The Romantic and the Real', p. 259.

16. Sidney Finkelstein, in *Massachusetts Review*, 3, p. 769.

17. Jean Frantz Blackall, *Jamesian Ambiguity*, p. 33.

18. William Veeder, *Henry James – the Lessons of the Master: Popular Fiction and Personal Style in the Nineteenth Century* (Chicago and London, 1975), p. 99.

19. Tony Tanner, in *Essays and Studies*, 16, p. 46.

20. Parker Tyler (in *Modern Fiction Studies*, 9, p. 127) makes a similar point, though unhappily formulated. With regard to Blackmur's much quoted 'nightmare nexus' of the artist's struggles as artist and as self, he comments: 'This "nexus" is quite unJamesian. James never left a struggle, in his fiction, in the balance . . . never established the conditions of a struggle without deciding their issue.' I agree in principle, except that 'deciding the issue' sounds too much like the umpire's task. James as artist has left many an 'issue' in the balance of his ambiguity, and instead of a decision has reached an artistic resolution.

21. The terms are Walter Isle's, although the aim is shared by many others – 'The Romantic and the Real', p. 249. Howells warned against such finalities: 'I am not going to try committing [Mr James] to conclusions he would shrink from'–'Mr Henry James's Later Work', pp. 14–15. Alas, few have followed his resolution. See Follett, quoted above (199). In Isle's view, 'James . . . gives us . . . the essence and accident of the world' and is also 'close to offering one of the major, twentieth-century solutions to the chaos of life – salvation through

art'–'The Romantic and the Real', pp. 263, 264. Robert Perlongo: ' . . . its final message seems to be a reaffirmation of life as a quantity to be valued for itself, and not merely for what the artist may make of it'. Salvation through life – as opposed to the ineptitude of art? And further: 'the book comes to have meaning as a chronicle of maturation' – '*The Sacred Fount*: Labyrinth or Parable?', *Kenyon Review*, 22 (1960), pp. 646, 647. Robert Andreach (in *Nineteenth-Century Fiction*, 17, p. 215) also detects a possible though gradual cure of the narrator towards maturity. J. A. Ward subscribes to the ' "salvation" theme', 'The Ineffectual Heroes', p. 320. And for G. H. Jones '*The Sacred Fount* . . . becomes James's most thorough expression of the philosophy of well-intended renunciation' – *Henry James's Psychology of Experience: Innocence, Responsibility, and Renunciation in the Fiction of Henry James, Series Pratica*, 79 (The Hague, 1975), p. 228.

22. Landon Burns (in *Texas Studies in Literature and Language*, 2, pp. 523–4), citing Follett, agrees with him: 'the flow of the fount would then be circular. . . . The question remains . . . about how much of this ideal symmetry actually exists and how much is the product of the narrator's fertile imagination.' Rather, the question remains how much of this perfect circular symmetry exists *textually*, and how much is the product of the *critic's* fertile imagination.

23. Philip Weinstein, *Henry James and the Requirements of the Imagination*, p. 109.

24. See, for example, Bernard Richards: '[James] makes himself as a novel writer, his characters and his readers share in the problem of the reception, the analysis and the expansion of data'. '*The Ambassadors* and *The Sacred Fount*: The Artist *Manqué*', in *The Air of Reality*, ed. John Goode (London, 1972), p. 220. Yet, like Weinstein, he mainly considers the narrator's likeness to the artist, which is partly due to his equation of 'data' with the events of the story, failing to expand the notion of 'data' and 'the problem' to the novelistic text. Ora Segal, deflected by her concern for the 'truth', fails to link the narrator's 'analytical' and 'interpretative activities' to her own – *The Lucid Reflector*, p. 149.

25. There may be a connection between this and some critics' objection to a vampiristic conception of sex, though they do not mind such a conception for creative and speculative imagination. Blackmur: 'the narrator could be any novelist, and the novelist could in the long run and in the same predicament be any man' – in *Kenyon Review*, 4, p. 346.

26. Bernard Richards, ' . . . The Artist *Manqué*', p. 219 (see also note 24 above). He virtually repeats this point, with the same problematical formulation, on p. 222.

27. For Walter Isle, the Romantic and the Real, appearance and reality, the true and the false, gradually become pairs of synonyms. Perlongo (in *Kenyon Review*, 22, pp. 646–7): 'life and art – appearance and reality – are confounded in [the narrator's] mind'. Laurence B. Holland counts as an exception with his subtler conception of appearance as part of reality, in *The Expense of Vision: Essays on the Craft of Henry James* (Princeton, NJ, 1964), p. 224.

28. Cf. Frank Kermode, *The Sense of an Ending* (New York, 1967), for a conception of 'fiction' that goes beyond a mere synonymity of 'prose literature'. Sidney Finkelstein (in *Massachusetts Review*, 3, p. 772) comes close to accepting such a conception of which there is no need to be ashamed, yet loses his nerve at the

last moment: 'If the narrator of *The Sacred Fount* has built only a "house of cards", then the structure of *The Wings of the Dove*, *The Ambassadors* and *The Golden Bowl* can also be described, wrongly to be sure, as a "house of cards".' It is not quite clear what the envisaged improvement on the 'house of cards' would be. James Reaney (in *University of Toronto Quarterly*, 31, p. 140) defends the respectability of fictions: 'If Mrs Brissenden is right, then not only the narrator is crazy but the whole world of human science may be crazy also, for it too consists of a palace of thought reared on just the sort of inductions the narrator is continually making, just his sort of hypotheses that lead to general laws'. Reaney is one of the few who is able, or takes the trouble, to follow the narrator's theory through to the end to find out if it 'works'; hence his views on the significance of Mrs Briss's last moves and apparent victories are similar to mine, except for his conviction of their truth.

29. Critics are prepared to consult the most ingenious sources rather than revert to the narrator's Word, the text. Thus Blackmur (in *Kenyon Review*, 4, p. 333) suggests 'other lights which must be turned on first and from quite far off; and of these the first is the light of the tale *Owen Wingrave*'. I hardly need point out that it would be difficult to turn this into a consistent method. Ralph Ranald (in *Nineteenth-Century Fiction*, 15, p. 241) thinks that to 'reach an understanding of the narrator, the reader must refer to other works of James, to see how similar characters and situations are treated'. Why not see how *this* character and *this* situation are treated? Arnold Hinchliffe: 'It will be valuable perhaps at this stage to move outside the novel' – in *Texas Studies in Literature and Language*, 2, p. 92. The problem is that if 'moving outside the novel' is permitted, there is no saying where it might take us. It has taken James Folsom (in *Modern Fiction Studies*, 7) to *The Faerie Queene*; Cynthia Ozick (in *Bucknell Review*, 11) to the New Testament; and Quentin Anderson to Henry James Sr. and the Junior's fear of the Father, *The American Henry James* (New Brunswick, NJ, 1959), p. 120, for example.

30. The complaint that 'we have no objective criteria to measure [the narrator's evidence] against' is too common to attribute to single critics. This particular one is from Robert Perlongo, in *Kenyon Review*, 22, p. 641, and deserves mention because the same writer nonetheless ventures to measure the net value of truth blindly: 'we have on our hands a record in which there may not be as much as a tenth part of truth' (p. 642). In connection with this lack of 'objective' information the detective is often brought in. To show the fallacy of this analogy I shall only quote Jean Frantz Blackall: '[James] was capable, we know, of teasing his reader's curiosity, for example by refusing to specify the object manufactured in Woollett, Massachusetts. . . . And, in general, most of his stories have something of the appeal and the pitfalls of the detective story for a reason indicated above, that the reader must work things out for himself and find his own way . . .' – *Jamesian Ambiguity*, p. 9. We are of course going to remain very frustrated detectives, since we will never find out what the Woollett article is, nor what was in Milly Theale's letter which landed in the fire, unread. This is why I have suggested the role of the judge in the courtroom, who analyses the witness's testimony, while we give up 'studying the bits of mud adhering to the boots' which Leon Edel recommends in his 'Introduction' (1959), p. 8. For we know mud as well as boots only from hearsay, which presents difficulties in the laboratory. In fact, Edel recom-

mends ' the manner of a lawyer or judge' almost in the same breath; he does not seem to see a significant difference.

31. Robert Andreach (in *Nineteenth-Century Fiction*, 17, p. 198) is one of the few who shows explicit awareness of this fact: 'We must bear in mind that we are two removes from the existential events of the weekend party'.

32. Cf. Ruth Bernard Yeazell, who discusses characters' avoidance of facts, thus entering the complexities of subconscious intention and conscious counter-intention. Yet despite the sophisticated discussion that follows, Yeazell starts out from a basis of absolute 'facts': 'the power of language to transform facts and even to create them seems matched only by the stubborn persistence of facts themselves' – *Language and Knowledge in the Late Novels of Henry James* (Chicago and London, 1976), p. 3. Such facts, for her, are the sexual liaison between Chad and Madame de Vionnet, of Charlotte and the Prince; and what is more, the 'fact' that Maggie discovers this 'fact'. Rather, Maggie discovers its possibility, and acts upon it. While one might argue that these are, *for the characters*, facts which only need revealing, or 'verification', there is no disputing that for us, the readers, they pertain for ever to the realm of inferences with no possibility of attaining the status of fact.

33. Ralph Ranald (in *Nineteenth-Century Fiction*, 15, p. 241), taking 'pretence' or 'deceit' or 'appearance' as the false signifier of a true signified in the manner we discussed, betrays his conception in his reference to the narrator's tale: 'the narrator may not always be telling the exact truth'. In other words, it is simply a bad selection, a representation of the truth with 'holes', or a bad paraphrase, so to speak; but the truth underlies it.

34. Wiesenfarth, in *Henry James and the Dramatic Analogy*, p. 102, argues that Mrs Briss's and the narrator's are 'equiprobable schemes'. They are perhaps 'equiprobable' in that correspondence to 'real events' which Wiesenfarth also finds irrelevant (p. 97); but the two systems are certainly not equally powerful, that is, explanatory. For the narrator's accounts, for instance, for Mrs Briss's last change of mind, her inconsistency, indeed, her 'system', while hers in no way accommodates his. Her 'explanation' is simply that he is crazy, a response always open to anyone facing a rival, but which is no judgement of his theory. But it is not true, as Wiesenfarth claims, that the two systems are derived 'from a single set of signs' (p. 103): for example, Mrs Briss's 'sign' that May Server is 'awfully sharp' is not a sign in the narrator's system, though her claim of that content becomes one. Nor does Mrs Briss work with the data concerning her own case.

35. There are too many who agree with Landon Burns (in *Texas Studies in Literature and Language*, 2, p.521) that the narrator is a 'prying reporter' or worse. The less slanderous judgements include Dorothea Krook's that the narrator is 'morally unqualified' for his observing and narrating task – *The Ordeal of Consciousness*, p. 194. Kenneth Graham thinks the problem is, above all, the novelist's and his 'act of creation-by-intrusion' – *Henry James: The Drama of Fulfilment* (Oxford, 1975), pp. 65–6. Cynthia Ozick, though asserting that the narrator is amoral rather than immoral, deems him 'without doubt a wretched busy-body' (in *Bucknell Review*, 11), p. 62. J. A. Ward manages to have it both ways, with the moralists and with Blackmur's conscience-hypothesis: 'On the symbolic level, then, the narrator is "the projected image of conscience", though on the literal level he is an overly curious snooper'. In *Kenyon Review*, 4, p. 326. Edel,

too, is as usual undecided, though with a definite inclination: 'But whether that obsession has reached a degree of morbidity in this book which becomes a kind of childish key-hole peeping at the guests . . . the reader must determine for himself'–'Introduction' (1959), p. 8. Among the defenders of the narrator are Ora Segal, *The Lucid Reflector*, pp. 149, 152; Sidney Finkelstein (in *Massachusetts Review*, 3), p. 769; Elliot Schrero (in *Modern Philology*, 68), p. 284; James Reaney (in *University of Toronto Quarterly*, 31), p. 138.

36. The exceptions are again less numerous: Parker Tyler (in *Modern Fiction Studies*, 9, p. 129) has a conception of 'art' and 'intelligence' as a creative force which is rare amongst 'fount' critics, realising that fiction, and art in general, cannot simply be a matter of 'real places' and 'the people who lived in them'. Yeazell, otherwise a laudable exception, cannot do without pairing 'artist' with 'liar': 'Despite her intense desire to know, [Maggie] must also suppress knowledge – even lie both to others and to herself. If Charlotte Stant and Kate Croy are liars who virtually become artists, Maggie Verver is an artist who is thus also a liar' (*Language and Knowledge*) p. 98. But to give her the benefit of the doubt, one may read 'liar' as between Jamesian quotation marks.

37. Quentin Anderson, in *The American Henry James*, also deals with 'emblems', p. 121, for example. James Folsom: 'the theme of vampirism in *The Sacred Fount* is basically symbolic of some aspect of the sin of Pride' (in *Modern Fiction Studies*, 7), p. 143. Apart from the stasis of such symbolism, such emblemistic thinking leads to the known 'essence' or 'final meaning' of the work. Wiesenfarth, who reads the novel as 'a study in logic and semiosis', unfortunately has a rather static conception of these: 'The *Fount* presents a limited number of . . . signs. . . . When all the signs are fitted into [the narrator's and Mrs Briss's] separate and symmetrical constructs, the novel ends. The narrator has used up all the signs available. . . . There are no more signs to use . . .' – *Henry James and the Dramatic Analogy*, p. 97. Rather than the fixed number of signs of Wiesenfarth, the narrator finds everything crying out for interpretation; and it is a matter of 'chains', if not indeed of fields of signifiers and signification which require, not a dictionary of symbols, but a dynamic principle of interpretation – what the narrator calls a 'law'.

38. The great exception is of course the thesis of Shlomith Rimmon already cited, which is a study in and a defense of ambiguity. A further notable exception is Joseph Wiesenfarth: 'If *The Sacred Fount* is to be read well . . . it is necessary to rest easy with ambiguity' – *Henry James and the Dramatic Analogy*, p. 98.

39. Charles T. Samuels, *The Ambiguity of Henry James* (Urbana, Chicago and London, 1971), p. 11.

40. Blackall, *Jamesian Ambiguity*, pp. 9–10.

41. Folsom, in *Modern Fiction Studies*, 7, p. 136.

42. Hinchliffe, in *Texas Studies in Literature and Language*, 2, p. 90.

43. Andreach, in *Nineteenth-Century Fiction*, 17, p. 199.

44. Christine Brooke-Rose, 'The Squirm of the True', p. 268.

45. Hinchliffe, in *Texas Studies*, 2, p. 89.

46. Ranald, in *Nineteenth-Century Fiction*, 15, p. 245. Folsom wonders what might be the difference between the detective and the 'psychologist', and determines that the latter has no justification 'other than private whim' (in *Modern Fiction Studies*, 7), p. 142. To mention just one other: the one works in the mind, the other in the mud.

47. Andreach, in *Nineteenth-Century Fiction*, 17, p. 212.
48. From *The Student's Manual* (1835), quoted by G. J. Barker-Benfield, *The Horrors of the Half-Known Life*, p. 176.
49. Among the religious we must count Ralph Ranald, who quotes St Augustine's *Christian Instruction* on unperverted, unharming love in order to unmask the narrator's travesty (in *Nineteenth-Century Fiction*, 15), p. 245.
50. S. Gorley Putt, *The Fiction of Henry James: A Reader's Guide*, (Harmondsworth, 1968: first published 1966), p. 230.
51. Howells, 'Mr Henry James's Later Work', p. 12.

Select Bibliography

WORKS BY HENRY JAMES

The Complete Tales of Henry James, ed. Leon Edel, 12 vols (London, 1961–4).

The Novels and Tales of Henry James, 24 vols (New York edition, 1907–9, first English edition, Macmillan, 1908–9).

The Sacred Fount, with an introductory essay by Leon Edel (London, 1959).

The Art of the Novel, ed. R. P. Blackmur (New York and London, 1962; first published 1934).

Hawthorne, ed. Tony Tanner (London, 1967).

The House of Fiction (London, 1957).

The Letters of Henry James, ed. Leon Edel, 4 vols (London, 1975, 1979 and forthcoming).

The Letters of Henry James, sel. and ed. Percy Lubbock, 2 vols (London, 1920).

The Notebooks of Henry James, ed. F. O. Matthiessen and K. B. Murdock (New York, 1947).

The Scenic Art, ed. Allan Wade (New York, 1957; first published 1948).

SECONDARY LITERATURE ON HENRY JAMES

Allott, Miriam, 'Henry James and the Fantastic Conceit', *The Northern Miscellany*, 1 (1953).

Anderson, Quentin, *The American Henry James* (New Brunswick, NJ, 1959).

Andreach, Robert J., 'Henry James's *The Sacred Fount*: The Existential Predicament', *Nineteenth-Century Fiction*, 17 (1962).

Appignanesi, Lisa, *Femininity and the Creative Imagination: A Study of Henry James, Robert Musil and Marcel Proust* (London, 1973).

Beach, Joseph Warren, *The Method of Henry James* (New Haven, London and Oxford, 1918).

Beach, Joseph Warren, 'The Figure in the Carpet' (1918), in *The Question of Henry James*, ed. F. W. Dupee (New York, 1945).

Blackall, Jean Frantz, 'James's *In the Cage*: An Approach through the Figurative Language', *University of Toronto Quarterly*, 31 (1962).

Blackall, Jean Frantz, *Jamesian Ambiguity and 'The Sacred Fount'* (Ithaca, NY, 1965).

Blackmur, R. P., '*The Sacred Fount*', *Kenyon Review*, 4 (1942).

Blackmur, R. P., 'In the Country of the Blue' (1943), in *The Question of Henry James*, ed. F. W. Dupee (New York, 1945).

Bloomfield, Morton W., ed., *The Interpretation of Narrative: Theory and Practice*, Harvard English Studies, 1 (Cambridge, Mass., 1970).

Booth, Wayne, *The Rhetoric of Fiction* (Chicago and London, 1961).

Bowden, Edwin T., *The Themes of Henry James* (New Haven, London and Oxford, 1956).

Brooke-Rose, Christine, 'The Squirm of the True: An Essay in Non-Methodology', *PTL*: vol. 1, no. 2 (April 1976).

Brooke-Rose, Christine, 'The Squirm of the True: A Structural Analysis of Henry James's *The Turn of the Screw*', *PTL*: vol. 1, no. 3 (October 1976).

Brooks, Van Wyck, 'Two Phases of Henry James' (1925), in *The Question of Henry James*, ed. F. W. Dupee (New York, 1945).

Brooks, Van Wyck, *The Pilgrimage of Henry James* (London, 1928).

Burns, Landon, 'Henry James's Mysterious Fount', *Texas Studies in Literature and Language*, 2 (1961).

Cambon, Glauco, 'The Negative Gesture in Henry James', *Nineteenth-Century Fiction*, 15 (1961).

Cargill, Oscar, *The Novels of Henry James* (New York, 1971).

Chatman, Seymour, *The Later Style of Henry James* (Oxford, 1972).

Colby, Frank Moore, 'In Darkest James' (1904), in *The Question of Henry James*, ed. F. W. Dupee (New York, 1945).

Croly, Herbert, 'Henry James and His Countrymen' (1904), in *The Question of Henry James*, ed. F. W. Dupee (New York, 1945).

Domaniecki, Hildegard, *Zum Problem Literarischer Ökonomie: Henry James' Erzählungen zwischen Markt und Kunst*, Amerikastudien, 38 (Stuttgart, 1974).

Dupee, F. W., ed., *The Question of Henry James* (New York, 1945).

Dupee, F. W., *Henry James*, The American Men of Letters Series (London, 1951).

Edel, Leon, *Henry James: The Untried Years 1843–1870* (London, 1953).

Edel, Leon, *Henry James: The Conquest of London 1870–1883* (London, 1962).

Edel, Leon, *Henry James: The Middle Years 1884–1894* (London, 1963).

Edel, Leon, *Henry James: The Treacherous Years 1895–1900* (London, 1969).

Edel, Leon, *Henry James: The Master 1901–1916* (London, 1972).

Edel, Leon, 'Introduction' to Henry James, *The House of Fiction* (London, 1957).

Edel, Leon, 'Introduction' to Henry James, *The Sacred Fount* (London, 1959).

Edel, Leon, 'An Introductory Essay' to Henry James, *The Sacred Fount* (New York, 1953); reprinted in *Henry James's Major Novels: Essays in Criticism*, edited and with an introduction by Lyall H. Powers (East Lansing, Mich., 1973).

Eliot, T. S., 'A Prediction in Regard to Three English Authors: Henry James; J. G. Frazer; F. H. Bradley', *Vanity Fair* (February 1924), reprinted in Dorothea Krook, *The Ordeal of Consciousness in Henry James* (Cambridge, 1962), p. 1 (only the part concerning Henry James).

Finkelstein, Sidney, 'The "Mystery" of Henry James's *The Sacred Fount*', *Massachusetts Review*, 3 (1962).

Follett, Wilson, 'Henry James's Portrait of Henry James', *New York Times Book Review* (23 August 1936).

Folsom, James K., 'Archimago's Well: An Interpretation of *The Sacred Fount*', *Modern Fiction Studies*, 7 (1961).

Ford, Madox Ford, 'The Old Man' (1932), in *The Question of Henry James*, ed. F. W. Dupee (New York, 1945).

Forster, E. M., *Aspects of the Novel* (Harmondsworth, 1962; first published 1927).

Gale, Robert, '*The Marble Faun* and *The Sacred Fount*: A Resemblance', *Studi Americani*, 8 (Rome, 1962).

Gard, Roger, ed., *Henry James: The Critical Heritage* (London, 1968).

Geismar, Maxwell, *Henry James and his Cult* (London, 1964).

Goode, John, ed., *The Air of Reality: New Essays on Henry James* (London, 1972).

Graham, Kenneth, *Henry James: The Drama of Fulfilment* (Oxford, 1975).

Hinchliffe, Arnold P., 'Henry James's *The Sacred Fount*', *Texas Studies in Literature and Language*, 2 (1960).

Hoffmann, Charles G., *The Short Novels of Henry James* (New York, 1957).

Holland, Laurence B., *The Expense of Vision: Essays on the Craft of Henry James* (Princeton, NJ, 1964).

Howells, William Dean, 'Mr Henry James's Later Work' (1903), in *The Question of Henry James*, ed. F. W. Dupee (New York, 1945).

Inglis, Tony, 'Reading Late James', in *The Modern English Novel*, ed. Gabriel Josipovici (London, 1976).

Isle, Walter, *Experiments in Form: Henry James's Novels 1896–1901* (Cambridge, Mass., 1968).

Isle, Walter, 'The Romantic and the Real: Henry James's *The Sacred Fount*', in *Henry James: Modern Judgements*, ed. Tony Tanner (London, 1968).

Jefferson, D. W., *Henry James and the Modern Reader* (Edinburgh and London, 1964).

Jones, G. H., *Henry James's Psychology of Experience: Innocence, Responsibility, and Renunciation in the Fiction of Henry James, Series Pratica*, 79 (The Hague, 1975).

Josipovici, Gabriel, ed., *The Modern English Novel* (London, 1976).

Kaye, Julian B., '*The Awkward Age, The Sacred Fount*, and *The Ambassadors*: Another Figure in the Carpet', *Nineteenth-Century Fiction*, 17 (1963).

Kenton, Edna, 'Henry James in the World' (1934), in *The Question of Henry James*, ed. F. W. Dupee (New York, 1945).

Krook, Dorothea, *The Ordeal of Consciousness in Henry James* (Cambridge, 1962).

Laitinen, T., *Aspects of Henry James's Style, Annales Acad. Scientiarum Fennicae. Dissertationes Humanarum Litterarum*, 4 (Helsinki, 1975).

Lebowitz, Naomi, '*The Sacred Fount*: An Author in Search of His Characters', *Criticism*, 4 (1962). Also in Lebowitz (1965).

Lebowitz, Naomi, *The Imagination of Loving* (Detroit, 1965).

Melchiori, Giorgio, 'Cups of Gold for *The Sacred Fount*: Aspects of James's Symbolism', *Critical Quarterly*, 7 (1965).

Ozick, Cynthia, 'The Jamesian Parable: *The Sacred Fount*', *Bucknell Review*, 11 (1963).

Parrington, Vernon Louis, 'Henry James and the Nostalgia of Culture' (1930), in *The Question of Henry James*, ed. F. W. Dupee (New York, 1945).

Perlongo, Robert A., '*The Sacred Fount*: Labyrinth or Parable?', *Kenyon Review*, 22 (1960).

Perosa, Sergio, 'Introduzione', *La fonte sacra*, translated by Sergio Perosa (Venice, 1963).

Phillips, Norma, '*The Sacred Fount*: The Narrator and the Vampires', *PMLA*, 76 (September 1961).

Pound, Ezra, 'Henry James' (1918), in *The Literary Essays of Ezra Pound*, edited with an introduction by T. S. Eliot (London, 1954).

Powers, Lyall H., 'Henry James's Antinomies', *University of Toronto Quarterly*, 31 (1962).

Powers, Lyall H., ed., *Henry James's Major Novels: Essays in Criticism* (East Lansing, Mich., 1973).

Putt, S. Gorley, *The Fiction of Henry James: A Reader's Guide* (Harmondsworth, 1968; first published 1966).

Raeth, Claire J., 'Henry James's Rejection of *The Sacred Fount*', *English Literary History*, 16 (1949).

Ranald, Ralph A., '*The Sacred Fount*: James's Portrait of the Artist Manqué', *Nineteenth-Century Fiction*, 15 (1960).

Reaney, James, 'The Condition of Light: Henry James's *The Sacred Fount*', *University of Toronto Quarterly*, 31 (1962).

Richards, Bernard, '*The Ambassadors* and *The Sacred Fount*: the artist manqué', in *The Air of Reality: New Essays in Henry James*, ed. John Goode (London, 1973).

Rimmon, Shlomith, 'Mutual Incompatibility: The Concept of Ambiguity, Illustrated from Some Novels and Stories of Henry James', PhD thesis (London, 1973), to be published shortly.

Roberts, Morris, 'Henry James's Final Period', *Yale Review*, 37 n.s. (1947).

Samuels, Charles Thomas, 'At the Bottom of the Fount', *Novel*, 2 (1968).

Samuels, Charles Thomas, *The Ambiguity of Henry James* (Urbana, Chicago and London, 1971).

Schrero, Elliot M., 'The Narrator's Palace of Thought in *The Sacred Fount*', *Modern Philology*, 68 (1971).

Sears, Sallie, *The Negative Imagination: Form and Perspective in the Novels of Henry James* (Ithaca, NY, 1968).

Segal, Ora, *The Lucid Reflector: The Observer in Henry James' Fiction* (New Haven and London, 1969).

Sherman, Stuart P., 'The Aesthetic Idealism of Henry James' (1917), in *The Question of Henry James*, ed. F. W. Dupee (New York, 1945).

Tanner, Tony, 'Henry James's Subjective Adventurer: *The Sacred Fount*', *Essays and Studies*, 16 (London, 1963). Also in Tanner 1965, revised; and in *Henry James's Major Novels: Essays in Criticism*, ed. Lyall H. Powers (East Lansing, Mich., 1973).

Tanner, Tony, *The Reign of Wonder* (Cambridge, 1965).

Tanner, Tony, ed., *Henry James: Modern Judgements* (London, 1968).

Terrie, Henry L., Jr., 'Henry James and the "Explosive Principle" ', *Nineteenth-Century Fiction*, 15 (1961).

Todorov, Tzvetan, 'Le secret du récit', in *Poétique de la prose* (Paris, 1971).

Tyler, Parker, 'The Sacred Fount: "The Actuality Pretentious and Vain" *vs.* "The Case Rich and Edifying" ', *Modern Fiction Studies*, 9 (1963).

Veeder, William, *Henry James – the Lessons of the Master: Popular Fiction and Personal Style in the Nineteenth Century* (Chicago and London, 1975).

Ward, J. A., 'The Ineffectual Heroes of James's Middle Period', *Texas Studies in Literature and Language*, 2 (1960).

Ward, J. A., 'James's Idea of Structure', *PMLA*, 80 (September 1965).

Watt, Ian, 'The First Paragraph of *The Ambassadors*: An Explication', *Essays in Criticism*, 10 (1960). Also in *Henry James: Modern Judgements*, ed. Tony Tanner (London, 1968).

Weinstein, Philip M., 'The Exploitative and Protective Imagination: Aspects of the Artist in *The Sacred Fount*', in *The Interpretation of Narrative: Theory and Practice*, ed. Morton W. Bloomfield, Harvard English Studies, 1 (Cambridge, Mass., 1970). Also in Weinstein (1971).

Weinstein, Philip M., *Henry James and the Requirements of the Imagination* (Cambridge, Mass., 1971).

Wiesenfarth, Joseph, *Henry James and the Dramatic Analogy: A Study of the Major Novels of the Middle Period* (New York, 1963).

Willen, Gerald, ed., *A Casebook on Henry James's ' The Turn of the Screw'* (New York, 1960).

Wilson, Edmund, 'The Ambiguity of Henry James' (1934–38), in *The Question of Henry James*, ed. F. W. Dupee (New York, 1945).

Yeazell, Ruth Bernard, *Language and Knowledge in the Late Novels of Henry James* (Chicago and London, 1976).

SELECT BIBLIOGRAPHY OF THE MAIN TEXTS USED

Barthes, Roland, 'Introduction à l'analyse structural des récits', *Communications*, 8 (Paris, 1966).

Barthes, Roland, 'An Introduction to the Structural Analysis of Narrative', trs. Lionel Duisit, *New Literary History*, 6 (1975).

Barthes, Roland *S/Z* (Paris, 1970).

Bogatyrev, P. and Roman Jakobson, 'Die Folklore als eine besondere Form des Schaffens', *Donum natalicium Schrijnen* (Nijmegen and Utrecht, 1929). Trs. into French by Jean-Claude Duport, in Roman Jakobson, *Questions de poétique* (Paris, 1973).

Chomsky, Noam, *Aspects of the Theory of Syntax* (Cambridge, Mass., 1969).

Cohen, G. A., 'Some Definitions', mimeograph.

Freud, Sigmund, *Studienausgabe*, vols. I–X, Conditio Humana (Frankfurt am Main, 1969–75).

Jakobson, Roman – see Bogatyrev.

Kermode, Frank, *Novel and Narrative*, The W. P. Ker Lecture (Glasgow, 1972).

Lacan, Jacques, *Ecrits, I and II* (Paris, 1966).

Lacan, Jacques, 'The Function of Language in Psychoanalysis', trs. Anthony Wilden, in Anthony Wilden, *The Language of the Self* (Baltimore, 1968).

Lugowski, Clemens, *Die Form der Individualität im Roman*, with an introduction by Heinz Schlaffer (Frankfurt am Main, 1976; first published 1932).

Olrik, Alex, 'Epische Gesetze der Volksdichtung', *Zeitschrift für Deutsches Altertum*, 51 (1909).

Propp, Vladimir, *Morphology of the Folktale*, ed. and intro. S. Pirakova–Jakobson, trs. L. Scott, *International Journal of American Linguistics*, Pt. 3, 24 iv, *Indiana University Center in Anthropology, Folklore and Linguistics Publication*, 10 (Indiana, 1958).

Propp, Vladimir, *Morphologie des Märchens*, ed. Karl Eimermacher, trs. Christel Wendt (Frankfurt am Main, 1975).

Segre, Cesare, *Semiotics and Literary Criticism*, Approaches to Semiotics, 35, ed. T. A. Sebeok (The Hague, 1973).

Wilden, Anthony, *The Language of the Self: The Function of Language in Psychoanalysis, by Jacques Lacan*, trs. with notes and commentary by Anthony Wilden (Baltimore and London, 1968).

Index